FASHION, DRESS AND POST-POSTMODERNISM

FASHION, DRESS AND POST-POSTMODERNISM

EDITED BY
JOSÉ BLANCO F. AND
ANDREW REILLY

BLOOMSBURY VISUAL ARTS
LONDON • NEW YORK • OXFORD • NEW DELHI • SYDNEY

BLOOMSBURY VISUAL ARTS
Bloomsbury Publishing Plc
50 Bedford Square, London, WC1B 3DP, UK
1385 Broadway, New York, NY 10018, USA
29 Earlsfort Terrace, Dublin 2, Ireland

BLOOMSBURY, BLOOMSBURY VISUAL ARTS and the Diana logo are trademarks of
Bloomsbury Publishing Plc

First published in Great Britain 2021
Paperback edition first published 2022

Cover design by Adriana Brioso
Cover image © Francois Guillot/AFP/Getty Images

A catalogue record for this book is available from the British Library.

A catalog record for this book is available from the Library of Congress.

ISBN: HB: 978-1-3501-1516-3
PB: 978-1-3502-1439-2
ePDF: 978-1-3501-1517-0
eBook: 978-1-3501-1518-7

Typeset by Newgen KnowledgeWorks Pvt. Ltd., Chennai, India

To find out more about our authors and books visit www.bloomsbury.com
and sign up for our newsletters.

CONTENTS

ILLUSTRATIONS

Figures

Table

NOTES ON CONTRIBUTORS

Caroline Bellios is Professor of Fashion Design and History at the School of the Art Institute of Chicago. Her current research ranges from nineteenth-century hair jewellery, embodiment and the transformative nature of touch, to the potential of fashion in the museum space, the memory space and as a platform for connection and inclusivity. With colleagues in her city, Caroline is a founder of the Chicago Fashion Lyceum, a new collaborative body for fashion discourse. She would also like to hear stories about your grandmother.

José Blanco F. is Professor and Chair in the Department of Fashion Merchandising and Design at Dominican University in River Forest, Illinois. His research focuses on dress and popular culture in the second half of the twentieth century, with an emphasis on male fashion. He is interested in fashion and visual culture in Latin America. José is the general editor of the four-volume encyclopedia *Clothing and Fashion: American Fashion from Head to Toe*. He has co-authored with Raúl J. Vázquez-López several articles and book chapters on Puerto Rican dress, costume and fashion.

Alla Eizenberg is part-time Assistant Professor in Parsons School of Design, New York, and is a PhD candidate at the Department of Design at Aalto University, Helsinki. Her research focuses on the meaning of the ordinary in fashion and the changing politics of sartorial signification in the sociocultural climate of the beginning of the twenty-first century.

Grant Klarich Johnson is a PhD candidate in the Department of Art History at the University of Southern California, a Joan Tisch Teaching Fellow at the Whitney Museum of American Art and a Jane and Morgan Whitney Fellow at the Metropolitan Museum of Art, 2019–20. His research focuses on contemporary art, fashion and performance. He has published on intersections including Marc Jacobs and Olafur Eliasson, and Prada and Rem Koolhaas. He is currently at work on his dissertation, *Sheila Hicks: Weaving to the World*, the first critical history of the prolific weaver and pioneer of global contemporary art.

Eun Jung Kang is adjunct Professor at Sungkyunkwan University, South Korea, in the Department of Fashion Design. Her multidisciplinary research interests include fashion theory, critical theory, political theory and modern social theory. She has published works on fashion studies, philosophy, sociology, visual culture, gender studies, art and cultural studies. Her most recent book is *A Dialectical Journey through Fashion and Philosophy* (2020).

Myles Ethan Lascity is Assistant Professor at Southern Methodist University in the Division of Journalism and is Director of the Fashion Media program. His research focuses on the intersection of fashion, communication and consumer culture. He is the author of *Communicating Fashion: Clothing, Culture and Media* (forthcoming), co-editor of the volume *Consumer Identities: Agency, Media and Digital Culture* (2019), and his research has been published in various journals, including *Fashion Theory* and *Fashion Practice.*

Nigel Lezama, a specialist in critical fashion and luxury studies and nineteenth-century French literature, teaches at Brock University, Canada. In May 2017, he co-organized the conference 'Nouveau Reach. Past, Present & Future of Luxury', in Toronto, Canada. Some recent works: 'Re-thinking Luxury in the Museum Fashion Exhibition' (2020) appears in *Luxury. History, Culture Consumption*; 'Status, Votive Luxury, and Labour: The Female Rapper's Delight' (2019) in *Fashion Studies*; and 'Mo' Money, Mo' Problems: Hip Hop and Luxury's Uneasy Partnership' (2018) in *The Oxford Handbook of Hip Hop Music Studies*. His co-edited volume *Canadian Critical Luxury Studies. Recentring Luxury* (2021) is forthcoming.

Marcia A. Morgado has retired after thirty-five years on the faculty of the fashion program at the University of Hawai'i at Mānoa. Her publications explore semiotics and contemporary culture theories as frameworks for analyses of the social and cultural meanings of dress. Her most recent paper, 'Mormons in Paradise: The LDS Centennial Aloha Shirt' will appear in *Fashion, Style & Popular Culture*, volume 8.

The Rational Dress Society is a counter-fashion collective founded by **Maura Brewer** and **Abigail Glaum-Lathbury** in 2014. Together they produce JUMPSUIT, the ungendered monogarment for everyday wear. Brewer received her MFA from the University of California Irvine and is a Whitney Independent Study Program Fellow. Glaum-Lathbury received her BFA from the School of the Art Institute of Chicago where she is currently Assistant Professor of Fashion

Design. JUMPSUIT has received several grants including a 2016 CEDF fellowship from the Center for Cultural Innovation in Los Angeles. It has been presented at venues including MoMA, the Museum of Arts and Design and Art in General in New York, and the MCA in Chicago. Press includes CBS National News, CBC's The Current, *Guardian* and *Paris Review*.

Andrew Reilly is Professor of Fashion Design and Merchandising at the University of Hawai'i, Mānoa. His research focuses on dress and appearance-related issues of gender and sexuality. His recent books include *Crossing Gender Boundaries: Fashion to Create, Disrupt, and Transcend* and *Introducing Fashion Theory: From Androgyny to Zeitgeist.* He is the editor of *Critical Studies in Men's Fashion.*

Dennita Sewell is the founding Professor of Practice at Arizona State University's BA Fashion program and served as Phoenix Art Museum's curator of fashion for nearly two decades. She has organized more than fifty exhibitions on subjects ranging from motorcycle jackets to haute couture designers. Her publications include *Isabelle de Borchgrave: Fashioning Art from Paper*, *Fashion Independent: The Style of Ann Bonfoey Taylor* and *Extending the Runway: Tatiana Sorokko Style.*

Iqra Shagufta Cheema is a doctoral candidate in the Department of English at the University of North Texas. Her research interests focus on postmodernity and postmodernism, South Asian postmodernist literature, postmodernist feminism and Islamic feminism.

ACKNOWLEDGEMENTS

José Blanco F. and Andrew Reilly wish to express their deep gratitude for each of the authors for their time and efforts to researching and writing their chapters. They also wish to thank the anonymous reviewers for the thoughtful and constructive comments, as well as the staff at Bloomsbury Visual Arts, especially Yvonne Thouroude.

Andrew thanks Marcia Morgado for her advice and mentorship at the beginning of his career and her initial exploration of post-postmodernism and dress. He also thanks his friends and family for their continued support, especially his dog Holly.

José wants to acknowledge the input received about this topic in conversations with friends and particularly faculty and students at Dominican University and thank, once again, Raúl J. Vázquez-López for his support and help with editing every one of his projects in the last nineteen years.

INTRODUCTION

Andrew Reilly

Two hundred years ago the Industrial Revolution ushered in mass production and increased the availability of manufactured clothing against a backdrop of shifting gender relations and social practices. One hundred years ago clothing trends in the West were dictated by famed designers who created styles for their elite clientele against a backdrop of social and cultural rules and expectations that governed appearances. Sixty years ago, those rules were upended, questioned and reformulated as street style and the Youthquake changed the landscape of fashion and style. Today, we see globalization, technology, branding and excessive consumption changing the purposes, uses and creation of clothes.

The zeitgeist, or sprit of the times, reflects the cultural, social and technological milieu at a given point and place in time. Dress, and especially fashion, is a reflection of the zeitgeist by virtue of who wears what, when, why and how. Dress, the totality of appearances, including body modifications and supplements (Roach-Higgins and Eicher, 1992), can become fashion, a trend among groups of people for a particular length of time until its popularity dissipates and vanishes. Fashion is seen as reflecting the modern, the contemporary, the here-and-now and the zeitgeist in three broad eras known as modernity, postmodernity and post-postmodernity.

The European modern era is divided into early and late periods. The early period beginning in the sixteenth century included notable changes such as the European Renaissance, European voyages and conquering of lands in the 'New World' and a move from magic, myth and speculation to scientific methods; the later modern era is widely recognized as having roots in the Industrial Revolution which heralded an era of manufacturing and industrial capitalism and saw the emergence of mass production, social equality movements, unionization and mass media (Dunan, 1964; Habermas, 1983; Snyder, 1988; Vattimo, 1988; Seidman, 1990).

The modern Western fashion industry is an outcome of the late modern period via mass production of clothing (Wilson, 1985) and served as social capital to mark social class and to display wealth and status. Fashion, in this context, was explained most notably by Simmel's (1904) Trickle-Down Theory which posited style change as a function of imitation and differentiation where the uppermost class wears a style or item of dress that is copied by the adjacent lower class, which is then adopted by subsequently lower classes, at which point the uppermost class originates a new style and the cycle begins anew. Of course, other theories also explained fashion change during this time; for example, Theory of the Shifting Erogenous Zones (Laver, 1937, 1969) and Historical Continuity theory (Kroeber, 1919). Fashion also served a conspicuous consumption motivation for the new, emerging middle and upper classes to display their new-found wealth through clothes, jewellery, make-up and accessories (Veblen, 1992). Fashion in the modern context was defined by rules and regulations of how to dress and behave based on one's gender, class and occupation. Manuals, books and advice columns provided guides for appropriate garments to wear for different seasons; proper colour and pattern combination; and suitable ratios of balance and proportions to one's figure. As a result of mass production, department stores, like Bon Marché in Paris, Harrods in London and Macy's in New York City, emerged in the last century to showcase a bevy of luxurious, desirable goods to consume.

However, by the middle of the twentieth century the rules that allegedly governed society were being questioned and started to break down, in what has become known as the postmodern era. Events included the assassinations of civil rights leaders, the emergence of neocapitalism and national independence movements around the world that were against a backdrop of racial, gender and sexual civil rights movements that questioned and challenged the establishment. Morgado (1996) connected tenets of postmodernism – rejection of authority, suspicion of narratives, death of progress, end of history and regime of the simulacrum (e.g. Jameson, 1984; Connor, 1989; Lyotard, 1990; Baudrillard, 1994) – to explain dress and fashion trends that included irony, recycled looks, violation of aesthetic rules, pastiche, parody and appearance for the sake of appearance rather than for symbolism or meaning. Ensembles of this time merged high-end and low-end garments, vintage reproductions and appropriated elements from racial, ethnic, sexual and disadvantaged groups of people. Fashion trends were now also explained by the Trickle-Up Theory (Field, 1970) as street style often became the inspiration for the fashion industry (Polhemus, 1994) and business focused on creating brand identities to link lifestyle and values to their consumer products (Okonkwo, 2007).

And again, as the last millennium gave way to a new one, scholars identified new facets of life and society that were dramatically different from before. Markers of this new era included globalization, Web 2.0, attention to the impact of humans upon the environment and rampant consumer debt. What to call this new era varied according to the scholar. Bourriaud ([1998] 2002, 2009) called it *altermodernism* and characterized it as resistance against standardization and commodification as well as the erasure of the artist's identity in works of art.

Lipovetsky (2005) called it *hypermodernity* and characterized it as excessive consumption mixed with anxiety and fear. Samuels called it *automodernity* (2008) and characterized it as combining digital technology with human autonomy. Kirby (2009) called it *digimodernism* and characterized it as haphazard, fluid and multiple authored. Eshelman (2008) called it *performatism* and characterized it as double framing, transcendence and erasure of cultural categories. Vermeulen and van den Akker (2010) called it *metamodernism* and characterized it as expressed in naivety and idealism. Morgado (2014) used the term post-postmodern as an all-encompassing moniker and applied these theses and concepts to dress. As a result she speculated that features of this new era include: sustainable and ethical textiles and fashions; mass customization where consumers can create unique products from a preselected assortment of features; excessive fashion consumption combined with anxiety over the environment and personal debt; cyborg fashion; haphazard aesthetics; collaborations between upscale and downmarket brands and retailers; blurred distinctions between fashion and art; and gender-nonconforming appearances.

Although some scholars have begun to explore the connection between post-postmodern theory and dress, there is still much more to learn and understand. *Fashion, Dress and Post-postmodernism* seeks to investigate this line of inquiry further and offers chapters that explore topics of time and meaning, expensive ordinary clothes, frenzied aesthetics, contemporary branding practices, South Asian political–religious–cultural dress practices, film and fashion, novel fashion exhibitions, counter-fashion, and self-reflection.

To begin, Marcia A. Morgado's chapter, 'Fashion phenomena and the post-postmodern condition: Inquiry and speculation', is reprinted to provide the reader with an overview of five prominent post-postmodern theories and their possible relationship to dress and the fashion industry. Her work is referenced throughout this book and provides a starting point for many of the following chapters.

In 'Fashion, subjectivity and time: From Deleuze's transcendental empiricism to Lipovetsky's hypermodernity', Eun Jung Kang explores the current unrestrained state of fashion and argues that due to the disintegration of traditional social structures, like class, people are unsure of, and in search of, their identities. She invokes Deleuze's argument that the mind is a 'collection of ideas' and the self a collection of habits, which are related to time. But if all is repetition, how does something new emerge? Kang further invokes the concepts of imagination, boredom and accelerated time and links them to Lipovetsky's views on hyperconsumption. She argues that fashion not only provides the newness the self seeks via pleasure and novelty but also allows consumers a moment of autonomy by searching for experience in an era when time is very limited and everything is characterized as urgent.

In 'With no twist: The metamodern sartorial statement of Vetements', Alla Eizenberg uses van den Akker and Vermeulen's (2010, 2015) concept of metamodernism to analyse the French fashion house Vetements. Eizenberg argues that 'If the postmodern deployment of the ordinary … intended to defy, metamodern fashion, in contrast, romanticizes it, underlining its rich cultural significance and the emotional value resonating with the drive for unity, inclusivity, and sincerity that once again become relevant', and she uses designer renditions of wardrobe staples (e.g. T-shirts, jeans) as evidence. In her analysis of Vetements, Eizenberg questions why the ordinary has become luxury and makes connections to Soviet communism, collective memory and class.

Like Eizenberg, Nigel Lezama also analyses brand aesthetics in 'Intensified: Alessandro Michele's hyperaesthetic at Gucci'. Lezama invokes Jeffrey Nealon's critique of the economy in the current era and Lipovetsky's hypermodern thesis and notes the complex and seemingly random styling of garments, use of historic and syncretic symbols, and reimagination of the Gucci logo, which characterize Michele's work 'at Gucci [and] draws from the brand's archives and codes, as well as global fashion history and style tribe practices'. And that 'it is the juxtaposition and intercalation of these codes that deregulates the social meaning of the commodity, in an analogous way to capital's deregulation through the financialization of the economy'.

Myles Ethan Lascity also utilizes Lipovetsky's hypermodern thesis in 'Hypermodern branding: The case of Uniqlo', but turns his attention to the fast fashion giant. How can global fashion companies compete in a time when trends last mere weeks and the time to identify, design, source, manufacture, distribute and market new items may be longer than the trend itself? Lascity argues that fast fashion can work in fast-changing times by focusing on simplicity, quality, comfort and technologically advanced textiles, while also employing marketing that is localized and socially aware. Note how this links to Eizenberg's chapter on staple/ordinary clothes becoming luxury items.

Iqra Shagufta Cheema also employs Lipovetsky's hypermodern argument as well as Bourriaud's altermodern and Samuel's automodern theses in 'Post-postmodernity and South Asian Muslim women's fashion'. Shagufta Cheema argues that the post-postmodern era provides more agency in dress choices for Muslim women. With a history of colonialization and Western appropriation of Indian and Pakistani clothing, she posits that South Asian women fuse contemporary and traditional dress styles (past and present, European and Asian) to restore dignity to the clothes and people. This practice also provides women the ability to contest with institutional patriarchy and to express their individuality. Shagufta Cheema also highlights that global brands are exploiting the South Asian Muslim labour markets while at the same time catering to Middle Eastern Muslim markets.

Grant Johnson turns our attention to film and fashion in 'Lights, camera, fashion: From designer to director in Tom Ford's *A Single Man* and *Nocturnal Animals*'. Using Eshelman's (2008) concept of performatism, Johnson analyses

Tom Ford's directorial and sartorial expressions arguing that both films employ Eshelman's locked-frame narrative device with the designer-director as god-like author who imbues his characters and sets with tasteful sartorial judgements. According to Johnson, these have more than a passing resemblance to Ford's own life. Johnson highlights the nature of camp, queer sensibilities and 'how fashion evidences, constructs, and complicates greater definitions of cultural authorship' at a time when boundaries between fiction and life are blurred or downright eradicated. This chapter provides a solid addition to the link between dress and performatism and also connects to the next chapter via the role of authorities.

In 'Seeing selves: The absent body in the museum and the work of exhibition maker Judith Clark' Caroline Bellios analyses how contemporary fashion exhibitions by Judith Clark move beyond the traditional static display of garments on mannequins. Bellios details how Diana Vreeland radically changed fashion exhibitions in the postmodern era from chronology to spectacle, and that the inventive present-day methods practiced by Clark move beyond 'the ambivalence of postmodernity' to employ engagement with clothes by conjuring 'viewer's personal associations and memories, [and] their willingness to bring part of themselves to the story essential to creating a new multivalent language for fashion exhibitions'.

In 'The Post-postmodern fashion exhibition', Dennita Sewell continues to tie post-postmodern theory to fashion exhibitions with an overview of noteworthy installations that represent theories covered in this book including altermodernism ('The Future Is Now', 'Scraps: Fashion, Textiles and Creative Reuse', 'Fashioned from Nature'), hypermodernity ('Dior: Form Paris to the World'), performatism ('Balenciaga: Shaping Fashion', 'The Fashion World of John Paul Gaultier: From Sidewalk to Catwalk'), automodernity ('Iris van Herpen: Transforming Fashion', 'New Nomads') and digimodernism ('blog.made: addressing fashion', 'Items: Is Fashion Modern?'). She adeptly ties Morgado's analysis of post-postmodern fashion to museum exhibitions and concludes with 'Ultracontemporary', an exhibition that encompasses all five of these theoretical concepts. Sewell's work 'support[s] pause for thought about the contribution of fashion exhibitions to the cultural zeitgeist of the 21st century' and how the meaning and interpretation of fashion are changing.

In 'Counter-fashion as critical practice', Abigail Glaum-Lathbury and Maura Brewer of The Rational Dress Society argue that 'counter-fashion is a strategy for developing alternatives to the current fashion system' which produces a continual outpouring of new clothes despite the ecological and human disasters that result. They highlight their own work with an ungendered monogarment (JUMPSUIT), unisex clothing by Fawn *Kreiger* (OUTFIT), Sky Cubacub's personalized creations (Rebirth Garments) and Marloes ten Bhömer's experimental shoes as alternatives to the current system. These examples reflect features of the post-postmodern condition. Morgado (2014) speculated that sustainable and ethical fashion is an extension of altermodernism (Bourriaud, 2009). Specifically, Bourriaud argued against standardization and commodification, and while Glaum-Lathbury and Brewer's monogarment and Fawn Kreiger's collections are standardized in their design, they argue they can be adapted to different body types and they are not commodified; rather they are intended to reduce waste and promote sustainability. JUMPSUIT, OUTFIT, Rebirth Garments and Marloes ten Bhömer's shoes also reflect the concept of performatism (Eshelman, 2008) as erasure of cultural categories such as sex, gender, class and ability.

And finally, co-editor José Blanco F. explores how the theories of post-postmodernism apply to his life in 'Entropy, fashion and post-postmodernism: Auto-ethnography of a book editor'. Blanco F. uses a self-reflective method to apply the frameworks to his experiences from growing up in Costa Rica, moving to the United States as a student, learning how to perform his Latin identity in his new home and now as an associate professor. Through this he employs van den Akker and Vermeulen's (2010) metamodernism, Bourriaud's (2009) altermodernism, Lipovetsky's (2005) hypermodernity and Eshelman (2000–1) performativity. He ties together these theories, concepts and frameworks with this book's chapters as a way to explore his own identity and lived experience.

In all, *Fashion, Dress and Post-postmodernism* provides a beginning point for the further study of the emerging era and its relationship to how, why and who adorns the body and the sociocultural forces that influence and reflect such decisions. We hope that this collection will inspire students and researchers to explore post-postmodernism in the study of dress and fashion and provide critiques and scholarship on this new epoch.

References

Baudrillard, J. (1994), *Simulacra and Simulation,* Ann Arbor: University of Michigan Press.
Bourriaud, N. ([1998]/2002), *Relational Aesthetics* (Trans. Simon Pleasance and Fronza Woods), Dijon, France: Le Presseus Dureel.
Bourriaud, N. (2009), *Altermodern*, London: Tate.
Connor, S. (1989), *Postmodern Culture: An Introduction to Theories of the Contemporary*, Oxford: Basil Blackwell.
Dunan, Marcel (1964), *Larousse Encyclopedia of Modern History, from 1500 to the Present Day*, New York: Harper & Row.
Eshelman, R. (2000–1), 'Performatism, or the End of Postmodernism', *Anthropoetics*, 6 (2).
Eshelman, R. (2008), *Performatism or the End of Postmodernism,* Aurora, CO: Davies Group.
Field, G. A. (1970), 'The Status Float Phenomenon: The Upward Diffusion of Innovation', *Business Horizons*, 13(4): 45–52.

Habermas, J. (1983), 'Modernity – An Incomplete Project, trans. S. Ben-Babib, in H. Foster (ed.), *The Anti-Aesthetic: Essays on Postmodern Culture*, 3–15, Seattle, WA: Bay Press.

Jameson, F. (1984), 'Postmodern, or the Cultural Logic of Late Capitalism', *New Left Review*, 146: 53–92.

Kirby, A. (2009), *Digimodernism: How New Technologies Dismantle the Postmodern and Reconfigure Our Culture*, New York: Continuum International.

Kroeber, A. (1919), 'On the Principle of Order in Civilization as Exemplified by Changes in Fashion', *American Anthropologist*, 21: 235–63.

Laver, J. (1937), *Taste and Fashion*, London: Dood Mead.

Laver, J. (1969), *Modesty in Dress: An Inquiry into the Fundamentals of Fashion*, Boston: Houghton Mifflin.

Lipovetsky, G. (2005), *Hypermodern Times*, Cambridge, MA: Polity Press.

Lyotard, J.-F. (1990), 'The Postmodern Condition', in J. C. Alexander and S. Seidman (eds), *Culture and Society: Contemporary Debates*, 330–41, Cambridge: Cambridge University Press.

Morgado, M. (1996), 'Coming to Terms with Postmodern: Theories and Concepts of Contemporary Culture and Their Implications for Apparel Scholars', *Clothing and Textiles Research Journal*, 14 (1): 41–53.

Morgado, M. A. (2014), 'Fashion Phenomena and the Post-postmodern Condition: Enquiry and Speculation,' *Fashion, Style & Popular Culture* 1 (3): 313–39.

Okonkwo, U. (2007), *Luxury Fashion Branding: Trends, Tactics, Techniques*, New York: Palgrave Macmillan.

Polhemus, T. (1994), *Streetstyle: From Sidewalk to Catwalk*, London: Thames & Hudson.

Roach-Higgins, E., and J. B. Eicher (1992), 'Dress and Identity', *Clothing and Textiles Research Journal*, 10 (4): 1–8.

Samuels, R. (2008), 'Auto-Modernity after Postmodernism: Autonomy and Automation in Culture, Technology and Education', in T. McPherson (ed.), *Digital Youth, Innovation, and the Unexpected*, 219–40, Cambridge, MA: MIT Press.

Seidman, S. (1990), 'Substantive Debates: Moral Order and Social Crisis – Perspectives on Modern Culture', in J. C. Alexander and S. Seidman (eds), *Culture and Society: Contemporary Debates*, 217–35, Cambridge: Cambridge University Press.

Simmel, G. (1904), 'Fashion', *International Quarterly*, 10: 130–50.

Snyder, J. R. (1988), 'Translator's Introduction', in G. Vattimo (ed.), *The End of Modernity: Nihilism and Hermeneutics in Post-modern Culture*, vi–lviii, Cambridge: Polity Press.

Van den Akker, R., and T. Vermeulen (2015), 'Utopia, Sort of: A Case Study in Metamodernism', *Studia Neophilologica*, 87: 55–67. Available online https://tandfonline.com/doi/full/https://tandfonline.com/doi/full/10.1080/00393274.2014.981964 (accessed 2 June 2018).

Vattimo, G. (1988), *The End of Modernity: Nihilism and Hermeneutics in Post-modern Culture*, Cambridge: Polity Press.

Veblen, T. (1992), *The Theory of the Leisure Class*, London: Transaction.

Vermeulen, T., and R. van den Akker (2010), 'Notes on Metamodernism', *Journal of Aesthetics and Culture*, 2. Available online http://www.aestheticsandculture.net/index.php/jac/article/view/5677/6304 (accessed 15 December 2012).

Wilson, E. (1985), *Adorned in Dreams: Fashion and Modernity*, Berkeley: University of California Press.

1

FASHION PHENOMENA AND THE POST-POSTMODERN CONDITION: INQUIRY AND SPECULATION

Marcia A. Morgado

References to the idea that we live in postmodern times are ubiquitous. Indeed, the term *postmodern* appears to be indiscriminately applied to virtually anything and everything. My Google search for the word in May of 2013 resulted in 10,400,000 hits and, among multitudinous other things, included references to postmodern bibles, texts on postmodern curriculum development, advertisements for postmodern kitchens and culinary preparations, postmodern urban planning guides, postmodern pornography and images purporting to depict postmodern families and postmodern pets. The search phrase 'postmodern fashion' alone generated 2,580,000 hits.

Scholarly works on postmodernism describe elements of its expression in art, architecture, literature, film, television, music and photography. And fashion figures prominently in the scholarly works as well (e.g. Baudrillard, 1976; Connor, 1989; Harvey, 1990). Appearance features such as intentional challenges to traditional aesthetic codes, disordered combinations of styles and fabrics, and disregard for traditional construction features and/or their relation to the body are interpreted as expressions of postmodern *rejection of authority* and *suspicion of narratives*. The influence of street styles and subcultures in setting fashion trends is understood as postmodern references to the *death of art* and *rejection of authority*. Looks and styles recycled from earlier periods are proposed as examples of postmodern assumptions regarding the *death of progress*. And appearances constructed on pastiche (i.e. imitation), parody and irony, along with concerns for image and appearance for their own sake, are interpreted as postmodern expressions of the *regime of the simulacrum* and the *random play of signifiers* (e.g. Morgado, 1996).

But a new body of theoretical work proposes that the postmodern era is waning – that conditions that characterized postmodernism are giving way to new circumstances and that a new cultural ethos is replacing the postmodern condition or is coming to occupy a place within or beside it. *Post-postmodern* is a catchall term for a variety of arguments that propose the end of the postmodern era and that describe new conditions as the defining influences on contemporary culture and social life. Because fashion figures prominently in theories of postmodern culture and because the postmodern characteristics associated with fashion appear to clearly substantiate Blumer's thesis that fashion reflects the spirit or zeitgeist of the times (1969: 283), I asked, What do theorists who propose the rise of post-postmodern culture have to say about fashion, style and appearance? And how do contemporary fashion phenomena reflect an emerging post-postmodern ethos? In this chapter I describe aspects of post-postmodern theory as detailed in the arguments of prominent theorists, and I extrapolate from these to speculate on how current fashion phenomena might be interpreted as reflecting a post-postmodern condition.

From postmodernism to a post-postmodern condition

Theories that address contemporary culture as representing a postmodern historical period are predicated on the idea that major transformations in social practices, economic conditions and artistic expressions have displaced the values, assumptions, behaviours and expressions that characterized the historical period identified with modernism. Two complementary theses address the underlying circumstances that precipitated the transformation from modern to postmodern times. One suggests that novel technologies and an altered socio-economic system gave rise to a new social order that broke with characteristics that defined modernism. The other proposes that a new, highly developed stage of capitalism resulted in global homogenization, fragmentation and altered ways of experiencing time and space and that this provided the bases on which postmodern culture rests (Best and Kellner, 1991: 3). These circumstances are played out in a postmodern cultural ethos characterized by a new recognition and valuing of diversity, multiculturalism, marginalized people and viewpoints, and a consequent denial of the values, truths, knowledge and ways of thinking that characterized white, male-dominated, Western culture in the modernist period.

A different set of conditions underlies the arguments of those who posit theories around the theme of an alternative or post-postmodern condition. Theorists point to a gamut of global crises, disruptions, upheavals and challenges that characterize the present and that signal a new cultural climate: a perilously endangered ecosystem, the threat of global climate change, global financial crises and an apparent inability to control financial systems, unstable political regimes, the collapse of global political centres and shifting geopolitical boundaries, the polarization of ethnicities and social classes, widespread adoption of genetic manipulations, advances in information and communications technology in general and the pervasiveness of Web2 platforms and the blogosphere in particular (e.g. Lipovetsky, 2005; Vermeulen and van den Akker, 2010).

A new vocabulary is also embedded in arguments surrounding the new cultural paradigm. The term *post-postmodern* is one of at least a dozen labels evident in scholarly works that address a new cultural milieu and/or that serve as tongue-in-cheek appellations for arguments regarding a new cultural ethos. Among these are: *altermodernism* (Bourriaud, 2009), *off-modernism* (Boym, 2010), *semi-post-postmodernism* (Davis, 2010), *trans-utopianism* (Epstein, 1997), *performatism* (Eshelman, 2008), *post-millennialism* (Gans, 2000), *digimodernism* (Kirby, 2009a), *pseudomodernism* (Kirby, 2006), *hypermodernity* (Lipovetsky, 2005), *automodernity* (Samuels, 2008), *post-postmodernism* (Turner, 1995) and *metamodernism* (Vermeulen and van den Akker, 2010).[1] Of these, popular culture scholar Alan Kirby identifies five as the foremost theories of the post-postmodern (2010): Bourriaud's thesis on *altermodernism*, Lipovetsky's proposal on *hypermodernity*, Eshelman's discussion of *performatism*, Samuels's argument on *automodernity* and Kirby's own argument on *digimodernism*.

In the discussion that follows I summarize the five theories identified by Kirby as the foremost post-postmodern works, and I provide examples of each theorist's application of theory to relevant creative works or cultural practices. I extrapolate from these materials to suggest how contemporary fashion phenomena (i.e. fashion-forward trends in clothing, accessories, appearance styles and related consumer behaviours and marketplace practices) might be interpreted as expressing the post-postmodern characteristics addressed in each theoretical account. Extrapolation is necessary because, from the outset, a conundrum is evident: although fashion, style and appearance figure prominently in theories surrounding postmodernism, and although some scholars write that post-postmodern theory tends to focus on 'peripheral' and 'seemingly trivial' issues such as fashion (Ritzer and Yagatich, 2012: 104), fashion – as incoming trend or popular dress form – is rarely addressed in the works on post-postmodernism that Kirby identifies. While all five theorists describe aesthetic or otherwise expressive characteristics of a post-postmodern cultural milieu, examples are drawn from virtually every field of creative endeavour other than contemporary trends in dress and appearance. Features of painting, photography, architecture, literature, film, TV, video games and social media are addressed (e.g. Bourriaud, 2009; Boym, 2010; Davis, 2010; Kirby, 2009a; Vermeulen and van den Akker, 2010). But nothing is said of how the expressive characteristics of post-postmodernism play out in popular forms of dress and appearance.

Sustainable and collaborative fashion as altermodern practice

Altermodernism is the name Bourriaud assigns to an emerging 'modern' culture and to a form of artistic practice through which that culture is both formed and expressed (2009: 37). His thesis, initiated in *Relational Aesthetics* (1998/2002) and developed in *The Radicant* (2009) and in the *Altermodern* exhibition he curated for the Tate Triennial in 2009, is that the primary goal of altermodern artistic practice is to further the dissipation of postmodernism while creating a new cultural space for the development and appreciation of a global art.

According to Bourriaud, the primary influences on contemporary life are globalization, commodification and standardization. Altermodern art resists the pressure to accept these conditions; it acts as 'a weapon against cultural standardization' (2009: 76). This is accomplished through works that exhibit global cooperation by making meaningful connections between artistic traditions (30); that 'enable disparate elements to function together' (43); that 'transcend existing cultural codes' (40); and/or that indicate that the artist is engaged in the breakdown of rigid identities – identities that reveal nationality, social class, culture, geography, historical origin and/or sexual orientation (43).

The *radicant* is a metaphor Bourriaud employs to address the altermodern artist's approach to work in the context of globalization. A biological term, it describes plant species, such as ivy, that spread by digging new roots to absorb nutrients from the soil as they move to inhabit new locations (1). The altermodern artist, Bourriaud says, is a nomad, a wanderer, an immigrant, a tourist, an experimenter, an explorer who grows by advancing 'in all directions on whatever surfaces present themselves' (51). This artist is continuously engaged in spontaneous, dynamic, heterogeneous invention, negotiation and experimentation, uprooting and grafting the self (either physically or virtually) to create works that result from their interactions and temporary acclimations to any geographic, chronological or cultural context (1; 52). The artist and the resulting works accomplish this by being 'more mobile than global capitalism' (52).

Among artists Bourriaud identifies as engaged in altermodern practice is one whose work involves manipulations of appearance. Marcus Coates creates installations and videos wherein he performs, becomes or otherwise takes the role of a shaman engaged in interactions with animals and birds in their natural habitats. The interactions involve Coates in using heads, hides and the stuffed bodies of these creatures as robes, headpieces and accessory-like elements integrated with his own contemporary clothing. In this garb he engages in communication with the natural world, replicating the movements and vocalizations of the animals whose parts he wears and whose spirits he engages.

Coates explains these performances as consultations through which he asks for and then interprets advice he receives from the animals on human problems and global issues (Griffin, 2007). An example, included in the Tate Triennial *Altermodern* exhibition, is Coates's 2008 composition *Firebird, Rhebok, Badger and Hare*. Here Coates is attired in sunglasses, a stuffed badger worn as a headdress and the head of a hare protruding from the zippered front of an iconic Adidas firebird track suit (Figure 1.1). At the Tate this work appeared in a video clip that was filmed in the office of an Israeli mayor, where Coates's performance

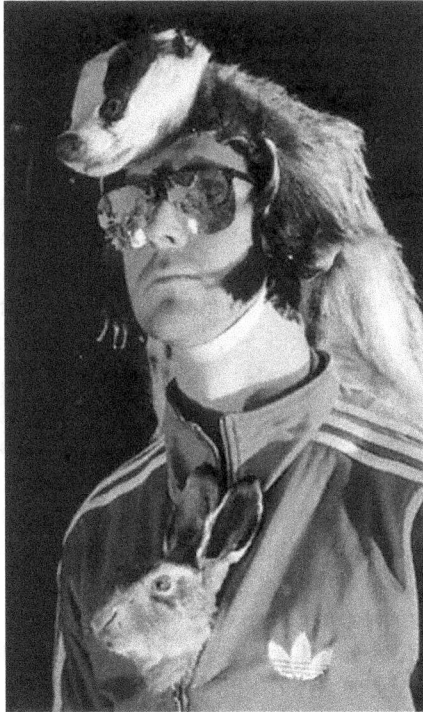

Figure 1.1 Marcus Coates, Firebird, Rhebok, Badger and Hare, 2008. Coates's work draws from his avocation as a naturalist and his concerns with learning and translating from the natural to the human environment. The social and environmental sensitivity evident in his artwork reflects characteristics Bourriaud attributes to the altermodern artistic practice. Parallel fashion phenomena are evident in contemporary concerns for sustainable fashion, organic textiles and environmentally friendly dyes. Image courtesy of the artist and Kate MacGarry, London.

was intended to generate advice from animal spirits on how the mayor should deal with the problem of youth crime (Whitby, 2009: 2).

Coates's work is visually bizarre: it appears to valorize the slaughter of wild animals for human garb. And viewing the video clip wherein he acts out and vocalizes shamanistic ritual (available at http://www.youtube.com/watch?v=BfBgWtAlbRc) is shocking in its suggestion of savage, primitive rites and sacrificial animals. However, these are surface images, and they are misleading. Coates is an ardent ornithologist, a naturalist and a deeply reverent and spiritual individual; his techniques are intended as a means of connecting with living animal and human spirits, of learning and translating from the natural to the human world. While some critics find his work reflects 'the superfluous nature of much contemporary art' (Whitby, 2009: 2), others read it as a subtle and sensitive means of generating reflection on the resolution of human issues and on the artist as 'problem solver' in the public sphere (Griffin, 2007: 3). Thus, his work illustrates Bourriaud's thesis of the altermodern artist as a voyager, an experimenter, a collaborator; as one who makes meaningful connections across traditions, who is engaged in negotiation and productive compromise and who enables disparate elements to work together.

I suggest we consider contemporary commitments to environmentally sensitive practices in the fashion industry, the development of sustainable fashion design programmes in higher education and rising interest in environmentally friendly fashion on the part of consumers as phenomena that parallel Coates's sensitivity to the natural environment and Bourriaud's thesis on negotiation, global cooperation and collaboration among disparate factions as evidence of altermodern practice. Concerns for sustainable fashion, the production of organic textiles and environmentally friendly dyes, the recycling and reuse of fashion apparel, and corporate policies on fair trade clothing depend on practices that are largely antithetical to the interests of global capitalism, and these fashion-related efforts speak to Bourriaud's proposal that an objective of altermodern practice is to build resistance to the effects of globalization.

In an earlier work, *Relational Aesthetics*, Bourriaud (1998/2002) introduces another idea that, while not directly addressed in the altermodern thesis, was influential in its development (Whitby, 2009: 2) and may be interpreted as relevant to post-postmodern fashion phenomena. Here he writes that *relational* art is a contemporary (i.e. 1990s) practice that is focused on 'the invention of models of sociability' (28). Sociability is a matter of building relationships: collaborations between the artist, the art works and the observers or viewers of these. He proposes that in relational art, viewers are a critically important component and that the works must be considered the result of collaborative relationships between artist and observers (15). These relationships are fostered in situations wherein the artist subdues or erases his/her presence by creating art that in no way reveals his/her geographic, cultural or social identity, thus leaving viewers to determine the meaning of the works. As an example, Bourriaud points to the works of Felix Gonzalez-Torres, a Cuban American artist, who is described as having 'largely distanced himself from identity politics and from any attempt to determine a reading of his work based upon (his) being gay or Hispanic' (McNamara, 2008). He uses simple, everyday materials and subjects, attempts to eliminate any indication that he has constructed the piece and invites audience participation by calling his works *untitled*. Thus, he leaves viewers to determine the works' meanings. Typical examples are his multiple versions of two ordinary, synchronized, side-by-side wall clocks.

A parallel can be drawn with current mass customization practices in the fashion industry. The internet offers a multitude of websites that invite creative shoppers to participate in the design of personal items by selecting from an array of preset style elements and colours that can be manipulated by the shopper. The result is neither an original artistic endeavour on the part of the consumer nor a unique undertaking on the part of company designers. Rather it is a shared undertaking. For example, New Balance-US (n.d.), an athletic shoe manufacturer, invites shoppers to '(m)ix and match colours on 15 separate areas of the shoe, using millions of different colour combinations'. Ypsilon, a specialty prom and pageant dress operation, offers young women the choice of thousands of interchangeable dress bodies, fabrications, necklines and sleeve styles through which to create individualized garments (Ypsilon Dresses, n.d.), and Wedding Dress Creator offers preset options for 'millions of possible combinations' of necklines, midriffs, silhouettes, lengths and colours (Design your wedding dress on-line, n.d.). The resulting constructions may be interpreted as akin to Bourriaud's thesis that relational artworks come about as shared activities, rather than result from an individual artist's effort.

Hypermodern fashion logic

In *The Empire of Fashion*, a text that preceded his publication on hypermodernity by a decade, Lipovetsky ([1987] 1994) argues that his theoretical account of fashion as a vehicle for the growth and support of democratic values and institutions has more explanatory power than does the proposition that fashion's primary function is to demonstrate social rank, status and class distinctions. Important for our purposes are two subsidiary themes developed in this early work: One is his suggestion that fashion has come to be the defining feature of contemporary social life. He writes, 'Fashion is no longer an aesthetic embellishment, a decorative accessory to collective life; it is the key to the entire edifice' (6), an edifice characterized by fashion-like qualities such as seduction, irrationality, superficiality, artificiality, evanescence, transience, ephemeralness and frivolity, qualities that 'have become the organizing principles of modern collective life' (6). A second theme emerges in what Lipovetsky describes as the paradoxical nature of our fashion-centred lives. In some cases paradox involves a simultaneity of seemingly incompatible social phenomena, such as an increase in large-scale poverty simultaneous with a phenomenal abundance of goods and services (246). In other cases paradox surrounds the displacement of one set of individual and social concerns for another. For example, he couples what he interprets as a decreasing interest in clothing fashions with an obsessive concern with body image, youthfulness, beauty, thinness and health and the goods, services and industries that have grown up around these: diets, health foods, health clubs, personal trainers, home exercise equipment, sports, skin creams, plastic surgery (244). It is these two themes – fashion-like characteristics of attractiveness and evanescence as 'the organizing principle' of contemporary life (6) and the accompanying paradoxes – that are the basis of Lipovetsky's more recent thesis on hypermodern times.

Lipovetsky's *Hypermodern Times* (2005) is the theoretical piece that Kirby (2010) identifies as one of the foremost theories of post-postmodernism. In the *Hypermodern Times* work, Lipovetsky's thesis is based on what he refers to as the principles of fashion, the fashion system and the logic of fashion (2005: 36–7). But in this text the references are not to contemporary dress forms. Rather, he uses characteristics associated with fashion as suggested in the earlier text – fashion as metaphor and the fashion process as a model – to describe how commercial practices; products and services; media techniques and contents; and consumer interests, concerns, behaviours and (adopted) identities have generated a post-postmodern 'mania for consumption' (32). The key features of hypermodern culture are 'galloping commercialization' (31) and excessiveness of everything (32). Hypermodernity is a 'society of hyperconsumption' (83). And it is driven by the principles of fashion: ephemerality, novelty, seduction, accelerated obsolescence and a passion for the new. Even non-economic aspects of life – personal identity, family, religion, work, education, sex and ethics – are driven by a fashion-oriented consumption mentality (84).

In hypermodern times, the pleasures derived from consumption are great, and people consume in excess to derive those pleasures. But paradox follows. The hypermodern individual is fraught with fear, anxiety, worry and insecurity: anxiety about pollution, the environment, climate change, the destruction of biodiversity (36–7); fear about global terrorism, natural and economic catastrophes, and personal health (39); insecurity about jobs and qualifications, about income and the possible loss of income. These, writes Lipovetsky, are the conditions of hypermodern times.

It is not difficult to consider our concerns with fashion in terms of Lipovetsky's thesis.

Excess, overabundance, frivolity and even irrationality characterize the plethora of available products and much of our behaviour in the marketplace.

Bejewelled cases and sparkling charms adorn cell phones, and add-on magnetic crystals add opulence to lampshades. Adorable fashion outfits – dresses, shorts, sweaters, T-shirts, hats, flannel hoodies and raincoats – are designed, marketed and purchased for dogs, along with jewelled collars – both faux and real. A dynamic, new industry with supporting university programmes in pet product design and marketing (e.g. Fashion Institute of Design, n.d.) stimulates frivolous expenditures on apparel and accessories for animal companions. In human accessory markets, oversized handbags and shoes are awash in decorative details: hardware, toggles, buckles, studs and eyelets; tassels, chains and fringe; multiple closures, multiple pockets and multiple straps. Embroidery, lacings, contrasting leathers, varied textures and multiple vivid colour combinations all suggest an abundance of excessive design details that align with a condition of excess.

In terms of the human garb, industry analysts report US apparel sales of $199 billion in 2011, an increase of 4 per cent over the previous year and greater than the sales of books, movies and music combined. E-market analysts report that '(o)nline sales of apparel and accessories are now growing faster than any other ecommerce product segment' (Apparel drives US retail ecommerce sales growth, 2012). Philpott (2012) reports that, in 1985, Americans bought an average of thirty-one items of clothing a year. But by 2012, that number had increased to sixty items per year. Other reports indicate that the average woman owns seven handbags (Lester, 2011), seven pairs of jeans (O'Reilly, 2010) and seventeen pairs of shoes (Hellmich, 2011). A columnist for *College Candy* writes, 'Gosh, jeans shopping is exhausting (because) we need a special pair of jeans for every (and I mean *every*) occasion: fat jeans, comfy jeans, old jeans, skinny jeans, more skinny jeans, going-out jeans, jeans for heels, jeans for flats, casual jeans, and trendy jeans' (Ten [10] pairs of jeans in every girl's closet, The, 2011). A spokesman for the NPD Group, Inc., a market research company that tracks data on consumer apparel purchases, reports that a condition described as the 'frugal fatigue phenomenon' appears to have materialized, as consumers have 'finally got(ten) back to building their wardrobes again' (Marshal Cohen, cited in NPD reports on the U.S. apparel market, 2012).

Excessive consumption of fashion-related items is certainly motivated by the pleasures of buying, owning and wearing, and these pleasures speak to the hedonistic impulse that Lipovetsky posits as characteristic of the contemporary ethos. When we consider that concerns for natural resources and the health of the ecosystem are also identified as conditions of post-postmodern culture, it's not difficult to project that hyperconsumption leads fashion-oriented consumers not only to experience pleasure in their purchases but also to feel anxious, fearful and concerned about their personal impacts on the environment.

Another contemporary form of excess with regard to fashion is evident in recent reports that indicate key fashion businesses such as H&M, Victoria's Secret and Walmart now make a practice of slashing, punching holes in and otherwise trashing their surplus inventories in order to prohibit stale-dated garments from reaching secondary markets (Riley, n.d.). Thus, we might amend Lipovetsky's thesis by aligning accelerated wastefulness and extraordinary resource abuse with post-postmodern fashion phenomena.

Fantasy fashion and sign appropriation as performative art

Eshelman's papers (2000/2001; 2005/2006; 2007/2008) and his text (2008) on performatism are concerned with identifying features of contemporary works of art, architecture, literature and film that characterize what he describes as a 'whole new epoch that is opposed to post-modernism and … is gradually coming to replace it' (2007/2008: 1). The elements that constitute *performative aesthetics* include interlocking frames, theistic plotlines, simple-minded subjects and manipulated interpretations. Eshelman's descriptions of these are slippery and obscure, and they are not evenly applied across artistic forms. However, his thesis is more-or-less easily grasped when considered in the context of familiarity with a typical performative work. Eshelman's clearest example is Yann Martel's novel *Life of Pi*, the film version of which is an adequate substitute. A summary of that work is followed by a discussion of the elements that constitute the aesthetics of performatism.

The central character in Martel's novel is Pi, a deeply spiritual, pan-religious young man disposed towards experiencing life as a series of phenomenal challenges and wondrous natural events. He has two stories to tell about the conditions that ensue when he is set adrift in a lifeboat with a zebra, an orangutan, a hyena and a Bengal tiger following a violent storm at sea. In one version, he recounts an uplifting and implausible tale of 227 days of terror, bravery, faith and courage at devising means of keeping the tiger fed and keeping himself alive in the face of both horrifying and wondrous natural and supernatural events. Challenged with the unlikely truth of the story, he provides a brutal and likely accurate second version wherein the animals are replaced with other humans who tear each other apart. He concludes by asking the challenger whether he prefers the beautiful, improbable story or the ugly truth. Eshelman's theoretical construct suggests that the first version of Pi's story is the one interpreters must accept.

The elements essential to performative aesthetics are *double framing*, *theistic plotlines* resolved through *transcendence*, *simple-minded subjects* with *authorial power* and interpretations manipulated by means of *locked frames*.

Double framing is an aesthetic device that facilitates a particular interpretation of works of art. It consists of an *outer frame*, or thesis, and an *inner frame*, which refers to the story or action. The *outer frame* contextualizes the action or the narrative. It is obviously artificial, implausible or absurd and generally involves some kind of conflict or violence (2008: 3). In Eshelman's *Life of Pi* example, the outer frame is the predicament into which Pi is violently thrown. The *inner frame* is the action described in the narrative; it is constructed so as to 'reduce(s) human behaviour to what seems to be a basic or elementary circle of unity with nature and/or with other people' (2008: 4). In Pi's story the inner frame is the narrative that describes encounters with horrendous lightning storms, lashing rain, mountainous waves, schools of flying fish, hordes of meerkats, carnivorous algae and a human predator, along with an abundance of extraordinary visual marvels and miraculous feats.

The narratives are constructed on *theistic plotlines*; they revolve around belief in the existence of a god (not necessarily Western or monotheistic) who created the world. One of five themes governs the plots: playing god; escaping from a frame; returning to the father (or mother); transcending through self-sacrifice; and perfecting the self (13). The action turns on the ability of the subject to transcend the context in which s/he is embedded. *Transcendence* may occur vertically, through passage to a higher level; horizontally, by sidestepping to a different frame; or holistically, by 'getting the right fit between subject and frame' (2000/2001: 13). In any event, it involves an aesthetic experience that generates a sense of beauty or feelings of goodness and human love. In *Life of Pi*, the dominant theme is escaping from a frame – that frame being the continuous life-threatening conditions into which Pi is thrown. The plotline, obviously theistic, revolves around Pi's spiritual nature: his pantheistic beliefs, prayers, inspirations and miraculous visions and the youngster's extraordinary accomplishments. Transcendence is central to the storyline: Pi transcends the horrendous and more plausible account of his experience by reframing it as an uplifting success story.

The central characters of performative works are *simple-minded subjects*; they are dumb, dumbed down (2000/2001: 3–4), opaque or dense (2008: 37). They appear oblivious to the contexts in which they are embedded and/or to be characterized by a kind of metaphysical optimism that sets them apart from the disturbing character of a context. Simple-minded subjects reveal their stories through first-person authorial narration: 'a narrator equipped with powers similar to those of an all-powerful, omniscient author forces his or her authoritative point of view upon us in what is usually a circular or tautological way' (2008: 19). The subjects also have *authorial power*, in that they can 'manipulate time, space, and causality for their own benefit' (2000/2001: 6). Pi's youth, religiosity, wonderment and unfailing optimism suffice as characteristic of a simple-minded subject, and his tale is clearly a fantasy that encourages readers to suspend disbelief.

In performative works the inner and outer frames (i.e. the thesis and the plotline) interlock to control how the viewer/observer/reader interprets the work. The *locked frames* manipulate or otherwise coerce interpreters to give up common understandings or to challenge previously understood categories. Further, the lock manipulates interpretation to the extent that the interpreter must believe in the narrative or image, even though s/he knows it is bizarre and irrational. In sum, Eshelman proposes that performative works 'demonstrate with aesthetic means the possibility of transcending the conditions of a given frame' (2008: 12). Although multiple reviewers of both Yann Martel's novel and Ang Lee's film version of the book are highly critical of Eshelman's proposition and refuse to suspend disbelief (e.g. Bradshaw, 2012; Kim, 2012), Eshelman maintains that interpreters must accept Pi's improbable, but beautiful tale rather than the horrendous, but more plausible account.

How might we extrapolate from Eshelman's thesis on performativity and its example in *Life of Pi* to parallel fashion phenomena? If we confine our extrapolation to the idea of the double frame with its artificial, absurd or implausible context and to the use of simple, dumbed-down characters with authorial power, and if we interpret the idea of transcendence in a more liberal way, it is possible to consider a recent fashion phenomenon in terms of Eshelman's analytic frame. The short film, *Electric Holiday*, a Christmas 2012 collaboration between Barneys New York and the Walt Disney Company (2012), is a performative work that revolves around the narrative theme of perfecting the self.

Projected on LED tiles that covered two stories of the exterior of Barneys high-end Madison Avenue store, the film features Disney cartoon characters reimaged as glamorous fashion models, and high-profile fashion industry celebrities reimaged as cartoon characters. The outer frame, or context, is Paris Fashion Week, as daydreamed by Minnie Mouse who gazes longingly at a Lanvin dress in a shop window. The context is doubly artificial; it's a non-realistic representation of an imagined locale in the mind of an anthropomorphized mouse. The inner frame, or action, involves the characters in preparing for, arriving at, participating in, observing and/or recording a Paris couture show.

The central character, the always adorable Minnie, might well be the poster child for optimism. In her dreams she is a fashion celebrity garnering the attention of the paparazzi and other high-fashion notables, all reimaged in caricature. With a sprinkling of magic supplied by Tinker Bell, Minnie imagines herself and her comic companions transformed into high-fashion models replete with idealized physical attributes and presentation styles and wearing couture designs on the Paris runway: Minnie in Lanvin, Mickey in Balenciaga, Daisy in Dolce & Gabbana and Goofy in Balmain (Iredale, 2012; Gallaher, 2012). The visual storyline and presentation techniques are clever and amusing, the cartoon characters charming, the caricatures delightful. And the story is, after all, a fiction. The resolution of the narrative is altogether satisfying and uplifting: when Minnie lets go of the dream, lovable Mickey appears bearing a kiss and a garment bag containing the Lanvin dress. And when Minnie dons the garment and looks into a full-length mirror, she is delighted with her 'real' appearance. At this moment, the inner and outer frames lock, allowing Ms. Mouse a moment of transcendence.[2]

More relevant to our concerns is Eshelman's discussion of the installation art staged by Italian-born, Los Angeles artist Vanessa Beecroft. Eshelman (2007/2008) describes Beecroft's installations as formulaic presentations, usually composed of a number of professional female models whose appearances have been unified through the use of body paint, wigs, makeup, nudity or identical outfits or clothing items. Beecroft arranges these living, mannequin-like figures in closed spaces, such as galleries or upscale fashion stores, and instructs them to hold their positions for hours at a time and not to interact with anyone (4). The performative features that Eshelman identifies in these works are the double frame, the erasure of categories through which the subjects can be interpreted and the direction in which an attempt is made to manipulate viewer response. In these works the outer frame appears to be either the space in which the installation is constructed or the psychological space wherein cultural information is carried. And the experience of transcendence involves the letting go of particular cultural categories rather than the experience of spiritual enlightenment. Eshelman maintains that the category erased in these performative works is not 'the constructedness of gender, but the constructedness of sex' (4). That is, the works challenge interpretation because the artist desexualizes her subjects.

Beecroft's works reference fashion in multiple ways. One is that reviewers interpret her performance pieces as replicating the aesthetics of a fashion photo shoot that has turned into a 'troubling flesh and blood spectacle' wherein models 'wear(ing) little more than garish wigs and killer heels (are) arranged in carefully composed clusters' (Making of colour guard: the Wallpaper* and Vanessa Beecroft collaboration, 2011). A second involves her collaboration with cutting-edge fashion houses such as Prada, Tom Ford and Imitation of Christ, which provide the fashion accessories and garments that Beecroft often uses in multiple replication as elements of her work (e.g. Thurman, 2003; Vanessa Beecroft, n.d.). And a third is in the novel twist she has imposed on relationships between art and fashion by staging her performance pieces in upscale specialty stores. We are accustomed to seeing collaborations that result in the works of upscale designers featured in museum and gallery shows. Less familiar, and perhaps post-postmodern in character, are collaborations such as those between Beecroft and fashion retailers that result in an artist's work showcased in the windows of fashion stores (Figure 1.2).

The challenges to and erasures of common cultural categories that Eshelman identifies with performative works are evident in contemporary appearance forms that effectively erase the male/female opposition. These new, dramatic looks combine typical masculine visual markers such as facial hair with very feminine appearance signs such as fluff and ruffles, peter pan collars and killer heels. Here there is no attempt at an androgynous mix, a blending of categories

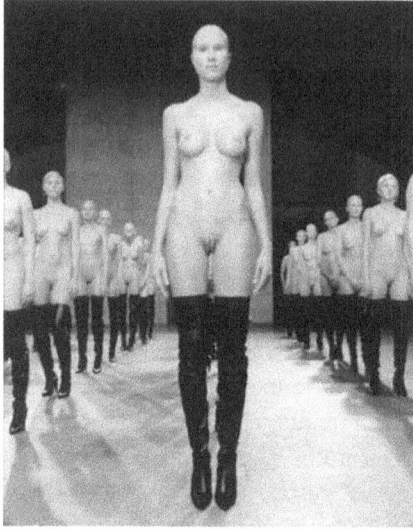

Figure 1.2 Vanessa Beecroft, VB45-007, DR, 2001. Eshelman identifies installations by Vanessa Beecroft as exemplifying characteristics of performatism. He posits that interlocking frames (i.e. context plus content) challenge viewers to disregard conventional cultural categories such as sex. But Beecroft's work also speaks to the heightened blurring of conventional boundaries between art and fashion. Image courtesy of Vanessa Beecroft.

Figure 1.3 A promotional photo shoot for the new Marc Jacobs beauty line at Sephora. The mix of obvious masculine and traditionally feminine visual markers is consistent with Eshelman's proposition regarding the challenge performative aesthetics brings to traditional understandings. © François Nars.

or the production of elegant dandy imagery. Rather, the combination of male and female signs works to destabilize the very idea of gender. Consider the recent Marc Jacobs photo shoot: a portrait shot of the obviously male designer effecting a typical female portrait pose, his masculine features enhanced with beautifully made up eyes, bright red lipstick and nail polish (Figure 1.3).

Or consider the daring looks assembled by Gregg Asher for his role as personal shopper on the Lifetime TV reality series *Million Dollar Shopper*. Clearly this is no attempt at cross-dressing, disguise, irony or humour. Rather, the appearance asks viewers to accept a masculine figure in dress and appearance forms designated as feminine (Figure 1.4).

Figure 1.4 Gregg Asher in a sequined Lanvin tunic, white Marc Jacobs trousers and Miu Miu high-heel sandals at the 2011 Art Ball sponsored by the Dallas Museum of Art. Asher's appearance style, which involves a mix of conventional masculine visual markers with conventional feminine appearance signs, parallels the challenge to commonly accepted categories that Eshelman identifies as an element of performative aesthetics. © My Sweet Charity.

Techno-fashion imagery as expression of automodernity

Samuels (2008) argues that the crucial element in automodern culture is the 'unexpected collusion' (228) of two opposing social forces: digital technology and human autonomy. His paper focuses on the effect that digital technology has on how 'digital youth' think and learn, and the issues this raises for educational methods. Samuels finds that immersion in contemporary technologies – personal computers, apps, digital games, iPods, blogs, Twitter, cell phones, remote-controlled TV, instant messaging and worldwide live chatting – as well as in the 'cultural realms' of the internet, movies, TV and advertising, in association with the prevalence of multi-tasking, has fostered a psychology that is not responsive to an educational model that relies on book learning, memorization and individual effort.

As an example, Samuels describes watching his 15-year-old nephew work on a paper for his high school English class. The assignment is to individually prepare a five-paragraph essay on a novel the class has just completed reading. Simultaneously open on the youngster's computer are Microsoft Word and a chat room wherein classmates are sharing their working drafts, a list of websites wherein the novel is discussed and an instant messaging programme that repeatedly signals incoming notes. The youngster is also consulting the novel, which is open on his desk. When questioned about who should ultimately be credited with completing the assignment, the youngster reminds Samuels that he is only collaborating on the research; that he still has to write the paper on his own. But he is simultaneously downloading a movie and is also engaged in playing an online interactive game with players from around the world. Samuels writes, 'He is thus multitasking at the same time as he is using multiple media to write his paper and entertain himself. If this scene is typical for many digital youth in the developed West, then these students may come to school with a radically different conception of writing and technology than their teachers have' (1–2).

The aspect of Samuels's argument that is relevant to the discussion of fashion is the thesis that the interaction between digital youth, digital technologies and contemporary media has resulted in a radical restructuring of what were previously assumed to be opposing social forces (219). Samuels writes,

> to understand the implications of how digital youth are now using new media and technologies in unexpected and innovative ways, we have to rethink many of the cultural oppositions that have shaped the Western tradition since the start of the modern era. To be precise, we can no longer base our analysis of culture, identity, and technology on the traditional conflicts between the public and the private, the subject and the object, and the human and the

machine. Moreover, the modern divide pitting the isolated individual against the impersonal realm of technological mechanization no longer seems to apply. (219)

Samuels's point is that for those immersed in contemporary technology, these sets of oppositions are not experienced as oppositions. Rather, technological automation is experienced as a vehicle of empowerment through which digital youth express their independence. Thus, the traditional opposition between automation and human endeavour has been undermined. Additionally, engagement in multitasking alters distinctions between work and play, while instant messaging (on an independent assignment) reconfigures distinctions between self and other. Furthermore, redistributing materials retrieved from the internet through chat rooms and emails upsets distinctions between public and private, while copying, pasting and sharing those materials without citing sources suggests an undermining of assumptions regarding property rights and plagiarism.

The most realistic examples of automodernity as expressed in fashion appearances are textiles, garments and accessories that integrate contemporary technology with wearable items. Sometimes referred to as cyborg or techno fashion, these include such things as fabrics infused with insecticides and sunscreen, garments that integrate solar cells, fibre-optic threads, LED lights, graphics and magnetic switches, and personal items such as computers, iPhones and GPSs strapped to the body or embedded in shoes and worn as accessories.

Visually arresting parallels with automodernity are also evident in the burst of creativity apparent in do-it-yourself appearances, accessories, home décor and artwork that has grown out of the appearance forms associated with cyberpunk and its steampunk derivative. Cyberpunk appearances are dark, sombre and are predicated on the theme of post-industrial dystopia with an attendant breakdown of the social order. They include elements of futuristic cyber-technology coupled with elements of punk and Goth. Steampunk appearances are likewise based on ideas involving human–technology interactions. But these appearance forms speak to the past, rather than the future. The general parameters involve a blend of neo-Victorian, neo-Edwardian and military styles accented with parts and pieces of retro technology (La Ferla, 2008: 2). Described as a profoundly romantic 'aesthetic expression of a time-traveling fantasy world inspired by the extravagantly inventive age of dirigibles and steam locomotives, brass diving bells and jar-shaped proto-submarines' (2), a steampunk appearance might consist of a gentleman's waistcoat with military trousers accessorized with aviator goggles, an antique flight helmet and a ray gun. Or corseted, bustled, balloon-sleeved gowns and high-button shoes accessorized with jewellery fashioned from recycled watch cogs (Figure 1.5). This paradoxical mix of the

Figure 1.5 Steampunk appearances, with their unusual blend of neo-Victorian, neo-Edwardian and military styles accented with parts and pieces of retro technology, reflect Samuels's thesis that digimodernism dissolves the opposition between automation and human endeavour. Wave Gotik Treffen, photo by Alexander Schlesier, Leipzig/Germany. Available at www.steampunker.de.

mechanical with the human and the historical with fantasy time travel appears nicely aligned with Samuels's description of automodernity's radical restructuring of opposing forces.

Digimodern fashion appearances, blogs and collaborations

Kirby's work addresses the 'exhaustion of postmodernism' (2009b) and its gradual replacement with new cultural and artistic forms predicated on the widespread adoption of digital technologies. His name for the emerging epoch is *digimodernism*, and he proposes that its revolutionary nature is most evident in Web 2.0 platforms – that is, in technology that allows user interaction with texts (e.g. video games, Wikipedia), or with each other (e.g. Facebook, Twitter, chat rooms, message boards, blogs), or that involve user-generated text (e.g. YouTube, self-publishing sites) (2009a). Kirby finds that the impact of digimodernism on aesthetics is emerging, but not yet clear. In its 'purest' form the content of digimodern texts is still 'up for grabs' (2009b), but it has the recognizable traits of evanescence, onwardness, haphazardness, fluidity, boundlessness and multiple authorship (2009a).[3]

It is not difficult to find parallel instances of haphazardness in contemporary appearances, one of which appears to be based on seemingly random mixes of garment styles, colours, textures and patterns. A recent edition of the fashion magazine *Elle* advises readers to 'Forget all the rules your mother taught you about coordinating an outfit. This is the season of the mismatch. Pile on clashing patterns and colours – the more aggressive, the better. Just don't tell Mom' (Dressing in the dark 2013: 196). Although the mixed and unmatched look is far more visible now than in the past, the dressing in the dark aesthetic has been with us for almost twenty years and is more clearly identified as a postmodern rather than a post-postmodern characteristic (e.g. Morgado, 1996).

On the other hand, the wildly imaginative, highly varied, seemingly cacophonous, yet carefully contrived imagery of Japanese street styles exhibit a novel and spectacular form of seemingly haphazard but nonetheless carefully constructed costume as street dress. Images variously play on mismatched sneakers, laces, stockings and tights; funky hats and handbags; outrageously mussed and coloured hair; bright, plastic beads and stuffed toys repurposed as charming fashion accessories; and brilliantly mismatched colours, textures, prints and garment styles. The exaggerated performance function of fashion and style, in conjunction with the haphazard visual effect of the presentations and the novel costume-as-street-dress approach, moves beyond the postmodern mixed and unmatched aesthetic and may be more aptly described in terms of digimodern or post-post-postmodern expressions (Figure 1.6).

Additionally, the introduction of decorative, bling-encrusted cases that have turned personal technology devices such as cell phones and tablets into the latest fashion accessories speaks to an instance of fashion as a reflection of digimodern concerns. Writing in a current edition of *Fast Company*, a business magazine that focuses on technology, business and design, reporter Daniel Rasmus writes that '(f)ashion now infuses the technology market' with 'cases that reflect lifestyle preferences, harmonize with clothing, and complement personality' (2013). At the January 2013 International CES consumer electronics and technology trade show in Las Vegas, Rasmus reports seeing 'hundreds, if not thousands, of cases, stands, button covers, skins, and other items to decorate and embellish' personal technology devices. These not only 'reflect current fashion, (but also) reflect the names of the upscale design house' (such as Louis Vuitton, Gucci, Jimmy Choo, Chanel, Alexander McQueen, Dior, Prada and Fendi) and the personality and lifestyle preferences of contemporary consumers. Rasmus notes that the latest addition to techno devices as fashion accessories

Figure 1.6 The charmingly haphazard visual effect and exaggerated use of fashion as costume in Japanese street styles reflect the evanescence, haphazardness, fluidity, boundlessness and perhaps even the multiple authorship that Kirby identifies with digimodernism. These unique expressions move beyond the postmodern mixed and unmatched aesthetic and may be more aptly described as post-post-postmodern expressions. Image © Tokyofashion.com.

is Lily Kwong's new LK accessory line, which features 'interchangeable bracelets that wrap around the edge of an iPhone 5 to bathe it in leather, gold or Swarovski crystal'. Prices for the combination case and bracelet start at $449 (2013).

The phenomenal growth of fashion blogs and the extraordinary influence of fashion bloggers also resonate as characteristic of digimodernism. Up-to-the-moment commentary, critique and photos of personal style, street styles, runway fashions and shopping and vintage finds are not only highly competitive with traditional fashion reporting media for both readership and trend-spotting leadership but have also altered fashion reporting techniques, the focus of fashion coverage and the character and prestige of key figures in fashion journalism and other fashion promotion venues. The immediacy and novelty of the observations, personal commentary and fashion images initiated by independent bloggers have both inspired and necessitated the addition of blog spots to the content of electronic editions of traditional fashion magazines and news reports and have made independent fashion blogs must-read material for fashion industry professionals. The focus of fashion runway coverage now includes the pre-show action – the uniquely attired posers outside the runway venues and the celebrity bloggers awarded front-seat positions in the shows (Menkes, 2013: 2–3). Among the most celebrated and visible personalities in the fashion limelight are bloggers such as Tavi Gevinson, who began an independent blog in 2008 at age 11, and Bryan Grey Yambo, who, under the pen name Brianboy, began blogging from home in Manila at age 24. Both have turned their blogs into big businesses with substantial corporate ties.

Bloggers have also initiated a new kind of content on fashion posts. Suzy Menkes, long-time fashion reporter and fashion editor for such papers as the *New York Times* and the *International Herald Tribune*, writes that in her early days of journalism, the 'mantra' she learned was 'It isn't good because you like it; you like it because it's good' (2013: 5). But bloggers have very different reporting objectives. Menkes writes that for bloggers 'judging fashion has become all about me: Look at me wearing the dress! Look at these shoes I have found. Look at me loving this outfit in 15 different images! Fashion has to some extent become mob rule' (2013: 5). But bloggers are now ubiquitous, and this is a regime to which the industry caters. Multiple mainstream publications now offer annual blogger awards. For example, *Marie Claire – UK*, a celebrity, fashion and beauty news publication, reports receiving thousands of nominations for their 2013 fashion blogger award (Best Fashion Blog and Twitter Feed Longlist, 2013). And *Signature9*, an electronic magazine that covers fashion, lifestyle, design and popular culture trends, reports reviewing some 5,000 current fashion blogs before selecting the 99 most influential for 2013 (Ninety-nine [99] Most Influential Fashion & Beauty Blogs, The, 2013). And *Cosmopolitan – UK* reports selecting its current Blog Award winner from over 43,000 entries (Cosmo Blog Awards 2013 Shortlist – Vote Here, 2013).

Other fashion-related phenomena parallel Kirby's description of the digimodern characteristic he calls *multiple authorship*. These involve novel collaborations across previously antithetical industry sectors – between upscale designer brands and downmarket retailers and between upscale and downmarket retailers.

An early collaboration between a luxury designer and a downmarket retailer occurred in 1983, when Halston initiated a collaboration that, to many in the fashion industry, signalled the inevitable demise of the upscale brand. Sold exclusively at JC Penney, the Halston III label was the first licensed fashion line to be developed by a high-end designer for a mass market retailer. The pairing proved unsuccessful. More recently, Isaac Mizrahi's collaboration with mass merchant Target appeared to be a clever marketing scheme designed to rescue the upscale line from bankruptcy. But the practice is now common, and more recent collaborative efforts between designer licensed brands and mass-market retailers are ordinary market expansion strategies, rather than attempts to salvage brands from possible demise. Vera Wang's Simply Vera collection is an exclusive line at the discount-priced Kohl's. Alexander McQueen, Zac Posen, Rodarte, Liberty of London and Jason Wu have all entered into cooperative arrangements with Target. The Missoni limited collection for Target, introduced in 2011, is reported to have sold out in a matter of minutes in several of the retailer's locations and to have generated so much online business that its website crashed multiple times (Kelly, 2011).

A collaborative effort without precedent in the fashion industry is the 2012 launch of a collection of designer apparel and home goods that was simultaneously promoted by and available from the luxury retailer Neiman Marcus and the mass market Target stores. The collection is promoted as appealing to their 'overlapping and cross-shopping' customer base and consists of identical merchandise carrying the names of high-end designers such as Tory Burch, Tracy Reese, Oscar de la Renta, Marc Jacobs and Carolina Herrera, with the goods available in the merchandise assortments of both Neiman Marcus' and Target's brick and mortar sites, as well as their online stores (Connor, 2012). These unusual industry collaborations might reasonably be interpreted as consistent with Kirby's thesis on the collaborative character of digimodern culture.

Salient elements of post-postmodern theories in theoretical works authored by Bourriaud, Lipovetsky, Eshelman, Samuels and Kirby and extrapolations from these to parallel fashion phenomena are summarized in Table 1.1.

Table 1.1 Post-postmodern characteristics and extrapolation to fashion phenomena

Theorist and Relevant Works	Theory	Salient Characteristics	Possible Parallel Fashion Phenomena
Bourriaud (2009), *The Radicant*. Bourriaud (2002), *Relational Aesthetics*	Altermodernism	• Artist resists standardization and commodification; fosters global culture in opposition to multiculturalism; engages in productive compromise • Artist's presence is submerged as works invite viewer/observer collaboration	• Sustainable fashion; organic and environmentally friendly textiles • Mass customization: preset options allow e-market consumers to collaborate in the design process

Theorist and Relevant Works	Theory	Salient Characteristics	Possible Parallel Fashion Phenomena
Lipovetsky (2005), *Hyper-modern Times*	Hypermodernity	• Hyperconsumption accompanied by anxiety and fear	• Excessive consumption of fashion goods; anxiety regarding environmental and/or personal consequences • Wastefulness: resource abuse
Eshelman (2008), *Performatism, or the End of Post-modernism*	Performatism	• Double framing; simple-minded, optimistic subjects; theistic plots; locked frames; transcendence • Erasure of cultural categories such as sexual orientation	• Cartoon characters portray fashion as vehicle for transcendence • Blurring distinctions between art and fashion • Integrated masculine and feminine appearance signs
Samuels (2008), *Auto-modernity after Postmodernism: Autonomy and Automation in Culture, Technology, and Education*	Automodernity	• Blending of digital technology and human autonomy • Challenge to assumptions re: property rights and plagiarism	• Techno and cyborg fashion integrate technology and apparel • Cyberpunk and steampunk appearances combine future and/or past techno-elements with punk, Goth and/or historic garb
Kirby (2009a), *Digimodernism: How New Technologies Dismantle the Postmodern and Reconfigure Our Culture*	Digimodernism	• Haphazardness • Multiple authorship • Infantilism	• Haphazard mixes of styles, prints, colours and textures • Cell phone and tablet cases as fashion accessories • Fashion blogs and bloggers democratize fashion reporting • Novel collaborations: upscale designers and downmarket retailers; upscale and downmarket retailers

Conclusion

Discussions of fashion, style and appearance have high visibility in scholarly works concerned with postmodernism. But some scholars posit that the postmodern period is exhausted, that new circumstances have altered the values, assumptions and behaviours that characterize contemporary life and that a new cultural paradigm has emerged. No consistent label has been devised for the emerging ethos, although the term *post-postmodern* is often used to represent it.

I examined works by Bourriaud, Lipovetsky, Eshelman, Samuels and Kirby, who are identified as the foremost theorists of post-postmodernism, and found attention given to fashion only as its use as metaphor for fashion-like characteristics such as superficiality, seduction and rapid obsolescence (i.e. Lipovetsky, 2005); in discussion of personal appearance only as a characteristic of the expressive mode of one particular artist (i.e. Bourriaud, 2009); and as an aspect of fashion business only in the use of a retail window display of an art installation (i.e. Eshelman, 2007/2008). Thus, I extrapolated from the theoretical works to speculate on how current expressions in fashion, appearance and related consumer behaviours and marketplace practices might be interpreted as reflecting a post-postmodern condition.

Some of my attempts to correlate fashion phenomena with theory fall short:

- Heightened consumption of fashion and fashion-related products is clearly evident, and the data regarding dress-related expenditures and the growth of new fashion products and markets directly tie into Lipovetsky's thesis on excess consumption (2005) as the primary feature of hypermodern times. However, accelerated consumption of fashion goods is identified as a characteristic and necessary correlate of postmodern *fast fashion*, the production and distribution strategy that provides a continuous stream of new fashion trends to replace the fashion-value of existing goods very quickly and at very low prices (Harvey, 1990: 156–285). Thus, the attempt to identify heightened consumption of fashion-related goods as a characteristic of post-postmodernism fails.

- While novel upscale–downmarket collaborations across fashion business and industry parallel Kirby's thesis on collaborative digimodern works (2009a), these are not more peculiar than was the decades earlier move of fashion retailers into product development and manufacturing, and the addition of fashion retailing to the business of apparel design and production. Nor are contemporary business collaborations particularly different from the postmodern 'cross shopper', who happily patronizes discount malls and mass market chain stores, as well as upscale retail operations.

- Although offered tongue-in-cheek, the extrapolation to the animated Disney/Barneys *Electric Holiday* video does appear to conform to the aesthetic characteristics Eshelman identifies with performatism (2008). But these traits have long been characteristic of animated films directed to juvenile audiences. Furthermore, it is difficult to escape reading the film as entirely predicated on irony – an interpretation that Eshelman clearly dismisses relative to performative works (e.g. 2000/2001).

Others of the extrapolations from post-postmodern theories to fashion phenomena are more convincing:

- The cooperative endeavours between fashion houses and consumers, as evidenced in mass customization 'Design your own' options available on internet sites, along with heightened consumer consciousness and industry practices directed towards sustainable and environmentally friendly fashion reasonably parallel the collaborative endeavours and global consciousness elements Bourriaud identifies with altermodernism.

- The retail practice of intentionally destroying surplus inventories in order to eliminate the possibility that stale-dated garments will reach secondary markets is relatively consistent with Lipovetsky's thesis regarding excessive consumption as a characteristic of hypermodern times. Of particular note here is that fashion changes now occur so rapidly that existing inventories may be considered stale dated when garments are little more than thirty to ninety days old.

- An increased blurring of distinctions between art and fashion, as evidenced in collaborations between artists and fashion designers and in the reconceptualization of retail spaces as venues for exhibiting artwork, appears consistent with Eshelman's thesis regarding performative works as sites wherein distinctions among commonly accepted cultural categories are erased.

- Contemporary appearance forms that integrate, without altering, contradictory masculine and feminine appearance signs provide additional support for both Eshelman's thesis on performativity and Bourriaud's proposition on altermodernism. Both point to the idea that post-postmodern aesthetics work to undermine rigid notions of identity and commonly understood cultural categories.

- Cyborg/techno fashions that literally integrate contemporary technology with textiles, garments, and accessories directly speak to Samuels's proposition (2008) regarding automodernity's radical restructuring of human relationships with technology. And cyberpunk and steampunk appearances, with their unusual integration of design and accessory elements predicated on futuristic cyber- or retro-technology and coupled with elements of punk, Goth and/or Victorian and Edwardian fashions, also nicely align with Samuels's automodernity thesis.

- Although the seemingly haphazard mix of styles, colours and prints evident in contemporary fashion appearances clearly mirror elements that Kirby associates with digimodern aesthetics, this expression in fashion is likely an exaggeration of similar postmodern appearance features. However, the introduction of decorative cell phone and tablet cases as fashion accessories is novel and in keeping with Kirby's ideas regarding an emerging digimodern culture.

- It is certainly the case that bloggers, with their impact on fashion trends, their elevation to celebrity status, their influence on mainstream fashion media and the integration of blogs with mainstream fashion enterprise, support Kirby's proposition that user-generated texts such as blogs are a distinctive feature of the new cultural ethos.

In sum, the extrapolations suggest that there is reasonable evidence that contemporary fashion phenomena reflect characteristics described in Bourriaud's thesis on altermodernism, in Eshelman's description of performative aesthetics, in Lipovetsky's discussion of hypermodern times, in Samuels's premises on automodernity and in Kirby's proposition on digimodernism.

Ample criticism is directed towards theories regarding the postmodern precursor of post-postmodernism. In addition to assessments of postmodernist theories as vacuous and unintelligible (Dawkins, 2003) and as ill-defined and inappropriately applied to everything, critics point to the lack of consistency among varied postmodern theories, the contradictions within these, the absence of grounded concepts, the breadth of subjects claimed as exhibiting postmodern characteristics, the lack of historical grounding for the premises and largely about the boredom that has followed on overuse of 'postmodern' as a buzzword (e.g. Davis, 2010). Neither is the idea that a post-postmodern sensibility has replaced postmodernism widely embraced. Critics argue that there has not been any real change from either the conditions that fostered or the characteristics that describe postmodernism and that present conditions simply appear to be some kind of intensification of the postmodern condition accompanied by 'the same old anti-historic academic bullshit' (6).

On the other hand, some who postulate the emergence of new post-postmodern conditions report that its features and ramifications are not yet clear (e.g. Bourriaud, 2009; Kirby, 2010). And whether we are witnessing the emergence of a new post-postmodern historical period, an intensification of postmodernism or the continuing development of modernity, it does appear that Blumer's thesis on fashion as a reflection of the zeitgeist (1969) remains operable.

Blumer's thesis is predicated on the idea of fashion as a process rather than a dress form. He posits that the recurring introduction of new models and the subsequent popularity of these is most clearly evidenced relative to (women's) dress, but that fashion is a generic feature, and perhaps 'one of the most significant mechanisms' of contemporary culture (283). The 'fashion mechanism' (282), he writes, is most likely to operate in circumstances wherein the introduction of new, competing forms is common; people are 'responsive to changes taking place in (the) world' and are interested in and open to embracing new social forms (286); and wherein prestige figures who promote or adopt the new forms are evident (287). Blumer's criteria neatly address characteristics that not only typify contemporary fashion-forward trends in clothing and appearance styles but also speak to consumer behaviours, marketplace practices and industry activities that surround contemporary fashion phenomena.

This chapter originally appeared in 2014 in *Fashion, Style and Popular Culture*, 1 (3), 313–39.

Notes

1 Oxford don Alan Kirby describes *post-postmodernism* as 'a vile term consecrated by Wikipedia' (2009a: 40).

2 *Electric Holiday* generated a hue and cry from critics who found the refashioned body images of cartoon characters inappropriate and insensitive, who were disturbed by the alteration of childhood icons and who faulted the film with sending the wrong messages to children.

3 Kirby additionally identifies *infantilism* as an obvious trait of digimodern culture, citing the form and content of contemporary film, popular music and television as particularly noxious (2009a: 124–65; 131).

References

Apparel drives US retail ecommerce sales growth (2012), eMarketer Newsroom, 5 April. Available online http://www.emarketer.com/newsroom/index.php/apparel-drives-retail-ecommerce- sales-growth (accessed 2 November 2012).

Baudrillard, J. (1976), *L'echange Symbolique et la Mort* [*Symbolic Exchange and Death*], Paris: Gallimard.

Best Fashion Blog and Twitter Feed Longlist (2013), *Marie Claire*. Available online http://www. marieclaire.co.uk/news/fashion/533781/best-fashion-blog (accessed 1 August 2013).

Best, S., and D. Kellner (1991), *Postmodern Theory. Critical Interrogations*, New York: Guilford Press.

Blumer, H. (1969), 'Fashion: From Class Differentiation to Collective Selection', *Sociological Quarterly*, 10: 275–91.

Bourriaud, N. (1998/2002), *Relational Aesthetics*, trans. S. Pleasance and F. Woods, Dijon, France: Les presses du réel.

Bourriaud, N. (2009), *The Radicant*, trans. J. Gussen and L. Porten, Berlin: Sternberg. Available online mission17.org/documents/NicolasBourriaud_Ch1altermodernity_pp25-77.pdf (accessed 10 February 2013).

Boym, S. (2010), 'The Off-Modern Mirror', *efflux*. Available online http://wws.e-flux.com/journal/the-off-modern-mirror (accessed 27 October 2012).

Bradshaw, P. (2012), 'Life of Pi – Review', *The Guardian*, 20 December. Available online http://www.guardian.co.uk/film/2012/dec/20/life-of-pi-review (accessed 29 January 2013).

Connor, E. (2012), 'Neiman Marcus-Target Designer Collection Launches on Saturday', *The Record*, 1 December. Available online http://www.northjersey.com/shopping/181647711Neiman_Marcus-Ta (accessed 1 December 2012).

Connor, S. (1989), *Postmodernist Culture: An Introduction to Theories of the Contemporary*, Oxford: Basil Blackwell.

Cosmo Blog Awards 2013 Shortlist – Vote Here (2013), *Cosmopolitan*. Available online http://www.cosmopolitan.co.uk/blogs/cosmo-blog-awards-2013/ (accessed 12 October 2013).

Davis, B. (2010), 'The Age of Semi-Post-Postmodernism', *Artnet*, 5 May. Available online http://www.artnet.com/magazineus/reviews/davis/semi-post-postmodernism/5-15-10.asp (accessed 12 October 2012).

Dawkins, R. (2003), 'Postmodernism Disrobed', in R. Dawkins, *A Devil's Chaplain*, 47–53, Boston, MA: Houghton Mifflin.

Design your wedding dress on-line (n.d.), *Wedding Dress Creator*. Available online http://www. weddingdresscreator.com (accessed 31 October 2012).

Dressing in the dark (2013), *Elle* XXVIII 7, no. 33: 196.

Epstein, M. (1997), *The Place of Postmodernism in Postmodernity*, after postmodernism conference. Available online http://www.focusing.org/apm_papers/Epstein.html (accessed 25 October 2012).

Eshelman, R. (2000/2001), 'Performatism, or the End of Postmodernism', *Anthropoetics*, 6 (2). Available online http://www.anthropoetics.ucla.edu/ap0602/perform.html (accessed 31 October 2012).

Eshelman, R. (2005/2006), 'After Postmodernism: Performatism in Literature', *Anthropoetics*, 11 (2). Available online http://www.anthropoetics.ucla.edu/ap1102perform05.html (accessed 20 January 2012).

Eshelman, R. (2007/2008), 'Performatism in Art', *Anthropoetics*, 13 (3) Available online http://www.anthropoetics.ucla.edu/ap1303/1303eshelman.html (accessed 19 January 2013).

Eshelman, R. (2008), *Performatism, or the End of Postmodernism*, Aurora, CO: Davies Group.

Fashion Institute of Design (n.d.), *Pet Product Design & Marketing* (course guide). Available online http://www.fitnyc.edu/3046.asp (accessed 2 March 2013).

Gallaher, V. (2012), *Disney Princess Looking Mighty Thin in This 'Runway' Video for Barneys*, 19 November. Available online http://geek-news.mtv.com/2012/11/19/Disney-barneys-electric-holiday (accessed 5 December 2012).

Gans, E. (2000), 'The Post-Millennial Age', *Chronicles of Love and Resentment* [aka *Anthro-Poetics: The Journal of Generative Anthropology*], 3 June, University of California, LA. Available online http://www.anthropoetics.ucla.edu/views/vw209.htm (accessed 11 September 2012).

Griffin, J. (2007), 'Marcus Coates', *frieze 108 June-August*. Available online hppts://www.frieze.com/issue/article/focus_marcus_coates/ (accessed 7 July 2013).

Harvey, D. (1990), *The Condition of Postmodernity*, Oxford: Basil Blackwell.

Hellmich, N. (2011), 'Women Fall Head over Heels for Shoes', *USA Today*, 15 March. Available online http://yourlife.usatoday.com/your-look/story/2011/03/Women-fall-head (accessed 2 November 2012).

Iredale, J. (2012), 'From the Magic Kingdom to Madison Avenue: Barneys to unveil "Electric Holiday"', 12 November, *WWD.com*. Available online http://www.wwd.com/retail-news/department-stores/from-the-magic (accessed 28 January 2013).

Kelly, C. (2011), 'Missoni for Target Sells Out in Stores, Crashes Website', *Style*, 14 September. Available online http://www.washingtonpost.com/lifestyle/style/missoni-for-target-sell (accessed 1 December 2012).

Kim, J. (2012), 'ReThink Review: Life of Pi – of Gods and Tigers', 26 November, *Huffington Post*. Available online http://www.huffingtonpost.com/jonathan-kim/rethink-review-life-of-pi (accessed 29 January 2013).

Kirby, A. (2006), 'The Death of Postmodernism and Beyond', *Philosophy Now*, November/ December 2012. Available online http://www.philosophynow.org/issues/58/The_Death_of_Postmodernism_And_Beyond (accessed 17 December 2012).

Kirby, A. (2009a), *Digimodernism: How New Technologies Dismantle the Postmodern and Reconfigure our Culture*, New York: Continuum International.

Kirby, Alan (2009b), *Digimodernism*, 11 August. Available online http://digimodernism.blogspot.com/2009/08/another-interview-i-gave-long-but- (accessed 14 December 2012).

Kirby, A. (2010), 'Successor States to an Empire in Free Fall', *Times Higher Education*, 27 May. Accessed online http://www.timeshighereducation.co.uk/story.asp?storycode=411731 (accessed 31 August 2012).

La Ferla, R. (2008), 'Steampunk Moves between 2 Worlds', *New York Times*, 8 May. Available online http://www.nytimes.com/2008/05/08/Dahion/08PUNK.hrml_r=0 (accessed 3 February 2013).

Lester, T. (2011), 'Average Woman Owns 7 Handbags', *Glamour*, 25 May. Available online http://www.glamour.com/fashion/blogs/salaves-to-fashion/2011/05/the-average (accessed 2 November 2012).

Lipovetsky, G. ([1987] 1994), *The Empire of Fashion: Dressing Modern Democracy*, trans. C. Porter, Princeton, NJ: Princeton University Press.

Lipovetsky, G. (2005), *Hypermodern Times*, Cambridge, MA: Polity Press.

Making of colour guard: the Wallpaper* and Vanessa Beecroft collaboration (2011), *Wallpaper.com*, 10 February. Available online http://wallpaper.com/video/fashion/making-of-colour-guard-the-wallpaper-and-vanessa- beecroft-collaboration/780751234001 (accessed 18 November 2013).

McNamara, A. (2008), 'Illegible Echoes: Felix Gonzalez-Torres, the Artist Spy', *Image & Narrative 22*, May. Available online http://www.imageandnarrative.be/inarchive/autofictin2/mcnamara.html (accessed 12 November 2012).

Menkes, S. (2013), 'The Circus of Fashion', *New York Times*, 10 February. Available online http://magazine.blogs.nytimes.com/2013/02/10/the-circus-of-fashion (accessed 31 July 2013).

Morgado, M. A. (1996), 'Coming to Terms with *Postmodern*: Theories and Concepts of Contemporary Culture and Their Implications for Apparel Scholars', *Clothing and Textiles Research Journal*, 14 (1): 41–53.

New Balance-US (n.d.), *New Balance Custom 574*. Available online www.newbalance.com/New-Balance-Custom (accessed 31 October 2012).

Ninety-nine [99] Most Influential Fashion & Beauty Blogs, The (2013), *Signature9*. Available online http://www.signature9.com/style-99 (accessed 1 August 2013).

NPD reports on the U.S. apparel market (2012), *PRWeb*. Available online http://www.prweb.com/releases/2012/3/prweb9343091.htm (accessed 2 November 2012).

O'Reilly, K. (2010), 'Poll Finds Women Own 7 Pairs of Jeans, but Wear only 4', *Thread NY*, 14 July. Available online http://www.nbc.com/blogs/threadny/THREAD-SmartShop-Poll-Finds (accessed 2 November 2012).

Philpott, T. (2012), 'What Not to Wear', *Mother Jones*, July/August: 68.

Rasmus, D. W. (2013), 'In Fashion, Tech Accessories Are the New Fragrance', *Fast Company*. Available online http://www.fastcompany.com/3009038/in-fashion-tech-accessories-are-the-new- fragrance (accessed 20 October 2013).

Ritzer, G., and W. Yagatich (2012), 'Contemporary Sociological Theory', in G. Ritzer (ed.), *The Wiley-Blackwell Companion to Sociology*, 98–118, West Sussex: Blackwell.

Samuels, R. (2008), 'Auto-Modernity after Postmodernism: Autonomy and Automation in Culture, Technology, and Education', in T. McPherson (ed.), *Digital Youth, Innovation, and the Unexpected*, 219–40, Cambridge, MA: MIT Press.

Ten [10] pairs of jeans in every girl's closet, The (2011), *CollegeCandy*, 10 July. Available online http://collegecandy.com/2011/07/10/the-10-pairs-of-jeans-in-every-girl (accessed 2 November 2012).

Thurman, J. (2003), 'Reckless Perfectionism', *New Yorker*, 17 March. Available online http://www.vanessabeecroft.com/New Yorker.pdf (accessed 18 November 2013).

Turner, T. (1995), *City as Landscape: A Post-postmodern View of Design and Planning*, London: Taylor and Francis.

Vanessa Beecroft (n.d.), *Artnet.com*. Available online http://www.artnet.com/artists/vanessa-beecroft/ (accessed 18 November 2013).

Vermeulen, T., and R. van den Akker (2010), 'Notes on Metamodernism', *Journal of Aesthetics and Culture*, 2. Available online http://www.aestheticsandculture.net/index.php/jac/article/view/5677/6304 (accessed 15 December 2012).

Walt Disney Company (2012), *Electric Holiday*. Available online http://www.youtube.com/watch?v=gd4GANMLess (accessed 5 December 2012).

Whitby, R. (2009), 'Tate Triennial: Altermodern', *Artvehicle 39*. Available online http://www.artvehicle.com/events/260 (accessed 7 July 2013).

Ypsilon Dresses (n.d.), 'Marketing Flyer'. Available online: www.YpsilonDresses.com (accessed 30 October 2012).

2

FASHION, SUBJECTIVITY AND TIME: FROM DELEUZE'S TRANSCENDENTAL EMPIRICISM TO LIPOVETSKY'S HYPERMODERNITY

Eun Jung Kang

This chapter addresses issues surrounding subjectivity, in particular empirical subjectivity that has a strong reference to desire, and the epistemological contingencies of subjectivity. The chapter seeks to contribute to post-postmodern debates on subjectivity in relation to time by resorting to Gilles Deleuze's transcendental empiricism and Gilles Lipovetsky's hypermodernity. Deleuze's transcendental empiricism provides a conceptual platform that helps us understand the relationship between fashion and subjectivity; that is, fashion as an eternal recurrence of the new and subjectivity as self-consciousness of the self. The elucidations of Deleuzian deconstruction of the thought processes proposed by Kant will lead us to grasp why the pursuit of something new in the form of fashion is closely entwined with the mode of life, from modernity to post-postmodernity. Lipovetsky's notion of hypermodernity reinforces the Deleuzian conceptualization of subjectivity, as the former is closely related to one's experience of time in a fast-paced mode of life that is expedited by the post-postmodern logic of urgency (Lipovetsky, 2005). The objective of this chapter is to discuss the process of subjectivity formation via Deleuze's empiricist metaphysics and Lipovetsky's post-postmodern social theory so as to illuminate fashion's role in the eras from modernity to post-postmodernity.

The connection between fashion and such concepts as subjectivity, individuality, and self-consciousness is among the most popular discussion topics in fashion studies. To illustrate, in *Fashion in Focus: Concepts, Practices and Politics* (2011), Tim Edwards maintains that the fashion consumer is 'a desiring subject who desires both objects and other subjects' and 'a desirer of alternative forms of subjectivity' (2011: 157–8). Observing today's multifarious fashion-related advertisements, one can hardly miss out on the fact that the pairing of fashion with the subject's desire is one of the most common tactics in marketing campaigns.[1] The advertising strategy that relies on fashion's strong association with the desire to locate an authentic self is far from irrelevant to contemporary philosophical debates on issues related to subjectivity that have evolved along with the progression from modernity through postmodernity to post-postmodernity. In an attempt to explore the relationships between the desirer and the desire for novelty, as well as between fashion and subjectivity, this chapter probes the topic of subjectivity in relation to time. Deleuze's rendition of the condition in which one's subjectivity is established helps us understand how fashion is interwoven with some critical issues and challenges surrounding the topic of time, while Lipovetsky's depiction of the attributes of hypermodern times assists us in comprehending existential questions in philosophy and grappling with the essence of fashion in the context of modern and post-postmodern issues, such as an experience of subjective crisis.

Deleuzian subjectivity, time and fashion

In order to explore the connection between fashion and subjectivity, a companion concept to modernity,[2] I will begin by investigating the topic of subjectivity under the lens of transcendental empiricism set forth by Gilles Deleuze, in that it will help us work with the relation between fashion and subjectivity as well as between the desire for objects and the desirer. The terms of inquiry are: (1) what Deleuzian subjectivity is in relation to time and (2) how fashion can be understood in terms of Deleuzian time. To this end, it is crucial to understand the crux of Deleuze's transcendental empiricism, about which a lot of debate has taken place in an attempt to decipher the meaning of the oxymoron of transcendental combined with empiricism. The distinction between thought and being, made on the basis of the concept of 'Difference' in Deleuze's *Difference and Repetition* (1994), provides a clear insight into his philosophy. Following Kant, Deleuze repudiates the logic of Cartesian dualism, in which the 'I think' makes the 'I am' equal to the thinking subject without justification. He then adopts Kant's transcendental approach to elucidate 'an *a priori* relation between thought and being' (1994: 85–6).

> The determination ('I think') obviously implies something undetermined ('I am'), but nothing so far tells us how it is that this undermined is determinable by the '*I think*': 'in the consciousness of myself in mere thought I am the *being itself*, although nothing in myself is thereby given for thought'. Kant therefore adds a third logical value: the determinable, or rather the form in which the undetermined is determinable (by the determination). This third value suffices to make logic a transcendental instance. It amounts to the discovery of Difference – no longer in the form of an empirical difference between two determinations, but in the form of a transcendental Difference between the Determination as such and what it determines; no longer in the form of an external difference which separates, but in the form of an internal Difference which establishes an *a priori* relation between thought and being. (Ibid.)

As indicated above, the Deleuzian transcendental does not pertain to differences found in external experiences, but reveals internal differences that cannot be fathomed in real experience. Accordingly, it questions the validity of association of the things or concepts that belong to the 'Same' or that are conventionally viewed as no different from each other. In line with this, the Deleuzian transcendental unfolds the relation between thought and being, instead of searching for the ontology of the mind. Indeed, this is where transcendental and empiricism are merged in a Deleuzian way, in which he draws a line between the epistemological and the ontological subject: 'The essence and the destiny of empiricism are not tied to the atom but rather to the essence of association; therefore, empiricism does not raise the problem of the origin of the mind but rather the problem of the constitution of the subject' (Deleuze, 1991: 31).

Running counter to Descartes and Kant, however, Deleuze believes that the *Cogito*, or *I think*, is an empirical being rather than an independent entity and the mind is given not as a system but as 'a collection of ideas' (ibid., 22–3). Therefore, he renounces the supremacy of the mind and the subject (ibid., 31). By responding to the question – 'how can I say "I"?' – another account of subjectivity in light of Humean empiricism[3] offers a clearer elucidation of Deleuzian empiricism regarding the self:

> We start with atomic parts, but these atomic parts have transitions, passages, 'tendencies', which circulate from one to another. These tendencies give rise to *habits*. Isn't this the answer to the question 'what are we?' We are habits, nothing but habits – the habit of saying 'I'. Perhaps, there is no more striking answer to the problem of the Self. (Deleuze, 1991: Preface to the English-Language Edition, x)

In order to figure out how habits constitute the self, it is imperative to look into Deleuze's notion of time, since habits are referred to as the basis of the synthesis of time. According to him, there are three stages in the synthesis of time, among which the first synthesis of time, the foundation of time, is habits constituting time as the present (Deleuze, 1994); while the second fundamental synthesis of time is memory that comprises time as a pure past; and the final synthesis of time is a phase in which the future is engendered as a form of 'eternal return' (ibid., 90). Deleuze further argues that all three syntheses are different modes of 'Repetition' (ibid., 94). Therefore, all is repetition. Consequently, a question arises as to how something new is hatched under this condition of Repetition, for it is nothing but an outcome of the temporary synthesis. Although Deleuze further explicates that it is imagination and habits that 'draw something new from repetition' (ibid., 73–6), this does not unravel why our habits of imagination pursue things that have yet to be seen or heard of and that are new. Even more complicated is that imagination is neither constant nor uniform, according to Deleuze (1991: 23). In addition, another question regarding imagination emerges. If imagination is inconsistent, how does something new come out of imagination without end, although intermittently, at some point? Indeed, how our habits of imagining beget a novelty on a continuous basis is another Deleuzian-like question, for it brings forth the issue of the constitution of imagination rather than of its origin, which is of internal differences of imagination.

Concerning *newness* and its formation, Deleuzian philosophy suggests that the logic of details does not contradict its overall argument. In other words, the answers for the questions I have raised can be found in transcendental empiricism. First, a novelty comes into being continuously with some interruptions owing not to imagination but to our habits that do repeat on the condition of Repetition. Remember that habits as the originary synthesis of time operate on the condition of Repetition; however, imagination itself does not. In addition, just as the mind is no more than a collection of ideas, like 'a collection without an album, a play without a stage, a flux of perceptions' (ibid., 22–3), so is imagination as Deleuze himself spells out: 'Nothing is done *by* the imagination; everything is done *in* the imagination. It is not even a faculty for forming ideas, because the production of an idea by the imagination is only the reproduction of an impression in the imagination' (ibid., 23). Second, inasmuch as experience makes impressions in the mind, in a strictly Deleuzian sense, the human desire for something new is due to a lack of experience. It is helpful to refer to Walter Benjamin's interpretation of Marcel Proust, who believed that our experience is contingent upon chance, thereby illustrating the inevitable fluctuation in terms of the amount of experience (Benjamin, 2003: 315–16). Using as an example the advent of newspapers, Benjamin expounds on how modern-day modes of communication, concise and clear in content but excessive in quantity, are attributed to the isolation of information from experience, resulting in an 'increasing atrophy of experience' (ibid.). Inspired by Austrian journalist Karl Kraus, Benjamin adds that even the brief journalistic style of newspapers as one form of linguistic habit 'paralyzes the imagination' of the reader (ibid.). Benjamin's observation clearly bears out the relation between experience and imagination during a time when individual experience was on the wane to the point of 'atrophy'. We are likely to be familiar with this state of being on the verge of void of experience, which is often called boredom. It is hardly groundless to relate boredom with the procreation of newness, for novelty is sought after in order to fill out the decreased stimuli in the mind caused by a lack of experience.

And yet, what makes boredom immensely critical in a philosophical discourse is the unique condition in which the subject is situated in relation to the deficiency of experience, although there is a myriad of information available to people through multiple sources. Borrowing from Elizabeth S. Goodstein, therefore, boredom is 'an experience of subjective crisis' (Goodstein, 2005: 5). It is under this circumstance that a subjective crisis takes place. I argue that transcendental empiricism is particularly useful in comprehending why and how existential questions are brought about while one is in a state of boredom. From the perspective of Deleuzian empiricism, the essential condition in which the Cogito questions about its being is not the subject that is 'preexisting' (Deleuze, 1991: 29) but the status quo of being destitute of experience in which the Cogito as an empirical being sets in, as Deleuze explains:

> The pure self of 'I think' thus appears to be a beginning only because it has referred all its presuppositions back to the empirical self. Moreover, while Hegel criticized Descartes for this, he does not seem, for his part, to proceed otherwise: pure being, in turn, is a beginning only by virtue of referring all its presuppositions back to sensible, concrete, empirical being. (Deleuze, 1994: 129)

Once the dearth of experience is apprehended, the 'I think' now questions the self, not just about the self itself, but about the self being in *that* situation. As opposed to Descartes's *Cogito*, which is constant such that it should never become bored, since it has its own autonomy, thought for Deleuze is subjected to the chance of being involved with experience, and he sometimes complains about the lack of sources of imagination. Hence, boredom is probably the best example that reveals the mechanism under which empiricism becomes transcendental, since questions regarding one's existence come out directly from the sensible, the experience of a lack of experience. All things considered, to seek after something new is essentially to look for the condition in which the *Cogito* confirms its subjectivity, thereby becoming the whole as an active self, not as a mere receptivity of intuition in the Kantian sense. In that account, pursuing fashion, which is *newness* par excellence in modern (and hypermodern) times, is no less meaningful in search of one's autonomy.

Lipovetsky's hypermodernity, individualism and fashion

The same theme resonates with Gilles Lipovetsky's observation on the seeking of novelty by means of consumption in our time. He argues that buying a new product is nothing but casting about for novelty and *the* paradigm by which hyperconsumption is in operation is fashion (Lipovetsky, 2005). As such, it is fashion that aptly discloses the mechanism of hypermodernity to which time is an essential condition entwined with the process of self-consciousness. As per Lipovetsky, the two phases during this time period are modernity and hypermodernity, which is a consummation of modernity or a second modernity (ibid.). For him, the expression *postmodern* is vague, since not only is postmodernity like something that receded from view without clearly identifying what had happened to us (ibid., 30), but it is also a changeover period (ibid., 34–5). He maintains that whereas modernity is characterized by the tendency towards a new ideological and political territory distancing away from the traditional system, what typifies hypermodernity is the acceleration of movement and change (ibid., 34), whose momentum grows over time to the point in which a sense of urgency haunts and daunts us (ibid., 50). Following Lipovetsky's line of thought, the touchstone by which to draw a line between modernity and hypermodernity is simply the degree of the pace of change, while the two stages are affected by the logic of incessant change, whose motor is fashion.

The key concepts and principles that represent the second stage of modernity, as defined by Lipovetsky, include democracy, human rights, the market and consumption.[4] As a matter of fact, they all can be boiled down to the concept of individualism, or put differently, they have assisted in furthering the development of individual autonomy in different areas of society. Noteworthy is the fact that when probing fashion, Lipovetsky (2002) avails himself of the concept of democracy coupled with consumerism and mass communications, not just resting on the vestimentary aspects of fashion only.[5] Throughout his book *The Empire of Fashion: Dressing Modern Democracy* (2002), Lipovetsky asserts that fashion has facilitated the growth of democratic ideals, individualist humanism, bourgeois market economy and the consumption of ephemera, thereby bringing about the advancement of individual autonomy. This helps us grasp why hypermodernity, which is nothing but an extension of modernity with an increased intensity in movement and change, is deeply connected with fashion, not just because individualism and newness are constitutive qualities of fashion, but also because fashion as the chief provider of newness has been an active actor in the progress of individual autonomy. Lipovetsky contends that fashion is closely related to the development of modern individualism and democracy by discussing the magnitude of individuality and of up-to-dateness in an era of democracy, *the* medium of propagandization and dissemination of whose value is fashion. As he puts it: 'Consummate fashion does not signify "the end of history" but the constantly renewed invention of democracy and the marketplace; it signifies the responsibility of citizens facing the construction of a future whose keys no individual now holds' (ibid., 251). By democracy he does not necessarily mean a government form or a political system in a narrow sense. Rather, the concept of democracy Lipovetsky deals with is none other than the social condition under which liberal, subjective autonomy finds its home. As mentioned by Lipovetsky himself, his adoption of this concept is an attempt to overcome the long-lasting theories of imitation and distinction which draw upon class difference in fashion studies of his time.[6] He claims that fashion as an agent of democracy hampered the dispersion of an elitist sartorial principle, while debilitating traditional values and behaviours in favour of the desire for novelty in association with an interest in the physical look (ibid., 19–20 and 31). In the same vein, for him, fashion stands against the model of immutable legitimacy of the past, while promoting the sense of the present and the new, since fashion is of the ephemeral, less of a display of wealth (ibid., 19–20). Lipovetsky expounds on how fashion has been instrumental to the equalization or democratization of existing conditions (ibid., 31), and its increasing power has also consolidated the cult of the here and now, the eulogy of the present and the prevalence of the aesthetics of the new (2005: 37). In the guise of empty newness, recurrence of the same and excessive veneration of ephemera, fashion has transformed the Western world over the course of modern and hypermodern times, leading to a paradigm shift from the supremacy of traditional values and social guidelines to individualist, democratic and worldly interests in happiness, pleasure and novelty (Lipovetsky, 2002: 71). Lipovetsky argues, therefore, that fashion is an embodiment of democracy as well as that fashion is an apparatus to the democratic revolution that has to do with equality, because fashion has dissolved the criteria of traditional social norms, made indistinct the demarcation between sublime and collective values and subjective individualism, and lent dignity to subjective pleasures (ibid., 72). What is most radical about his view on the relation between fashion and democracy is that it is with the influence of fashion that democracy has thrived, as he puts it: 'Under fashion's reign, democracies enjoy a universal consensus about their political institutions' (ibid., 7) and 'Viewed in a long-term perspective, fashion in its new status has to be interpreted rather as a phase and an instrument of the democratic revolution' (ibid., 72). Such companion concepts as democracy, human rights, the market and consumption, as illustrated by Lipovetsky, all combined together disclose the fact that over the course of modern and hypermodern times individual autonomy has been reinforced.

In order to identify the relation between time, consumption, fashion and subjectivity, which is the main subject of discourse of this chapter, I shall discuss why the feeling of insecurity is described as one critical aspect of hypermodernity by Lipovetsky.[7] The hypermodern subject is no longer bound by rigid ideologies and conventional values and practices; hence, he or she is responsible for finding his or her own identity, as compared with those who lived with fixed social conditions and class hierarchy to which how one defines oneself was subjected. Lipovetsky holds that what sustains hyperconsumption is existential anguish and the pleasure linked with change (2005: 52), intimating the linkage between subjective desire and one's experience of time as well as that between identity crisis and consumption. He further explicates that the hypermodern consumer desires to revitalize 'his or her experience of time' by means of attaining novelties and the desire manifested by the hypermodern consumer is 'a desire for perpetual self-renewal and the renewal of the present' (ibid.). This Kantian musing over the desire for never-ending reclaiming of the self in relation to time made by Lipovetsky reveals one important role fashion has played under hypermodern conditions. That is to say, fashion as a purveyor of newness has provided a model that works out on an interminable basis by which one can obtain relentless chances of self-assurance, although fugitive and fleeting. Fashion has long served as a basic model underlying the system of modern and hypermodern societies in terms of temporal movements as well as of consumerism, as Lipovetsky opines that consumption and mass communication are closely entwined with seduction and ceaseless movement, and the system of fashion proffers their momentum while establishing the present as the point of temporal reference (ibid., 36–7).

The hypermodern consumer and the subjective experience of time

It has to be highlighted that the hypermodern preoccupation with time can be construed as negative on account of the rarefaction of time.[8] Under the hypermodern logic, time is no longer ours. Time is increasingly detached from our control, while our management of time schedules each day has become of greater significance than ever before, so much so that temporal norms and standards virtually govern everyday routines. According to Lipovetsky, while modern capitalism is based on the economy of time, in hypermodern times everything is organized according to working time (ibid., 48). Such modern concepts as free time, leisure, holiday, working hours and retirement age all demonstrate the time-conscious social trends and mode of life that have been set firmly in our society (ibid., 48–9), while expressions like 'beat the deadline', 'time is money' and 'zero delay' (ibid., 39) disclose how time is being hypostatized, encapsulating our contemporary mind-set that is tied with temporal logic. Our constant dissatisfaction with the feeling of scarcity of time also affirms this hypermodern concern with and about time. As the upsurge of time-related issues and discord has increasingly dominated our life (ibid., 49), one has been staged to act upon the ever-accelerated movement of time. The expedited pace in life caused by our time awareness and our desire to keep up with the flow of time has brought with it a sense of urgency (ibid., 39 and 50); that is, one is forced to take action along with the movement of an ever-escalated sense of time. However, on a positive note, in hypermodern times people are situated to exercise choice and examine themselves because they are set free from tradition (ibid., 50), although not everyone processes this trait in a philosophical manner. Hyperbolically speaking, under the logic of the hypermodern, one is positioned to become an involuntary philosopher who has no idea what it is that he or she is to philosophize. It is in the domain of consumption in particular that the hypermodern subject makes individualized choices and gains subjective experience that is linked with the temporal movement. As Lipovetsky remarks, 'We need to think of hyperconsumption as an emotional rejuvenating experience, one that can start all over again an indefinite number of times' (ibid., 52). What is of great importance in comprehending the nature of the consuming individual governed by hypermodern logic is that the desire of the hypermodern consumer is nothing more than the desire to cognize his or her own self in time. This is why consumption, the search for experience, the desire for novelty, subjectivity, and time awareness all require investigating together when seeking the contingencies of the human subject in post-postmodern societies.

Conclusion

The elucidations made by both Deleuze and Lipovetsky on the topics surrounding time help us grasp the meaning not only of procuring experience in time, but also of a repetitive subjective experience through consumption as a venue by which one finds his or her subjectivity. This is not to say that each time we buy new things, a new existential awakening is to be achieved, as we often fail to reach this stage. The truth is that the more one is obsessed with grappling with the flow of time by means of buying new things, the deeper one is trapped in a form of accelerated time. Accordingly, the process of redeeming oneself from the state of unempirical self through endless consumption can be viewed as regressive. And yet, today one has room to practice one's autonomy by exercising choice or contemplating on oneself, as Lipovetsky points out (ibid., 50). It has to be emphasized that the pure act of seeking a new experience through consumption is concerned with our effort to confirm the existence of oneself, whereas hedonic consumption behaviour is hardly conducive to confirming one's subjectivity. The latter confuses the philosophical awakening of oneself with the mere emotional pleasure that is associated with a new product one has just bought, or it simply mixes all together. Experiencing novelty proffered by the supposedly relentless supply of new products more often than not makes it hard for us to have an existential experience of the self to the point at which one finds shopping vacuous and meaningless. But still this experience in time is closely related to the subjective desire to cognize oneself as an active self. Indeed, the path to the realization of the self that is expounded by Deleuze is no different. Consider his analysis on how we find subjectivity. According to him, it is through the simple act of habit which acknowledges the 'me' as the 'I' that we cognize the 'I', which is the self; therefore, we are all habits. The *repetitive* action, calling the 'me' the 'I', simply makes one come to arrive at one's subjectivity. This taken-for-granted habit hardly draws full attention unless one recoups its implications through conscious, existential endeavour. All in all, it can be said that any new experience that arouses our unempirical self on the basis of recurrence is an underlying structure that poses a possibility of subjective experience. The contingencies of subjectivity in the post-postmodern era, or whatever it is termed, still rest on time, which is even more elusive than ever. Time is an important constituent of both modern and post-postmodern eras. It also provides a clue as to the mechanism by which one conceives of oneself. Now one should be able to come to grips with why, during the post-postmodern era, the consumption of novelty, especially of fashion, is linked with individualism and humanist values as well as viewed as a matter of existential inquiry by some philosophers. Like habits that unceasingly come about in a spontaneous mode, fashion relentlessly operates in the most individualized, superficial and impulsive areas of life, providing an unremitting mechanical potential of redeeming the self from the nadir of undisrupted and dormant status.

Notes

1   For example, see Emma Banister and Margaret K. Hogg, Chapter 10. Consumers and their negative selves, and the implications for fashion marketing, ed. T. Hines, M. and Bruce, 2nd edn, *Fashion Marketing: Contemporary Issues*, (Oxford: Butterworth-Heinemann, 2007), 217–29.

2   The definition of *modernity* cannot be made without an exploration of the theme of subjectivity. Concerning this, see Harvie Ferguson, *Modernity and Subjectivity: Body, Soul, Spirit* (Charlottesville: University Press of Virginia, 2000).

3   Refer to David Hume's comment about subjectivity formation with respect to his Copy Principle in D. Hume, *An Enquiry Concerning Human Understanding* (Mineola, NY: Dover Philosophical Classics ([1748] 2004)), 10.

In short, all the materials of thinking are derived either from our outward or inward sentiment: the mixture and composition of these belongs alone to the mind and will. Or, to express myself in philosophical language, all our ideas or more feeble perceptions are copies of our impressions or more lively ones...

4 Refer to Gilles Lipovetsky, *Hypermodern Times* (Cambridge: Polity Press, 2005), 34.

The modernity of the second sort is the one which, at peace with its basic principles (democracy, human rights, the market) has no credible model to be set against it and never stops recycling within its own system the pre-modern elements that were once objects to be eradicated.

5 See Lipovetsky's own comment on this in Gilles Lipovetsky, *The Empire of Fashion: Dressing Modern Democracy*, trans. Catherine Porter (Princeton, NJ: Princeton University Press, 2002), 5 and 72.

On the other hand, I attempt to comprehend the rising power of fashion in contemporary societies, the central, unprecedented place it occupies in democracies that have set out along the path of consumerism and mass communications. (5)
Viewed in a long-term perspective, fashion in its new status has to be interpreted rather as a phase and an instrument of the democratic revolution . . . . Moreover, by attributing greater dignity to inferior phenomena and functions, by blurring the boundary between noble art and modest art, the empire of fashion helped promote equality. The dissolution of the hierarchy of genres and trades, which instituted theoretical equality among formerly heterogeneous realms, allows the celebration of fashion to appear as a manifestation of democracy, even though fashion arose in the name of distinctive difference within a world of privilege. (72)

6 In the epilogue of *The Empire of Fashion*, Lipovetsky says:

A theoretical updating was needed because the model of social distinction had proved unable to account either for the historical invention of fashion in the fourteenth century or for the major organizational, behavioral, and aesthetic mutations that orchestrated its historical development. I did not seek to deny the impact of competition for social rank on fashion; rather I sought to demonstrate that such competition has less explanatory value than the modern individualist ethic that has been present exclusively in the West for more than six centuries. (242)

7 See Lipovetsky, *Hypermodern Times*, 39–40.

The spirit of the time dominated by frivolity has been replaced by a time of risk and uncertainty. A certain carefree attitude has gone for good: the present is increasingly lived out in a sense of insecurity. (39)

8 See Lipovetsky's own remark on the rarefaction of time in *Hypermodern Times*, 51.

Modernity was built around the critique of the exploration of working time; hypermodern time registers a feeling that time is being increasingly rarefied.

References

Benjamin, W. (2003), *Selected Writings, 1938–40*, ed. Howard Eiland and Michael W. Jennings, trans. Edmund Jephcott, Cambridge, MA: Belknap Press of Harvard University Press.

Deleuze, G. (1991), *Empiricism and Subjectivity: An Essay on Hume's Theory of Human Nature*, trans. Constantin V. Boundas, New York: Columbia University Press.

Deleuze, G. (1994), *Difference and Repetition*, trans. Paul Patton, New York: Columbia University Press.

Edwards, T. (2011), *Fashion in Focus: Concepts, Practices and Politics*, London: Routledge.

Ferguson, H. (2000), *Modernity and Subjectivity: Body, Soul, Spirit*, Charlottesville: University Press of Virginia.

Goodstein, E. S. (2005), *Experience without Qualities: Boredom and Modernity*, Stanford, CA: Stanford University Press.

Lipovetsky, G. (2002), *The Empire of Fashion: Dressing Modern Democracy*, Princeton, NJ: Princeton University Press.

Lipovetsky, G. (2005), *Hypermodern Times*, Cambridge: Polity Press.

3

WITH NO TWIST: THE METAMODERN SARTORIAL STATEMENT OF VETEMENTS

Alla Eizenberg

The sartorial expressions of the second decade of the new millennium have been marked by the unprecedented presence of familiar, functional, everyday garments – for example, T-shirts, sweatshirts, hoodies and trackpants – that became ubiquitous not only on the streets but also on catwalks and in expensive retail outlets. Observing the proliferation of this type of clothing into high fashion and recognizing the transformation of this ordinary wardrobe into an active participant in the cultural and social discourse, this chapter analyses the changing politics of sartorial signification as a result of the emergence of the new cultural paradigm that comes to replace the waning postmodern state (Morgado, 2014). I argue that the rise of the familiar, the ordinary and the mundane in clothing in the beginning of the twenty-first century is a manifestation of a new sensibility shaped by a variety of trends across the cultural, socio-economic and political spectrum. In this chapter, I focus on the work of the young French high-fashion brand Vetements as exemplary of this shift. The brand is known for openly denouncing the principles fashion has been predicated on – the new and spectacular – instead promoting an approach that is grounded in the investigation and reinterpretation of the ordinary staples of the Western everyday wardrobe posing a challenge to the definition of fashion and reconsidering its meaning and value.

If the postmodern condition signalled a break with the modernist assumptions due to their loss of relevance and incoherence with the phenomena and sensitivities emerging in late-capitalism (Morgado, 1996: 42), the first decade of the twenty-first century was marked by a growing consensus about the obsolescence of the postmodern epoch (Morgado, 2014: 315). Theorists from a wide spectrum of disciplines agree that geopolitical and financial crises, environmental uncertainties and fast-changing information and communication technology are the key factors responsible for the emergence of a new cultural paradigm often referred by a general catch-all term called post-postmodern (Hutcheon, 2002: 165–6; Morgado, 2014: 314). I identify the rise of the ordinary clothes – common, familiar, accessible for all and aesthetically consistent over time – in high fashion as one among the most prominent and consistent sartorial expressions evolving during the same time period that the new cultural paradigm comes to the fore.

While some scholars believe that the postmodern is 'dead and buried' (Hutcheon, 2002; Kirby, 2009), others suggest it has not disappeared but has restructured into a new phase (Eshelman, 2008; Bourriaud, 2009; Nealon, 2012). Robin van den Akker and Timotheus Vermeulen can be regarded as proponents of the latter with their notion of metamodernism that seems to tap more acutely than many other theories into the distinct structural and emotional differences characterizing first decades of the twenty-first century (2010, 2015, 2017). They acknowledge the presence and impact of both modern and postmodern qualities at once in the new cultural realm where the coexistence of these contrasting notions recontextualizes the principles of and alters the qualities associated with each of these conditions. Metamodernism is defined as an oscillation 'between a modern enthusiasm and a postmodern irony, between hope and melancholy, between naïveté and knowingness, empathy and apathy, unity and plurality, totality and fragmentation, purity and ambiguity', prefix *meta*, an adaptation from the term *metaxis*, translating as 'between' (van den Akker and Vermeulen, 2010: 5–6). The objects that are capable of expressing such rich and oftentimes dialectical meanings are particular, they can hardly be found in the items whose existence is based on novelty alone which is often a characteristic of fashion. Hence, my attention turns to the ordinary, to the simple, functional and change resistant, considering the adoption of these garments into the fashion discourse as a metamodern expression of fashion.

Drawing on the concept of 'the structure of feelings' introduced by the British cultural theorist Raymond Williams ([1954] 2001) and described as 'a sentiment, or rather still a sensibility that many people share, that many are aware of, but which cannot easily be pinned down' (van den Akker and Vermeulen, 2015: 56), van den Akker and Vermeulen articulate metamodern as a manifestation, mostly an aesthetic manifestation, that is capable of expressing the structure of feelings of the contemporary time and space. The scholars identify three pronounced approaches that are becoming increasingly notable in the metamodern aesthetic phenomena: neoromanticism, new interest in Utopian perspectives, which they share with Raoul Eshelman (2008), and the 'new depthiness' (2010, 2015).

Drawing on the notions of neoromanticism, I argue that the appeal of the familiar staples of everyday represents a qualitative change in the perception of these clothes, not only changing their position in the sartorial hierarchy but underlining the expansion of what fashion can and attempts to represent.

Re-establishing the connection between fashion and clothes

Sartorial practices are always a cultural phenomenon expressing themselves through the clothes people wear in certain places during certain times, yet fashion is a particular case among these articulations. 'The Zeitgeist expressing itself in visible form' (Vinken, 2005: 41), fashion bears intrinsic ties to modernity and its unique qualities, and it is imperative to outline this connection in order to grasp the inevitability of the impact of the cultural changes on fashion and its function.

A complex notion, modernity is simultaneously a state, a cultural condition and an intellectual framework defined by the ideas of Enlightenment and the realities of industrial capitalism. While different sartorial practices historically existent around the world could potentially share similarities with what became known as fashion, for this discussion it is necessary to distinguish the phenomenon that emerged in the nineteenth-century European context and was a result of the radical changes happening in the economic, social and cultural domain at once. Elizabeth Wilson was among the first theorists to draw attention to fashion's intrinsic link to modernity, describing it as one of its 'direct outcomes, and ... one of its most accurate manifestations' ([1985] 2014: 3) capable of representing simultaneously the plethora of characteristics of the modern period. The ideas of humanism expressed themselves through the dichotomy of individualism and conformity of appearances (Simmel, [1901] 2004: 292), industrial potential drove the expansion of fashion into the influential cultural phenomenon due to mass production and the consequent accessibility of goods to more people (Wilson, [1985] 2014; Breward, 2000), capitalism found its incarnation in commodity fetishism creating the desire for endless consumption (Veblen, [1899] 2007: 340, Sombart, [1902] 2004: 316) and social mobility could be manifested through the newness of the dress style, as the temporal hierarchies characterizing fashion created a clear demarcation between the fashionable, in this respect, the current or of the moment, and the outdated (Van De Peer, 2014: 329). Since keeping pace with the latest vogue was dependent on pecuniary spending fashionability became a visual marker of belonging to the higher social strata. More than anything, however, fashion captured the restless nature of modernity (Gilroy, 1993: 16) represented by its intrinsic quality of the self-perpetuating change.

Here, the immanence of change and its cyclical nature come to signal the break between fashion – ever-changing intriguing novelty versus everyday clothes – the ordinary, the aesthetically consistent, familiar and unassuming that drove the conceptual distinction between fashion's association with desire and that of clothes with utilitarian necessity. Fashion required attention and compliance resulting in consistent replacement of the outdated garments with new ones. The ordinary was replaced only when it could no longer serve its function and, even then, oftentimes kept on lingering around the house or at the back of the closets as a material memory of the personal experience or another human being (Stallybrass, 1999: 29).

Gaining significance at the time of social mobility, fashion became a visual language to signal one's social standing in the ambiguous public interactions of the time, distinguishing between the seasons and between those who could afford the following of the latest vogue and those who could not. In order to create visual distinctions or, in Veblenian terms, the *conspicuousness* ([1899] 2007: 340), fashion creators like Worth, Poiret, Madam Grès took no interest in the common and mundane, rather they aspired to create a dream intended to separate their clientele from the repetitive everydayness and from the wardrobe representative of this experience. This tendency deepened the divide between the fashionable and the ordinary, creating the realm in which fashion appropriates all 'the distinct, superior, and specialized' elements of the sartorial spectrum, while ordinary clothes stand for 'what is left over', consistent with Lefebvre's definition of the everydayness (cited in Buckley and Clark, 2017: 7).

In the aftermath of the Second World War, the first signs of discontent with the modernist vision and opposition to its unquestionable belief in reason, progress and history began to manifest themselves in the sociopolitical upheavals of the 1950s. During those days youth, and not exclusively an established higher class, became an active and prominent participant in the cultural discourse in the West, epitomized in cinema with films like *The Wild One* (1953), *Rebel without a Cause* (1955) and literature (by authors like Françoise Sagan in France, J. D. Salinger in the United States). Youth drove to the fore different sets of values and ideals that prioritized freedom of expression and rejection of authority, actively shifting the canons of ethics and aesthetics. Most often clad in utilitarian clothes, the youth revolution illuminated garments and styles that were significantly different from those promoted by high fashion, privileging a variety of everyday working-class staples, including T-shirts and blue jeans in America, or fisherman's sweaters in France, over the typically considered class-, age- and gender-appropriate garb. Gaining popularity during this period, blue jeans, leather jackets and the modest undergarment, the T-shirt, began to establish their place among fashionable items.

The postmodern tendencies of the late 1970s came to signal a rupture of the assumptions dominating social and cultural discourses that took their root in modernity. A contested term, postmodern, is often applied to describe a plurality of ideas and tendencies, such as the distrust of grand narratives (Lyotard, [1979]

1984), concern with the technological mediation of experiences (Baudrillard, [1976] 1993) resulting in the alienation of a sign from its meanings and questioning of linear history (Foucault [1975] 1995), just to name a few. Yet, what unites those and other ideas under the title of postmodern theory is the opposition to the modernist vision and the aims to undo the dominant discourses by exposing the contingencies they are constructed upon. These tendencies manifested themselves across the broad spectrum of social and aesthetic fields including in sartorial practices. Here, the transformation of norms and values was quick to express itself through pastiche, parody and subversion of traditional aesthetic codes, as could be seen in 'the oppositional dressing' of punks (Hebdige, 2005: 125). In the 1980s these tendencies arrived to high fashion expressed through the unprecedented interest in street style that muddled the high and low categories of the dress code and the acceptance of the unfamiliar aesthetics introduced by the Japanese designers. The ordinary, the functional and the mundane were assigned a powerful role in the communication of difference, rejection of authority (Morgado, 2014: 314) and deconstruction of modernist norms and aesthetics (Vinken, 2005: 67). These were evident in the audacious assemblages of ripped jeans paired with tulle and lace, or corsets worn on top of chunky sweaters (Jean-Paul Gaultier Prêt-A-Porter Spring/Summer 1994, Paris; Vivienne Westwood Witches Collection/Autumn-Winter 1983–1984, London respectively), intended to bring fashion down and strip it off its pretentious elitist status through the pastiche and deliberate stylishness. Barbara Vinken captured these conscious and unconscious sartorial expressions coherent with the postmodern attitude by the term 'postfashion', meaning 'what comes after the "hundred-year fashion" (Lipovetsky, 1994) as its after-image' (Vinken, 2005: 35). Postfashion deconstructs the modernist premises of fashion, the way it defines class, gender and age; reveals fashion's artificiality; and exposes arbitrariness of the notion of taste (Vinken, 2005: 35).

By the 1990s, writes Malcolm Gladwell, 'things got turned over, and fashion became trickle-up' (1997: 78). The 'cool hunting', a creative and market research based on the discovery and appropriation of the urban subculture's trends and styles (Gladwell, 1997), impacted the relationship of fashion and the clothes excluded from the fashion realm (according to Valerie Steele, 2005), that is, the ordinary and the common constituting the baseline of streetwear. The styles conceived by the urban youth communities as means of self-expression were later named 'streetwear' by the mass-market manufacturers as an umbrella term to address the casual items comprising the styles. Those usually represented an amalgam of sportswear (clothes for athletic or outdoor activities), uniforms (mostly associated with military, or other disciplined or controlled environment) and workwear (durable clothes for performance of physical labour.) Due to the particular material qualities and cultural meaning some of the garments from these non-fashion categories gained popularity among wide groups of people regardless of their class, gender, race or ethnicity. They became so common and familiar that they were unnoticeable in the crowd despite the differences in the brands and the price tags. The simplicity, accessibility and ubiquity made those clothes into what I call the ordinary, the group consistent of jeans, T-shirts, track pants, sweatshirts and sneakers. Since the postmodern period they have been continuously present in or 'next' to fashion. For Martin Margiela, for instance, the ordinary staples served as a source for sartorial investigation of meaning, that is, the deconstruction experiments with a pair of jeans or a white shirt (Maison Martin Margiela, Spring/Summer collection 1992, Paris). While for Alexander McQueen the use of T-shirts was intended to create shocking juxtapositions of high and low forms, a clash of the immaculate tailoring with a basic familiar item (Spring 1997).

During the 1990s another important change occurred when the particular brands originating in streetwear began to accumulate cultural and symbolic capital due to their association with certain communities. The shift was particularly recognized with brands like Quicksilver (founded in 1969), Stüssy (1980) and Supreme (1994) that became synonymous with bold attitude of surfing and skateboarding, respectively. It was hip-hop culture, however, that created a powerful merger of ordinary and luxury items. Valerie Steele described the style as 'reflect[ing] the energy and resonance of the urban experience while omitting illusory signs that demonstrate the metamorphosis of the subaltern individual into street luminary' (Steele, 2005: 215). The combination of the material focus with the grim everyday revealed in the lyrics of hip-hop and rap created the idea of 'ghetto fabulousness', a style based on juxtaposition of 'fabulously' expensive objects placed in the context of the impoverished ghetto (Steele, 2005: 217). This effect was often achieved through the combination of the ordinary item of clothing with the luxury brand logo. By the late 1990s hip-hop style became associated with the oversized white T-shirts, basketball tops, baggy denim jeans, cargo pants often branded with the designer's logo, as well as Nike or Adidas sneakers. It is in the context of the hip-hop style that fashion brands started to produce the expensive versions of ordinary items, like Tommy Hilfiger with his logo-emblazoned baseball shirt and 'Uptown' jeans style in the 1990s.

Metamodern fashion: Romanticizing the ordinary

With the beginning of the new millennium the attitude towards the ordinary sartorial staples in fashion started to shift, expressing new sensitivities and aims. A good illustration for this change can be found in William Gibson's *Pattern Recognition* (2003), where the wardrobe of everyday garments became instrumental in the construction of the protagonist Casey Pollard as a person of sublime aesthetic sensibilities.

[She] gropes for her clothes. A small boy's black Fruit Of The Loom T-shirt, thoroughly shrunken, a thin grey V-necked pullover purchased by half-dozen from a supplier to New England prep school, and a new and oversized pair of black 501's, every trade mark carefully removed. Even the buttons on these have been ground flat, featureless, by a Korean locksmith in the Village, a week ago.

On the one hand, Gibson's sartorial choices harken back to the stylistic expressions of the 1990s, where the appropriation of the basic clothes represented a disdain for the aggressive policies of advertising and forced aesthetic forms, specifically exaggeration in design. On the other, however, it displays a new attitude towards the ordinary characterized by attention and romantic tenderness, which the author achieves through the use of words like 'thoroughly', 'carefully' or by adding an extra detail about a trip to a particular locksmith to treat the buttons. By combining something mundane, unworthy of attention with caring attitude towards this very thing, Gibson succeeds to fuse together the sense of disillusionment and idealism, creating an example of neoromanticism in regard to ordinary clothing, which according to Van den Akker and Vermeulen is a significant feature of the metamodern condition.

Drawing on the notion of Novalis that 'to romanticize is nothing but a qualitative heightening' (Novalis cited in van den Akker and Vermeulen, 2010: 8), I argue that the adoption of the sartorial staples into high fashion in the first decades of the twenty-first century is distinct and qualitatively different from the previous uses of this particular group of clothes based on its functional role. If the postmodern deployment of the ordinary, as mentioned earlier, intended to defy the principles of fashion, metamodern expression, in contrast, turns to the ordinary as a real-life reference in attempt to re-establish the relevance of fashion. By romanticizing it, metamodern fashion underlines the rich cultural significance of everyday staples and the emotional value resonating with the drive for unity, inclusivity and sincerity that once again become thought after. 'Postfashion' aimed to create an appearance that read as 'one is certainly not naked, but by no means "dressed"' (Vinken, 2005: 67) or, in other words, this pile of clothes layered upon the body is all fashion is. Metamodern, then, does not look to undermine the existence of fashion but attempts to reconnect it with the cultural paradigm of the time by challenging the meaning and the structure of the phenomenon without denying its merits.

These new sensitivities characterized by the appeal towards the ordinary and the mundane were pronounced in the hipster aesthetics of the early 2000s. Their wardrobes that comprised the familiar styles often originating in American workwear and including heavy-duty clothes made of twill cottons and canvas, often stone-washed and worn wrinkled, flannel lumberjack's plaid shirts and vintage T-shirts (Hill, 2015) shared commonalities with the dress codes of the Grunge scene of the 1990s. However, if grunge sartorial choice was driven by the urge to 'look … stripped down and raw' (Grayer Moore, 2017: 143), hipsters gave much attention to simple and ordinary garments, elevating them by a touch of connoisseurship. Hipsters attributed special value to the provenance of the clothes and their consumption was effected by the association of particular garments with the American heritage brands, like Levi's, Pendleton or Vans, that originally manufactured them, exhibiting the enthusiasm and irony coexisting in the same aesthetic gesture.

At the same time, fashion designers started to express interest in another area of the ordinary wardrobe, namely sportswear, the first example of which was the collaboration initiated by Yohji Yamamoto with Adidas that resulted in the launch of Y-3 in 2002. This model was later adopted by Alexander McQueen collaborating with Puma in 2005, Stella McCartney with Adidas in 2005 and Louis Vuitton with Supreme in 2018. After the launch of Y-3, Yamamoto explained that he was concerned about being called 'the maestro of fashion', 'I felt I came too far from the street. … So, I wanted to work with sneakers as a way of getting back to the street' (Gonsalves, 2014).

The absorption of the ordinary into high-fashion vocabularies continued to manifest itself throughout the first decades of the twenty-first century. Evidence of it can be found in the T-shirts and tight jeans worn by the bold-looking models chosen by Raf Simons (Fall 2001), the Kenzo sweatshirts designed by Humberto Leon and Carol Lim in 2011, and the heavy-duty hoodies from Vetements with the logo in the Champion font (Spring 2016). The presence of these clothes in the collections of high-fashion houses no longer confronts the rules of fashion and the sociocultural categories these typically represent. On the contrary, the fashion of the early twenty-first century turns to the ordinary to reconnect to the reality of the world, of the street and to regain relevance, be it in order to preserve its existence as an influential cultural phenomenon or to sustain its being a multibillion-dollar industry.

Additional examples of this approach can be seen in the heavily embellished tracksuits of the New York-based designer Maria Jahnkoy or in the chunky, resembling home-knitted hats chosen by Raf Simons to complement the glamorous evening gowns in his Fall 2018 collection for Calvin Klein and the work of Vetements that I discuss next. Here, the focus on the ordinary is consistent with the neoromantic tendency for 're-signification of "the commonplace with significance"' (2010: 10), similar to what van den Akker and Vermeulen have observed in art, becoming one of the more remarkable metamodern manifestations in fashion.

Vetements means clothes

Pondering the questions of the contemporary prominence of the ordinary in high fashion through the lens of metamodernism, a young, multinational design collective Vetements stands out as a compelling case for analysis due to its pronounced interest in the mundane everydayness and the resonance their work achieved with the fashion media and consumers. With the focus on Vetements and the case of the DHL T-shirt from their Spring 2017 collection, in particular, I articulate the correlation between the metamodern sensibilities and the various aspects of the brand's practice. My aim here is to consider why something as unassuming and ordinary as Champion hoodies, deconstructed jeans or a shipping company T-shirt have been received with such enthusiasm, recognized as fashion and consumed at the luxury goods price point. In addition, it is also an attempt to consider whether Vetements is different from other designers and brands, like Hood by Air founded in 2013, Off-White in 2012 or Jaquemus in 2014, who, at first glance, seem to apply similar methodology towards fashion making.

Started by Georgia-born, Antwerp-educated designer Demna Gvasalia and a number of his colleagues and friends, all of whom held design positions in the top tier of the Parisian fashion industry, the early gatherings conducted by the designers were more akin to an experiment in alternative aesthetics or, in Gvasalia words, 'a fun project', addressing the 'creative frustration' (Amed, 2016) experienced by the designers in their day jobs. Concerned by the detachment reigning in the fashion industry between the creative vision and the commercial (Amed, 2016), and the reality of the designers' own everyday, the clothes they made were 'not supposed to be a concept or a statement' but the things 'people want to wear' (Amed, 2016). Rejecting the idea of fashion as 'glamorous, unattainable or super exclusive' (Suleman, 2015), the collective opted for the blunt ordinariness of references, in clothes and experiences, seeing these as a source for connection, 'something people can relate to' (Suleman, 2015). As often referred to by the press, this vision translated into 'a list' (Socha, 2015; Suleman, 2015) of sartorial staples that included jeans, T-shirts, tracksuits, a number of uniform variations and hoodies that became a signature item of the brand.

With support from Gvasalia's younger brother Guram, who held a degree in strategic management from the London College of Fashion, the experiment evolved into a brand with an inconspicuous name that literally means clothes in French, further promoting the philosophy of its founders. After three seasons of their existence, Vetements became a prominent feature of the high-fashion media discourse, celebrated by fashion journalists (Amed, 2016; Fury, 2015, 2016a, 2016b, 2016c, 2016d; Mower, 2015, 2016a, 2016b, 2016c), distributed in more than one hundred high-end retailers around the globe and proving themselves able to withstand the fierce criticism from the opponents of their approach to fashion (Aronowsky-Cronberg, 2016; Rabkin, 2016).

In October 2015, the enthusiasm towards the brand among fashion professionals and consumers led to Gvasalia's appointment as the creative director of Balenciaga, the venerated Parisian fashion house. The press release issued by the Kering conglomerate, who owns the brand, explained the choice as the recognition of the contribution of Vetements to the contemporary perception of fashion as 'a sociological observation of the wardrobe's essentials' (Friedman, 2015). While the reasons for the nomination may vary, in the context of this chapter, I argue that the appointment underlined Gvasalia's acute sensitivity to the cultural climate of the first decades of the twenty-first century and the fact that the aesthetics Vetements promotes taps accurately into the structure of feelings representative of this moment in time.

Normcore, Vetements and the politics of the ordinary in fashion

In the short article 'Metamodernism: A Brief Introduction' Luke Turner argues that for 'a generation raised in the '80s and '90s, on a diet of *The Simpsons* and *South Park*, for whom postmodern irony and cynicism is a default setting, … a yearning for meaning – for sincere and constructive progression and expression – has come to shape today's dominant cultural mode' (Turner, 2015). In this context, the short-lived phenomenon of normcore becomes an important reference for this discussion. In the document that coined the term, normcore, to articulate the emerging cultural mode, the young forecasting agency K-hole argued that 'once upon a time, people were born into communities and had to find their individuality. Today people are born individuals and have to find their communities' (2013). The agency romanticized the low-key aesthetics of ordinary clothes: boxy shapeless jeans, oversized sweatshirts, gift shop baseball hats and old-school sneakers initiated by New York art school students. Quickly spreading across the major megapolises of the world, normcore expressed non-deterministic, unconcerned with authenticity aspirations of post-postmodern cultural realm, privileging empathy over tolerance and striving for belonging rather than differentiation (Duncan, 2014). This description also provides a rare example of the metamodern sensitivities that are characterized by the constant movement between the modern and the postmodern ideas of collectivity and individualism, irony and enthusiasm, totality and anti-authoritarianism (van den Akker and Vermeulen, 2010: 2). Understanding of normcore sartorial practice in the context of this ideological underpinning provides additional perspective on the romanticizing of the ordinary, the mundane, the non-individualistic as a sartorial platform for connection, sincerity, and belonging. K-hole writes, 'Normcore seeks the freedom that comes with non-exclusivity. It finds liberation in being nothing special' (2013). This statement echoes accurately Gvasalia's widely communicated claim that fashion 'is not to be in the fashion book …. It is just things that people want to wear' (Amed, 2016) that privileges simplicity over conceptual and aesthetic complexity.

Emerging during the very same time, 2013, it is apparent that normcore and Vetements responded to similar sentiment and were driven by the same aesthetic aspiration – to move away from postmodern apathy to metamodern empathy. And while the differences in price point of the clothes worn by normcore followers and Vetements clientele are noticeably different, I offer to focus here not on the consumer product per se but on aesthetics that stems from and responds to the same fragmented consumption-oriented cultural realm. Both normcore and Vetements have remained 'faithful to the milieu that they transform, but from which they also draw the force of their gesture' (Vinken, 2005: 65), both focusing not only on the same sartorial wardrobe but also highlighting the brands associated with them. For example, Normcore wore the Champion sweatshirts, and Vetements also collaborated with the brand (Figure 3.1). However, while normcore impacted fashion from the outside leading to its fast appropriation by the very system it criticized, Vetements, by default situated inside the fashion system, utilized the fashion platforms and discourse to legitimize this aesthetic proposition and turned it into something bigger than just a seasonal trend. The metamodern attitude of Vetements becomes clear in the attempt to transgress the fashion system without necessarily denying it, to be sincere in the place of smoke and mirrors.

The Oxford English Dictionary defines sincere as 'genuine, not perverted in any way, and uncontaminated' (OED online, 2019); various examples of this quality can be found in Vetements' actions. It is in the straightforwardness of Gvasalia's claim 'what we do is nothing new' (Amed, 2016), in cheerful reaction on the copying of Vetements raincoats printed 'Vetememes' (Friedman, 2016). In the Collaborations collection (Spring 2017) overtly celebrating the brands that originally produced each one of the staples Vetements continuously redesigns. And it is certainly in the choice of the items representative of what is found in the average closet that constitute their collections, 'a skirt, a pant, a bomber jacket' (Suleman, 2015).

It can be argued that Gvasalia's privileging of ordinary clothes is indebted to his exposure to those garments in different cultural systems – notably his Soviet upbringing in the later 1980s to early 1990s, where the deficit of most basic consumer goods made an 'Adidas tracksuit comparable with Lamborghini' (Fury, 2016d). Added to this was his adulthood in Western Europe, where the same garments were common, ordinary and hence passed unnoticed, as well

Figure 3.1 Yanis Vlamos, Vetements SS 2016 – green tracksuit with Vetements logo in Champion font. Courtesy of Vetements.

as his multiple research trips in the United States during his tenure in Maison Margiela and Louis Vuitton (Amed, 2016). The interactions with such garments in these distinctly different cultural contexts revealed the potentially different meanings and values embedded in them. Hoodies, tracksuits, jeans and T-shirts are simultaneously fetishized commodities – status markers, exotic symbols of the inaccessible West – material representation of the political system, the tropes of mundane everydayness and stamps of identity. The romanticizing of those garments means the romanticizing of the lived experiences behind the clothes, bringing visibility to communities and places that are often not considered to be inspiring, which in Vetements' case is achieved through elevation of the garments by their display in the context of high fashion. The result is a parade of oversized hoodies (all the collections) often featuring teenage-maximalist-inspired graphics like 'May the bridges I burn light the way' (Fall 2016) or simply references to a popular culture trope, that is, *Titanic* or *Star Wars* (both from Spring 2016). There are also delicate full-length floral print dresses (Fall 2015, Spring 2016, Fall 2016), deconstructed blue jeans (Fall 2015) and Soviet school uniform dress (Fall 2016).

Even though such approach sometimes may be criticized as appropriation, the brand does not see it as a conflict, the blunt copying is its way to bring real and genuine into the fashion discourse, and it is so much so that often 'it [is] difficult to see where the runway ends and reality begins' (Fury, 2016b).

These examples share a similar, hard-to-determine flavour, restlessly moving between irony and empathy, sarcasm and enthusiasm, expressing in fashion what van den Akker and Vermeulen, as well as other scholars noted in contemporary art, cinema and literature (2017). Here, the romanticizing of the simple familiar garments happens by way of embedding them with a personalized touch or a collective memory. The effect is twofold, on the one hand opening the possibility to relate, to contextualize the clothes within one's own past, while, on the other, preserving the commonplace and approachable qualities. And it is in this slightly paradoxical way that these garments become active agents driving the sense of belonging, of collectivity. In van den Akker and Vermeulen words, this process 'redirects the modern piece (*fashion*) by drawing attention to what it cannot present in its language, what it cannot signify in its own terms (*clothes*)' (2010: 10). The 'structure of feelings' revealed by Vetements is indebted to their ability to draw the attention of the fashion discourse back to clothes, highlighting the unspectacular, mundane garments as a depository of tactile, emotional and semiotic meaning, the perspective long missing from the fashion domain. The interest of the brand in the ordinary suggests that the notion of fashion as spectacular and outstanding is reductive, and by trying to redefine it against its own premise they offer an alternative perception of what fashion can be. The renowned trend forecaster Li Edelkoort was quick to recognize this attempt, in her comment she commends Vetements for 'the focus on the essence of clothes' (Socha, 2015), noting that their practice is bigger than just a trend and will eventually lead to a new structure in fashion. 'This is about more reconstruction than deconstruction', she summarized echoing the metamodern aspirations described by van den Akker and Vermeulen.

Raoul Eshelman too supports this perspective in his *Introduction to Performatism, or the End of Postmodernism*, where he argues that the newly emerging aesthetic is concerned with 'a fundamental assumption about how signs relate to things' (2008: X). In this case, it is the relationship between fashion, a sign, and clothes, material things, that is under investigation in Vetements practices, and it is through the process of romanticizing of the ordinary, the material and the familiar that this connection is attempted to be re-established.

The peculiar case of the DHL T-shirt

On 1 October 2015, a man wearing a bright yellow T-shirt, featuring the red DHL logo across the chest, visually identical to the one worn by DHL couriers across

Figure 3.2 Yanis Vlamos, Vetements SS 2016 – the DHL T-shirt.
Courtesy of Vetements.

the globe, opened Vetements show during Spring 2016 fashion week in Paris (Figure 3.2). Through the analysis of the event and the dissociated components that it was made of, the history of the garment, the sociocultural context of its being a uniform of a courier and the fashion discourse it was placed in, I aim to demonstrate the metamodern qualities of Vetements' practice.

The T-shirt

One of the more common, basic and unassuming items of clothing, the T-shirt started as a knitted or sewn undergarment made of plain and soft cotton or wool. Usually sleeveless or with short sleeves, its purpose was to protect the body from the rougher outer garments often made of unrefined fibres, to absorb sweat and provide heat and comfort due to the characteristics of cotton or wool cloth. While the widely accepted theory is that T-shirt first appeared as a part of the UK Royal Navy uniform (Antonelli and Millar Fisher, 2017), according to the study of sociologists Betsy Cullum-Swan and Peter Manning (1994: 419), in America the item of clothing serving as undershirt was originally made at home for the members of the household, remaining a strictly private garment for private spaces. With industrialization, T-shirts started to be mass-produced but still preserved the intimate character of the undershirt. Wearing T-shirts in public was a transgressive act as epitomized by Marlon Brando's performance in the cinematic production of Tennessee Williams's *A Streetcar Named Desire* in 1951. During this period, the T-shirt gained its first cultural signification as a garment representative of the post-war atmosphere of disillusionment that confronted the blue-collar male returning home (Cullum-Swan and Manning, 1994: 420). Tightly stretched on the muscular body, dirty with sweat, the T-shirt became representative of raw physical masculinity as well as eroticism (Lippe, 2009: 6). This marked the beginning of the T-shirt's cultural evolution as an outer garment containing meanings beyond its functionality, capable of communicating information about the identity of the wearer (Cullum-Swan and Manning, 1994: 421), turning the T-shirt into the semiotic sign of social communication. During the 1960s T-shirts became more ubiquitous due to the general liberalization of Western societies. In these years the T-shirt evolved into an embodied message board, through which the wearers communicated their beliefs and ambitions associating themselves with the logos, slogans or other graphic material printed on the garment (Neal, 2014: 187). The transgressive attitude characterizing the postmodern cultural climate did not escape the T-shirt. Torn, mutilated and decorated with shocking graphics, it became a prominent part of the punk repertoire, becoming a powerful agent for 'communication of a significant difference' (Hebdige, 2005: 259). The accessibility, easy and cheap production and comfort made the T-shirt from its early days into an essential element of many professional uniforms associated with physical activity, including security jobs, production line manufacturing or couriers and delivery personnel. Essential, yet an ordinary and modest item of the sartorial closet, the T-shirt is a carrier of rich 'cultural biography' (Kopytoff, 1986: 67) that contains (or reveals) a complex trajectory of changes in the cultural logic of the West since modernity until the beginning of the twenty-first century.

The uniform – brand, labour, mobility

The explanation provided by Gvasalia about the idea to design a T-shirt similar to the one sported by the couriers of the shipping company is unabashedly straightforward. According to the designer, the interaction with the courier company became a recurring motif of the everyday routine in Vetements studio. 'DHL seemed to be more a part of my life than anything else', explained the designer, 'so I thought, why isn't it in the show?' (Cochrane, 2016). Extrapolating the perception of fashion as a reflection of the everyday experiences, Vetements' avoidance of any conceptual pretence becomes a concept in its own right, and indeed a telling one.

In fact, the California-founded company referenced in the garment, DHL (the name is the abbreviation of the founders' initials Dalsey, Hillblom and Lynn), became the world's largest logistics company, after it was acquired by Deutsche Post in 2002 (Deutsche Post DHL Group, official website). Subsequently, it stands for globalization, as well as connection. The constant presence of the corporate in the life of cultural producers, in this case fashion designers, sheds light on the scale of fashion geographies revealing the long-distance communication routes between points of creative conception, production and distribution. Highly visible and recognizable, the uniform is associated with the physical labour of thousands of couriers around the world, which makes the garment accessible and easily relatable to. While sharing similarities, the use of familiar logo by Vetements is different from the appropriations conducted with other brand's logos. For instance, the use of McDonalds logo by Jeremy Scott for Moschino (Fall 2014) drove to the major split of opinions between those who saw it as a criticism and 'an unflattering comparison between fast food and fast fashion' (BOF, 2014) and those who understood it as an ode to a provocative sense of humour of Franco Moschino himself, in the best traditions of the postmodern irony. DHL is so prosaic and mundane that it does not create any negative sentiment, the only controversy here is the question, what is it doing on the catwalk and why is the price so high? And this is exactly what makes it different.

The direct, with no twist, use of the uniform supplies more evidence on the metamodern character of the design. While according to Naomi Klein, 'trend-setting cool kids' of the 1990s 'express[ed] their disdain for mass culture … not by opting out of it but by abandoning themselves to it entirely – but with a sly ironic twist' (Klein, 1999: 86), nowadays the tendency seems to be for no irony at all, exemplifying the sentiment different from postmodern. While the distinctions are delicate, they are not marginal, and the use of similar approach does not suggest the same meaning, as illustrated by the example of normcore mentioned earlier. The editor of *Creative Review* and author of *Board: Surf, Skate, Snow Graphics*, Patrick Burgoyne, supports this assumption in his comment to the *Independent:* 'This is straight up, perhaps now there is so much corporate control that the most subversive thing to do is to have the thing in the actual form' (Cochrane, 2016). And the strategy director of Wolff Olins interviewed for the same article calls it 'a shortcut to social realism', which brings this analysis back to the simple, yet rather meaningful reason provided by Gvasalia. The resonance created by the T-shirt underlines the depth of the everydayness and its potential for powerful message-making if studied with attention, showcasing the approach as one of the major contributions of Vetements.

The context

The appearance of the T-shirt in the show published on the official schedule of Paris Fashion Week is another significant detail. As described by Yuniya Kawamura (2004), the French fashion system is a highly selective affair, consolidated under one trade organization, Federation de la Haute-Couture et de la Mode, who is the main gatekeeper of this hierarchical field. 'Entries into these organizations are exclusive and difficult' in order to preserve the powerful position of the French fashion on a global scale (Kawamura, 2004: 53–4). The choice of the venue, however, was far less exclusive, being staged in a large Chinese restaurant in Belleville on the outskirts of Paris, a choice bearing similarities with the unconventional show locations of Martin Margiela, that is, the Spring 1990 show in a derelict neighbourhood playground or Autumn 1992 presented in Salvation Army depot.

The fact that the model wearing the shirt was the famous photographer and fashion designer Gosha Rubchinskiy emphasizes the disjuncture between three social positions that converge in the garment. First, the blue-collar employee of the DHL company, referenced by the uniform. Second, the model, who could hypothetically be read as a courier if he were not walking in the clearly determined site of the show, is instead a fashion celebrity, who in this case serves as to reinterpret the T-shirt moving it from mundane workwear into fashionable commodity. And third, a potential customer representing a different social milieu characterized by high economic standing which would enable him/her to spend US$240 on a T-shirt. Here, the modest piece of clothing representative of hard physical labour is transformed into a coveted fashion item through the process of romanticizing embodied (or materialized/exemplified) by the recognizable but unassuming personality of Rubchinskiy.

The simplicity of the DHL T-shirt walking down the exclusive runway underlines another qualitative distinction between the postmodern and the metamodern sentiment. While the former is rooted in cynicism and sarcasm leading to apathy and withdrawal, the latter is light-hearted and humble, drawing empathy. Even though the shirt is slightly altered in design by the red stripe running across the back and fit, the bright colours of the garment and the graphics are dominant enough to make a fashion statement without a need to purchase the original Vetements product, creating an ambiguous mix, where the T-shirts from Vetements, from the DHL website priced at US$6.50 and a myriad of copies available online for prices ranging from US$20 to $100 (Cochrane, 2016) intermingled on the streets and on Instagram feeds. On the one hand, Vetements' aesthetic statement acknowledges the logo culture dominating the industry from the beginning of the millennium and challenges the hierarchies associated with the brand names, be it in fashion or the corporate world. If wearing the logo-branded clothes is in fashion, suggests Gvasalia, it might as well be the logo of DHL (Finningan, 2016). On the other hand, it leverages the power of fashion discourse to elevate something ordinary and mundane, to create an impossible and brief confusion between high-fashion clientele and the blue-collar labourer and to ignite the desire for clothes that until recently were rather unnoticeable due to their prosaic ordinariness, not to mention fashionable. The effect here is the oscillation between the crude critique of the fashion system with its pretentious exclusivity, through 'hyperrealism' (Cartner-Morly, 2018) to the naiveté of the sincere humour that continuously questions why not; one is rational with conscious intent, another emotional, yet both in different ways explore what fashion might be. Hence, the controversial gesture of opening the show with the prosaic item of clothing bearing the corporate logo of the ordinary brand is metamodern in all of its qualities.

Vetements are not original in the controversy surrounding their practices, which might recall Duchamp's signed urinal, *Fountain*, placed in an art gallery in 1917 and Margiela's garments made of the linings from vintage dresses from his Spring 1996 collection, just to name a few. What is different is this new type of ambiguity in the message, one that criticizes (the postmodern) and embraces (the modern), ironic and sincere. All the elements of the fashion show are present in the appearance of the DHL T-shirt – designer, clothes, runway, model – but each one of them is relatively alien to the other, creating a situation that 'floats in a zone that is both instantly recognizable, because it reminds one of all these earlier traditions, but also strange, since its logic adheres to no tradition in particular' (van den Akker and Vermeulen, 2015: 59). This brings to the surface a rich vocabulary of meanings and associations that do not fit right together, though, nor do they collide but rather coalesce in the metamodern amalgam, negotiating the meaning through the continuous process of oscillation. The unrealistic constellation of ideas that are unrelated or even alien to one another is idealistic, impossible and often problematic, but it is daring and it does resonate with the public given the emotional response it receives either from the fans of Vetements aesthetics or by its vocal critics.

Conclusion

In *The Restless Image: A Sociology of Fashion* German theorist René Koenig argues that fashion 'is a general social institution, it affects and shapes individuals and society as a whole' (1973: 40), and at the same time it is a cultural phenomenon and a material object reflective of the zeitgeist of the time (Vinken, 2005: 41). Hence, the cultural production of fashion simultaneously is a result of the cultural climate and has an impact on it. While the post-postmodern condition is shaping, the theories and ideas are still in active interaction, yet the metamodern perspective is particular and important in the way that it engages with the intangible aspects of aesthetic and emotional experiences.

The neoromantic perspective van den Akker and Vermeulen find so prominent in cultural expressions at the beginning of the twenty-first century, on the one hand, follows the traditional definition of romanticism privileging 'emotional introspection', 'uniqueness, and dissimilarities' (Berlin, 1965: 14), while on the other focuses on very different experiences and objects, not traditionally associated with romanticism. As demonstrated above, both of these aspects are present in the work of Vetements, and this is what makes the case so pertinent for the discussion of post-postmodern expressions in fashion. Therefore, while the questions about the legitimacy of certain practices loom high over Vetements, I suggest it worth dwelling over the creative approaches, choices of garments brought to the fore and reactions evoked by the brand before simply dismissing the case of the DHL T-shirt as appropriation.

There are reasons for the resonance the brand achieved, and these reasons are bound to the cultural condition of the beginning of the twenty-first century, to the 'structure of feeling' defining this historical moment. The yearning characterizing it is not for the past like in postmodern nostalgia, neither it is for authenticity but for sincerity. Fashion is not often associated with this quality, but the ordinary and the mundane items of the sartorial wardrobe are deeply engrained with it. Rich depositories of meaning, those clothes contain the elements of life experiences and the sensibilities related to those experiences, be it on the practical level – in their simple cut, durable materiality and comfortable fit – or on conceptual, what they represent – lifestyles, attitudes, geographies. The complex 'cultural biographies' of these clothes make them unique and their qualities increasingly acknowledged in the post-postmodern cultural realm inviting new ways for romantic expressions through clothes and expanding the definition of fashion.

References

Akker, R., and T. Vermeulen (2010), 'Notes on Metamodernism', *Journal of Aesthetics & Culture*, 2 (1). Available online https://www.tandfonline.com/doi/full/10.3402/jac.v2i0.5677 (accessed 2 June 2018).

Akker, R., and T. Vermeulen (2015), 'Utopia, Sort of: A Case Study in Metamodernism', *Studia Neophilologica*, 87: 55–67. Available online https://tandfonline.com/doi/full/https://tandfonline.com/doi/full/10.1080/00393274.2014.981964 (accessed 2 June 2018).

Akker, R., and T. Vermeulen (2017), 'Periodising the 2000s, or, the Emergence of Metamodernism', in R. Akker, A. Gibbons and T. Vermeulen (eds), *Metamodernism: Historicity, Affect and Depth after Postmodernism*, 1–19. London: Rowman & Littlefield.

Amed, I. (2016), 'Demna Gvasalia Reveals Vetements' Plan to Disrupt the Fashion System', *Business of Fashion, Intelligence*, 5 February. Available online https://www.businessoffashion.com/articles/intelligence/ demna-gvasalia-reveals-vetements-plan-to-disrupt-the-fashion-system (accessed 20 February 2016).

Antonelli, P., and M. Millar Fisher (2017), *ITEMS: Is Fashion Modern?* New York: Museum of Modern Art.

Aronowsky-Cronberg, A. (2016), 'The Revolution Will Be Branded Vetements', *Vestoj*. Available online http://vestoj.com/the-revolution-will-be-branded-vetements (accessed 22 May 2016).

Baudrillard, J. ([1976] 1993), *Symbolic Exchange and Death*, trans. I. Hamilton Grant, London: Sage.

Berlin, I. (1965), *The Roots of Romanticism*, Princeton, NJ: Princeton University Press.

Bourriaud, N. (2009), *Relational Aesthetics*, Dijon, France: Les Presses du Réel.

Breward, C. (2000), *Fashion*, Oxford: Oxford University Press.

Buckley, C., and H. Clark (2017), *Fashion in Everyday Lives: London and New York*, London: Bloomsbury.

Cartner-Morley, J. (2018), 'I Don't Think Elegance Is Relevant: Vetements' Demna Gvasalia, the Worlds Hottest Designer', *The Guardian*, 6 February. Available online https://www.theguardian.com/fashion/2018/feb/06/i-dont-think-elegance-is-relevant-vetements-demna-gvasalia-the-worlds-hottest-designer (accessed 13 May 2019).

Cochrane, L. (2016), 'Scam or Subversion? How a DHL T-shirt Became This Year's Must-Have', *The Guardian*, 20 April. Available online https://www.theguardian.com/fashion/2016/apr/19/dhl-t-shirt-vetements-fashion-paris-catwalk (accessed 13 August 2016).

Cullum-Swan, B., and P. K. Manning (1994), 'What Is a t-shirt? Codes, Chronotypes, and Everyday Objects', in S. H. Riggins (ed.), *The Socialness of Things: Essays on the Socio-Semiotics of Objects*. Berlin: De Gruyter Mouton.

Duncan, F. (2014), 'Normcore: Fashion for Those Who Realize They're One in 7 Billion', Cut, *New York Magazine*, 26 February. Available online https://www.thecut.com/2014/02/normcore-fashion-trend.html (accessed 5 October 2015).

Eshelman, R. (2008), *Performatism, or, the End of Postmodernism*, Aurora: Davies.

Finningan, K. (2016), 'Demna Gvasalia on Race, That DHL T-shirt and Why He Wouldn't Pay for His Own Designs', *The Telegraph*, 16 May. Available online https://www.telegraph.co.uk/fashion/people/demna-gvasalia-on-race-that-dhl-t-shirt-and-why-he-wouldnt-pay-f/ (accessed 13 October 2016).

Foucault, M. ([1975] 1995), *Discipline and Punish.* New York: Random House.

Friedman, V. (2015), 'Balenciaga Names Demna Gvasalia, Vetements Designer, as Artistic Director', *New York Times*, 7 October. Available online https://www.nytimes.com/2015/10/08/fashion/balenciaga-names-demna-gvasalia-vetements-designer-as-artistic-director.html (accessed 13 October 2016).

Friedman, V. (2016), 'Vetements Won't be Pouring Cold Water on the Parody Raincoat', *New York Times,* 31 March. Available online https://www.nytimes.com/2016/04/01/fashion/vetements-wont-be-pouring-cold-water-on-parody-raincoat.html?rref=collection/sectioncollection/fashion&action=click&contentCollection=fashion&region=rank&module=package&version=highlights&contentPlacement=3&pgtype=sectionfront&_r=1 (accessed 15 March 2017).

Fury, A. (2015), 'The Label Vetements Is the Most Radical Thing to Come Out of Paris in Over a Decade. So What's the Big Idea?' *The Independent*, 16 October. Available online www.independent.co.uk/life-style/fashion/features/the-label-vetements-is-the-most-radical-thing-to-come-out-of-paris-in-over-a-decade-so-whats-the-big-a6692211.html (accessed 13 October 2016).

Fury, A. (2016a), 'Demna Gvasalia Is Making Clothes That Are Meant to Be Worn', *W Magazine*, 8 March. Available online https://www.wmagazine.com/story/demna-gvasalia-vetements (accessed 13 October 2016).

Fury, A. (2016b), 'These Two Guys Are Changing How We Think about Fashion', *New York Times, T-magazine*, 11 April. Available online https://www.nytimes.com/2016/04/11/t-magazine/gucci-alessandro-michele-balenciaga-vetements-demna-gvasalia.html (accessed 13 October 2016).

Fury, A. (2016c), 'VETEMENTS: Fit Me Better Than My Favourite Sweater', *10 Men* (43), 13 April. Available online http://www.10magazine.com.au/men/vetements-fit-better-favourite-sweater// (accessed 13 October 2016).

Fury, A. (2016d), 'DEMNA', *Fantastic Man* (24): 202–13.

Gibson, W. (2003), *Pattern Recognition*, Berkeley: Penguin Publishing Group.

Gilroy, P. (1993), *The Black Atlantic: Modernity and Double-Consciousness.* London, New York: Verso.

Gladwell, M. (1997), 'The Coolhunt', *New Yorker*, 10 March.

Gonsalves, R. (2014), 'The Y Still Has It: The Masterful Japanese Designer Yohji Yamamoto Shows No Signs of Taking a Back Seat in his Fashion Empire', *The Independent*, 1 February.

Grayer Moore, J. (2017), *Street Style in America: An Exploration.* Santa Barbara, California: Greenwood Publishing Group. Available online http://ebookcentral.proquest.com/lib/newschool/detail.action?docID=4926414 (accessed 11 June 2019).

Hebdige, D. (2005), 'Subculture: The Meaning of Style', in K. Gelder (ed.), *The Subcultures Reader*, 121–31, London, New York: Routledge.

Hill, W. (2015), 'A Hipster History: Towards a Postcritical Aesthetic', *Critical Studies in Fashion and Beauty*, 6 (1): 45–60.

Hutcheon, L. (2002), *The Politics of Postmodernism*, New York/London: Routledge.

Kawamura, Y. (2004), *Fashion-ology: An Introduction to Fashion Studies*, Bloomsbury Publishing: ProQuest Ebook Central. Available online http://ebookcentral.proquest.com/lib/newschool/detail.action?docID=533063 (accessed 8 June 2019).

K-HOLE (2013), 'Youth mode: A Report on Freedom'. Available online http://khole.net/issues/youth-mode/http://khole.net/issues/youth-mode/ (accessed 10 October 2015).

Kirby, A. (2009), *Digimodernism: How New Technologies Dismantle the Postmodern and Reconfigure our Culture*, New York, London: Continuum.

Klein, N. (1999), *No Logo*, Toronto: Random House of Canada.

Koenig, R. (1973), *The Restless Image: A Sociology of Fashion*, trans. F. Bradley, London: George Allen & Unwin.

Kopytoff, I. (1986), 'The Cultural Biography of Things: Commoditization as Process', in A. Appadurai (ed.), *The Social Life of Things*, 63–94, New York, Cambridge: Cambridge University Press.

Lippe, R. (2009), 'Elia Kazan 1909 2009: A Man in Conflict', *Cineaction*: 6–7. Available online https://login.libproxy.newschool.edu/login?url=https://search-proquest-com.libproxy.newschool.edu/docview/216883005?accountid=12261 (accessed 20 June 2019).

Lipovetsky, G. (1994), *The Empire of Fashion*, Princeton: Princeton University Press.

Lyotard, J.-F. ([1979] 1984), *The Postmodern Condition: A Report on Knowledge*, trans. G. Bennington and B. Massumi, Minneapolis: University of Minnesota Press.

Morgado, M. A. (1996), 'Coming to Terms with Postmodern: Theories and Concepts of Contemporary Culture and Their Implications for Apparel Scholars', *Clothing and Textiles Research Journal*, 14 (1): 41–53.

Morgado, M. A. (2014), 'Fashion Phenomena and the Post-Postmodern Condition: Enquiry and Speculation', *Fashion, Style & Popular Culture*, 1 (3): 313–39.

Mower, S. (2015), 'Vetements Spring 2016 Collection Review', *Vogue* 2 October. Available online https://www.vogue.com/fashion-shows/spring-2016-ready-to-wear/vetements (accessed on 3 October 2015).

Mower, S. (2016a), 'Vetements Fall 2016 Collection Review', *Vogue* 4 March. Available online https://www.vogue.com/fashion-shows/fall-2016-ready-to-wear/vetements (accessed on 5 March 2016).

Mower, S. (2016b), 'Vetements Spring 2017 Collection Review', *Vogue*, 4 July. Available online https://www.vogue.com/fashion-shows/spring-2017-ready-to-wear/vetements (accessed on 7 July 2016).

Mower, S. (2016c), 'How Demna Gvasalia Is Revolutionizing Balenciaga from the Inside Out', *Vogue*, 18 August. Available online https://www.vogue.com/article/demna-gvasalia-balenciaga-artistic-director-vetements-cofounder-designer (accessed on 16 September 2016).

Neal, L. S. (2014), 'The Ideal Democratic Apparel: T-shirts, Religious Intolerance, and the Clothing of Democracy', *Material Religion*, 10 (2): 182–207.

Nealon, J. T. (2012), *Post-Postmodernism or, the Cultural Logic of Just-in-Time Capitalism*, Stanford: Stanford University Press.

OED online (2019), 'Sincere, Adj', Oxford University Press. Available online https://www-oed-com.libproxy.newschool.edu/view/Entry/180053?redirectedFrom=sincere (accessed 21 June 2019).

Rabkin, E. (2016), 'Vestoj X SZ: What Revolution? T-Magazine, Gucci, and Vetements', *StyleZeitgeist*, 16 April. Available online https://www.sz-mag.com/news/2016/04/vestoj-x-sz-what-revolution-t-magazine-gucci-and-vetements/ (accessed 15 November 2016).

Simmel, G. ([1901] 2004), 'Fashion', in D. L. Purdy (ed.), *The Rise of Fashion*, 298–309. Minneapolis: University of Minnesota Press.

Socha, M. (2015), 'Demna Gvasalia – His Own Rules', *WWD*, 18 November. Available online wwd.com/fashion-news/fashion-features/demna-gvasalia-balenciage-vetements-10279574 (accessed 13 October 2016).

Sombart, W. ([1902] 2004), 'Economy and Fashion: A Theoretical Contribution on the Formation of Modern Consumer Demand', in D. L. Purdy (ed.), *The Rise of Fashion*,,310–16, Minneapolis: University of Minnesota Press.

Stallybrass, P. (1999), 'Worn Worlds: Clothes, Mourning, and the Life of Things', in D. Ben-Amos and L. Weissberg (eds), *Cultural Memory and the Construction of Identity*, 2727-4444, Detroit: Wayne State University Press.

Steele, V., ed. (2005), 'Hip Hop Fashion', *Encyclopedia of Clothing and Fashion*, 2: 214–18. Detroit, MI: Charles Scribner's Sons.

Suleman, A. (2015), 'Demna Gvasalia on Vetements', *Balenciaga, and THE SYSTEM*, 032c (29). https://032c.com/demna-gvasalia-vetements-balenciaga-system (accessed 13 October 2016).

Turner, L. (2015), 'Metamodernism: A Brief Introduction', *Notes on Metamodernism*. Available online http://www.metamodernism.com/2015/01/12/metamodernism-a-brief-introduction/ (accessed 2 June 2018).

Van de Peer, A. (2014). 'So Last Season: The Production of the Fashion Present in the Politics of Time', *Fashion Theory*, 18 (3): 317–40.

Veblen, T. ([1899] 2007), 'Dress as an Expression of the Pecuniary Culture', in B. Malcolm (ed.), *Fashion Theory*, London: Routledge.

Vinken, B. (2005), *Fashion Zeitgeist*, Oxford: Berg.

Williams, R. ([1954] 2001), 'Film and the Dramatic Tradition', in J. Higgins (ed.), *The Raymond Williams Reader*, 25–41, Oxford: Blackwell.

Wilson, E. ([1985] 2014), *Adorned in Dreams*, London, New York: I.B. Tauris.

4

INTENSIFIED: ALESSANDRO MICHELE'S HYPERAESTHETIC AT GUCCI

Nigel Lezama

Since Alessandro Michele assumed creative control of the brand in January 2015, Gucci has transformed both the fashion cognoscenti and the ordinary consumer into bedazzled bohemians and radical ragpickers. In 2018, the Italian fashion and accessories company, owned by French luxury conglomerate Kering, became the world's top growing fashion brand, according to Interbrand's *Best Global Brands Report*, by crafting an altogether new fashion language, at least according to the fashion press. Indeed, Michele's aesthetic, elaborated in the brand's fashion shows, events, advertising campaigns, products and spaces, is discombobulating and beguiling in equal measure. To enter the Gucci universe is like falling down a globalized and cultural rabbit hole where high becomes low; big, small; ugly, strangely beautiful. It is this aesthetic aporia that makes Gucci one of the brands of the post-postmodern moment, characterized by a globalized economy in which economic growth is divorced from production, by a financial system that impoverishes the many to the benefit of the few (corporate entities and their key officers) and, importantly, by the problem of representation in a society of consumption; that is to say, an onerously indebted consumer class compelled to live *as if* wealth were real and consumption not a mortgage on the future (cf. Baudrillard, 1970). Michele's Gucci reaches both backward and forward, extends both up and down, uses elite and popular references, and enlightens and alienates the consuming public. In this way, the Italian creative director's aesthetic materializes the economic and social contradictions that have intensified since the full emergence of neoliberalism, in response to the world economic crises of the 1970s and 1980s (Nealon, 2012: 15) and culminating in globalization and the ensuing financial neocolonialism. The Gucci fashion paradox is profoundly productive and ultimately responsive to this cultural context.

Post-postmodernism, accordingly, can be read as an economically centred categorization of the current period, when the cultural, political and economic fields have coalesced to form a cultural politics of contradictory extremes. In the ideological west of consumer culture, individuals seem ever more liberated from habitus-driven practices, yet financial domination of the political field has rarely been more acutely experienced than in the far-reaching wake of the 2008 subprime mortgage crisis (Harvey, 2010). Great Britain's fitful exit from the EU; Donald Trump's election in the United States; the rise and radicalization of xenophobic, misogynist and racist groups; and the devolution of basic human rights led by the reactionary right, each expresses the dominance of late capitalist ideology and ensuing neoliberal thinking. However, the broad demand for reconciliation by previously marginalized sociopolitical, gendered and racialized groups, as well as the growing awareness of the ruinous impact of human intervention on the planet demonstrate that the current moment also inspires counterhegemonic practices and beliefs. Jeffrey Nealon's (2012) book *Post-Postmodernism or, the Cultural Logic of Just-in-Time Capitalism* uses Frederic Jameson's formidable dialectical analysis of the postmodernism of the 1980s as a model to interpret this postmillennial cultural sphere in which consumption, politics and identity intermingle to both positive and negative effect. Like Jameson thirty years prior, Nealon seeks to impose neither moral nor ethical readings on contemporary phenomena. Rather, *Post-Postmodernism* is Nealon's attempt to 'make post-postmodern sense' (Nealon, 2012: xii) in and of the contemporary moment.

How do Michele's Gucci and post-postmodernism find space in the same analysis? Gucci's growing global value is inextricably linked to the cultural conditions of its existence. That Michele's carnivalesque aesthetic could gain such cultural currency signals that it is not merely the Romantic myth of the isolated creative genius at the source of Gucci's success, but that Michele is working both in and with the contemporary moment to craft an aesthetic that is a 'sign of the times', an expression of the state of things that both unnerves and entices the individual, precisely because the post-postmodern period is simultaneously dire and hopeful. Gucci's codes may seem bewilderingly polyphonic. French philosopher Gilles Lipovetsky argues, in his engaging analysis, *Hypermodern Times* (2005), that the current moment has witnessed a shrinking of 'a teleological vision of the future' (43) in which the 'future lends itself to being manufactured in a hyperrealist way: science and technology in combination aspire to explore the infinitely great, the infinitely small, to reshape life, to manufacture mutants, to offer a semblance of immortality, to resurrect vanished species, to programme the genetic future' (ibid.). Michele's Gucci materializes a *hyperaesthetic*, a 'manufactured' and aporetic style, singularly volatile and expressing the 'erosion of the organizing power of collective norms'

(52). Yet once the heterogeneity of elements is isolated and analysed, it becomes clear that the brand's aesthetic fuses multiple vestimentary and cultural signifiers that the contemporary consuming public must decipher, now that credit-fuelled consumption has overtaken the dispositions of social origin and education that, historically, determined taste and social practices – what French sociologist Pierre Bourdieu termed 'habitus' in his foundational analysis *Distinction. A Social Critique of the Judgement of Taste* ([1979] 1984).

Essentially, by harnessing a multivalent and paradoxical symbology Michele's Gucci dresses the post-postmodern consumer who, according to Lipovetsky, 'is nourished both by existential distress and by the pleasure associated with change, by the desire to intensify and reintensify, without end, the course of daily life' (2005: 52). Key to Michele's aesthetic is his repurposing and remixing of subcultural signs to obscure original counterhegemonic messages and foreground a 'liberated' aesthetic message. Further – and perhaps most importantly –, Gucci's current moves both backwards and forwards. Through his use (and misuse) of the logo, Michele revisits the house's history all the while rewriting it to 'manufacture' its future. In the aggregate, Gucci's revitalization has recoded the brand for the contemporary consuming subject – the *hyperconsumer* – as Lipovetsky terms this post-postmodern subject in his analysis of contemporary consumption practices, 'La Société d'hyperconsommation' (2003).

Reaching down, pushing up

For an earlier period, Pierre Bourdieu and Yvette Delsaut chart the movement of players in the field of high fashion and ensuing shifts in consecration in their germinal work 'Le Couturier et sa griffe' (1975). Established fashion houses maintain and accumulate cultural, economic and symbolic capital by producing fashions that satisfy dominant class tastes. Young designers build their capital working as *créateurs* and *créatrices* in these austere and older houses that also acquire some of the lustre of the later generation. After accumulating sufficient social, economic and symbolic capital, these younger players establish their own houses, seeking consecration at the expense of their former employers. Bourdieu and Delsaut turn to the example of Christian Dior and Pierre Balmain, who, once having gained sufficient symbolic capital working for the older house of Lucien Lelong, leave to found their own eponymous houses that eclipse the founding designers' former fashion stable. Later still, a young Yves Saint-Laurent joins the house of Dior, where he builds his economic and symbolic capital only to leave in 1962 to found his own haute couture brand. Each movement is an agonistic shift to ensure consecration as *la dernière mode*.

While this capitalist and Darwinian movement in the field of fashion remains relatively paradigmatic, in the contemporary moment the field of fashion has undergone a number of transformations, offering the possibility of different trajectories. For example, a counterexample to the Bourdieusian movement of the field of fashion is Christian Lacroix's move from Patou in 1987 to his own eponymous house, which led not to consecration but rather to expulsion from the field. More recently, Riccardo Tisci's exit from Givenchy and appointment as creative director at Burberry is a move by the brand that exemplifies Bourdieu's logic. Whether or not the British brand is able to use this designer to rebuild its capital remains to be seen, as analysts have looked to the brand's stock valuation as a sign that success is not assured. Raf Simons's abbreviated stint at Calvin Klein, from August 2016 to December 2018, simultaneously demonstrates a similar Bourdieusian move as well as the fundamental difference of the fashion system from Bourdieu's time to the contemporary period. In the introduction to their timely edited collection *The End of Fashion* (2019), Adam Geczy and Vicki Karaminas invoke Saint-Laurent's valedictory speech in 2002 in which he declared 'I have nothing in common with this new world of fashion' (Geczy and Karaminas, 2019: 2). For these fashion scholars, Saint-Laurent's declaration is more than a swan song; it is an utterance on the new state of the field of fashion. By the millennium, the agents of consecration were no longer a coterie of select gatekeepers of class habitus – journalists, stylists, fashion buyers and social elites, but had been complexified by the entry of non-traditional players: bloggers, celebrities and social media influencers (cf. Rocamora, 2016). Further, the increasing financialization of the luxury fashion industry, as highlighted by Dana Thomas in her fascinating exposé *How Luxury Lost Its Lustre* (2007), as well as the rise of fast fashion and street style photography also functioned to fundamentally transform the fashion system. Bourdieu and Delsaut's inaugural study charts the field when its movement could still be characterized as 'trickle-down', a social working that Simmel parsed in his germinal study *Philosophie der Mode* ([1905] 2013). However, since the 1960s in the capitalist West, fashion subcultures have materialized their dissent through 'the construction of a style' (Hebdige, 1979: 3) and, later, asserted dominance economically, so that the fashion system's movement can no longer be characterized as top-down. In 1991, Karl Lagerfeld exemplified fashion's sea change by using hip-hop's subcultural codes for Chanel's Spring/Summer collection.[1] Lagerfeld adapted the fashion practices of this subculture to invigorate the long-established vestimentary codes of a traditional mainstay of the *haute bourgeoisie*. Chanel's adoption of hip-hop's codes can be likened to Bourdieu's elucidation of the field of fashion. There is a fundamental difference, however, in that an established fashion house adopting the codes of a subculture can give the appearance of being on the cutting edge, but there is little change in the real status of the marginalized group whose fashion practices have been annexed.

Michele's use of subcultural fashion tropes at Gucci is different. In the contemporary period, first, subcultures are no longer marginal in the way that punk or hip-hop, for example, was in the 1970s and 1980s. Further, integration of subcultural practices into the mainstream divests subcultural taste expressions of their political force, as Polhemus, in his meticulous reading of subcultural fashion practices, *Street Style* (1994), elucidates with his concept of style 'bubbling up'. However, in this 'bubbling up', value is nevertheless extracted from the perception of 'authenticity', the 'fantasized image of The Real Thing' (12), Polhemus asserts. Yet, in post-postmodernity, subcultural and dominant cultural fashions no longer aspire to some form of zero-degree authenticity (other than from a marketing perspective). 'It is undeniable that, in celebrating the pleasures of the here and now and the latest thing, consumerist society is continually endeavouring to make collective memory wither away, to accelerate the loss of continuity and the abolition of any repetition of the ancestral' (Lipovetsky, 2005: 57). Consequently, the power of dominant culture and its habitus have waned as the impact of democratic and individualist ideology is experienced more and more profoundly in social practices, albeit through the tightening grip of late capitalist and neoliberal ideology on the cultural sphere. Lipovetsky (2005) rightly suggests that dominant ideologies no longer carry the same weight as they once did. 'Hypermodern culture is characterized by the weakening of regulative power of the collective institutions and the corresponding way in which actors have become autonomous *vis-à-vis* group imperatives, whether these come from family, religion, political parties or class cultures. Hence the individual becomes more opened up and mobile, fluid and socially independent' (55). Michele's aesthetic refracts the dispersal of mass culture and the rise of individual style tribes and subcultures each *performing* their counter-normative stance from differing ideological vantage points. Gucci now clothes a post-postmodern subject living in the intensified present of a hyperconsumerist society.

> The fact remains that far from being locked up in a self-enclosed present, our age is the scene of a frenzy of commemorative activities based on our heritage and a growth in national and regional, ethnic, and religious identities. The more our societies are dedicated followers of fashion, focused on the present, the more they are accompanied by a groundswell of memory. (Lipovetsky, 2005: 57)

Michele's fashion practice folds past and future, dominance and subjugation, homogeneity and alterity into an intensified aesthetic – that is to say, a *hyperaesthetic* – that is mobile, polyvalent and fundamentally aporetic.

Chasing Gucci's White Rabbit

Michele's Fall/Winter Ready-to-Wear show 'The Alchemist's Garden: An Anti-Modern Laboratory', which launched Milan's 2017 fashion week, exemplifies the post-postmodern fragmentation of social identity that responds to the shrinking of class hegemony that Lipovetsky (2003) elucidates. Unlike, say, Frida Giannini's Gucci, monochromatic, conventionally sexy, responding to a dominant class habitus aesthetic and, accordingly, to a postmodern context in which ' "timeless classics" [gain] in popularity' (Polhemus, 1994: 9), Michele's Gucci leaves the buying public scrambling to decode social identity from the garments shown. Walking through a Plexiglas corridor that frames a looming, mirrored pyramid, models seem like travellers on a utopian spaceship. Certain looks, for example, the opening one, hinted at dominant class habitus: a calf-length, white skirt, adorned with gold glitter along its pleats, matching tights and a white Mary Jane pump, almost demure were it not for the pearl embellishments dangling from the straps. Michele paired this monochromatic ensemble with a white, short-sleeved bouclé blazer that featured a black knitted band at the sleeve, down the collarless front panels, and along the hem and the opening of the two patch pockets. The mid-thigh-length jacket was worn over a shorter, red crew neck sweater with the same black band at the neck and the hem. The jacket was belted with a thin red leather strap buckled with the brand's signature horsebit brass closure. To adorn the model's neckline, Michele added a series of five cascading pearl necklaces with a bejewelled broach closure. She also wore a white knitted hood, embellished with a red and white knitted poppy at the centre of the collarbone. The hood left the face exposed, like a balaclava (see Figure 4.1).

There were many more other-worldly looks that could have opened the show more spectacularly. However, as the introduction into Michele's world, this look is significant. Like the tardy rabbit who compels Alice down the rabbit hole, this outfit seems, at first glance, quite ordinary. In Carroll's tale, it is only once the rabbit pulls a pocket watch out of his waistcoat that Alice realizes the extraordinariness of the scene unfolding before her. Gucci's opening look, essentially a smart and conservative skirt suit adapted to the brand's codes, hints at the dominant taste of a more storied time. One could imagine the Duchess of Windsor in such an outfit. Revealing Michele's grasp of fashion history, the two-toned black and white jacket calls to mind Chanel's signature tweed jacket, a connotation only strengthened by the pearls that adorn the ensemble. Through the lens of fashion history, this outfit – at first glance – seems to express nothing extraordinary, like Alice and the rabbit, whose presence only surprises once the girl notices his waistcoat. Gucci's opening outfit may be made of luxurious materials, crafted by rarefied specialists and – sine qua non – expensive, but it is not in itself unexpected at a luxury fashion show. However, like Alice watching the tardy rabbit, the viewer is compelled to take a second, closer look as the extraordinary emerges from the seemingly ordinary.

The model's knitted balaclava and poppy, crowning a relatively staid ensemble, extracts this fashion from its evident class fraction positioning and points to alternative possibilities for skirt suits and pearls. At a practical level, the head

Figure 4.1 Autumn/Winter 2017 Ready-to-Wear Collection 'The Alchemist's Garden', Look 1, © Getty Images/Catwalking.

covering could be a nod to the contemporary modest fashion movement: this is a saleable garment that allows the wearer to be in the latest fashion, without transgressing personal mores. The accessory also connotes women's historical head coverings. The colour and simplicity hint at seventeenth-century Flemish women's coifs, for example. However, framed in the retro-futurist set design of 'The Alchemist's Garden', the bouclé balaclava, matching the relatively conventional skirt suit, gives the outfit an extraterrestrial flair, as all decoding possibilities – from the cultural to the historical to the science-fictional – converge. Michele's fashion aesthetic extends both forward and backward from the present. 'There is no degree zero of temporality, of a "self-referential" present consisting of radical indifference to what happened before and what will happen afterwards: the second kind of presentism that now rules our lives is no longer either postmodern or self-sufficient: it never ceases to open out onto something other than itself' (Lipovetsky, 2005: 41). In the introduction to their excellent study *Fashion and Modernism* (2019), editors Louise Wallenberg and Andrea Kollnitz foreground fashion's 'neomania'. The late nineteenth into the mid-twentieth century was the theatre of fashion's penchant for novelty, as the cultural moment sought to privilege progress, innovation and the avant-garde. The current period and its cultural production differ categorically in that notions, such as 'progress' and 'innovation' are no longer considered as uniquely positive drivers of social and cultural movement. Lipovetsky (2005) links this ideological redirection to society's 'secularization of modern representations of time, a process of disenchantment or modernization in the modern awareness of time itself' (42). Effectively, Michele opens his show with a look that annuls fashion time – the modernist (and postmodernist) teleology of newness for newness' sake – and prepares the viewing and buying public for his post-postmodernist alternate reality, where past and future converge to create the *hyperaesthetic* of an intensified (i.e. more dense) present. For Nealon, the post-postmodern period is characterized by an intensification, propelled by post-industrial capitalism's push to extract more profit from increasingly limited resources by 'money creating more money' (Nealon, 2012: 27), that is to say, in a model based on the financial market but brought to its full conclusion in the aesthetic and practices of contemporary Las Vegas. Whereas Jameson (1991), following Venturi, conceives of the city as the site of the collapse of distinction of high and low, and therefore fundamentally postmodern, Nealon's analysis pushes the collapse further as one of the economic into the cultural, making Las Vegas the capital of neoliberalist post-postmodernity.

In this new space, outside of fashion time, Michele's Gucci demonstrates the potential for a post-teleological aesthetic. Many brands take inspiration from fashion subcultures and global fashion practices for their collections. The most eclectic of brands, Dries Van Noten or Maison Margiela, for example, will look to a plethora of cultural practices or objects to build a given collection's story. While the story may shift from one season to another, the collection itself will express a unified message that speaks to a specific buying public. Remarkable in Michele's 'The Alchemist's Garden' is the confusion the designer integrates both at the level of the collection and in individual outfits. At the macro level, the Fall/Winter 2017 collection draws inspiration from divergent class fractions, style tribes and Western popular culture. There are looks that suggest the 1920s 'modern girl', 1950s rockabilly, 1970s glam rock, 1980s 'preppy' style, the femme fatale, cowboys, hippies, hip-hop, rockers, goth and punk. Other looks take inspiration from global fashion history: Geishas, the Belle Époque, the qipao, the Scottish Highlands and the leisure suit. The collection also nods to a 'Ziggy Stardust' futurism of the extraterrestrial with the designer's use of metallics, asymmetrical accessories and rhinestone-covered body and head stocking.

The Gucci Resort 2020 collection, entitled 'A Hymn to Freedom', which showed in the Capitoline Museums of Rome, continues Michele's heterogeneous and atemporal aesthetic (see Figure 4.2). In the darkened Renaissance space, filled with an alternating haunting electro soundscape that seemed to announce

Figure 4.2 Resort 2020 Collection, Look 57, © Getty Images Europe/Vittorio Zunino Celotto.

immanent apocalypse and redemption, Michele set up a narrow, labyrinthine runway. Lit by sparse spot and flashlights, lanky, ambisexual models stalked the runway dressed in roman tunics, glittering and breezy peasant dress, ecclesiastical-like robes, plain, muddy-coloured 1970s thrift shop finds and a number of logoed and signature-patterned separates, sets and accessories. The overall heterogeneity of looks is typical of Michele's merchandising eye. However, like the contemporary moment – both hopeful and dire – Michele's show expressed an uncanny timeliness. As American lawmakers actively attempt to disassemble twentieth-century attainments in women's fundamental rights through a worrying number of state-level bans on abortion, Michele's fashions declare support for women's autonomy and their bodily rights. Dressed in a billowy, white tunic, with loose smocking around the bicep opening into an accordion pleated bell sleeve, a pale female model with long black, messily braided and loose hair, seeming somewhere between Vestal Virgin priestess and countercultural hippy, walked the runway. Embroidered on the garment at the level of her hips was a paillette and beaded uterus, whose fallopian tubes ended in pink flowers. If the message of solidarity was not evident, on the back of another garment – a purple, double-G branded women's suit jacket with matching, ankle-length shirt – Michele emblazoned the well-worn 1970s slogan 'My Body, My Choice', making plain the collection's message of feminist solidarity. Alongside these empowering clothes, Michele also chose to introduce another iconic figure into the collection, Disney's Mickey Mouse, who appeared on a man's oxford shirt pocket, as part of a diamond pattern on a blousy, red men's sweater and on a number of handbags. The collection's pairing of a highly charged message countering masculine hegemony with the falsely affable icon of a global and globalized entertainment industry titan specializing in the creation of mediatized fantasies begs analysis. Lipovetsky (2005) argues for the thick ambivalence of the *hypermodern*. In this context, the yoking of the affirmingly individualist and the imposingly hegemonic, feminist first principles and a neoliberal rodent is a suitable pairing, which collectively signal 'the reign … of the immediate satisfaction of needs, but it is also that of a moral demand for recognition broadened to identities based on gender, sexual orientation or historical memory' (65). The presence of Mickey Mouse, the symbol of an imperialist entertainment industry, calls to mind Adorno and Horkheimer's scathing critique of the culture industry. The message of solidarity that Michele weaves into Gucci's politicized fashions speak to the personal freedoms that, unfortunately, still demand organized and collective action to protect, freedoms that the post-postmodern consumer can *endorse*, both literally and etymologically. Mickey's presence in the collection, however, is a call to order that foregrounds the corporate underpinnings of this fashion 'awakening' (following other 'woke' logos, like Maria Grazie Chiuri's 'We Should All Be Feminists' at Dior). 'In such settings, you don't so much *consume goods* as you *have experiences* where your subjectivity can be intensified, bent, and retooled' (Nealon, 2012: 31). Collective, social action, in post-postmodern fashion, while timely, is nevertheless a function of the culture industry.

Code surfing

However, Michele short-circuits cultural identification for the consumer by mixing disparate codes in a given look (see Figure 4.3). Returning to 'The Alchemist's Garden', for example, on an Asian model sporting a perfectly futurist hairstyle (or a Foujita bowl-cut, depending on one's perspective), Michele paired a royal blue American West-themed, highly embellished, cropped-sleeved plaid shirt with a loose-fitting, black PVC jean with vertical zippers at the hem. The model also wore black ankle boots with white laces, embellished with a red toe cap featuring a gold crescent and sword motif and a white snakeskin strip at the throat line and along both sides of the shaft. The boot was also adorned with a silver double-G ornamental buckle at the base of the toe cap. The overall effect

Figure 4.3 Autumn/Winter 2017 Ready-to-Wear Collection 'The Alchemist's Garden', Look 19, © Getty Images/Catwalking.

is harmonious, despite the heterogeneity of individual pieces originating from disparate style codes. A consumer pondering this outfit would have to parse the component elements in order to make aesthetic choices granting or discounting value, extracting a denotation or inferring a connotation in order to 'make sense' of Michele's exaggerated styling choices, made for a marketing event like the fashion show. Nevertheless, the creative director's bricolage, evident in this look, represents the reinvigoration of the brand through a renewed aesthetic.

The cowboy-inspired shirt holds obvious connotations of easy, supple masculinity. The cowboy, in *fashion* lore, is a storied persona emerging from two disparate films, John Schlesinger's (1969) *Midnight Cowboy*, starring Jon Voight, and James Bridge's (1980) *Urban Cowboy*, starring John Travolta. The cowboy conjures images of youth, innocence, virility and gay culture, finding apotheosis in Annie Proulx's (1997) short story *Brokeback Mountain*, adapted by Ang Lee for his 2005 film. The shirt's floral motif, done in beadwork and rhinestones, plays with gender connotations, but calls to mind the 1975 Glen Campbell country hit, 'Rhinestone Cowboy'. The shirt is supple, seemingly comfortable, but the pant, although not cut 'skinny', strikes as uncomfortable and stiff. Michele cites and reinvents the BDSM aesthetic through his choice of material and cut. The rubberized fabric suggests fetishism but is tempered by the looseness of the fit. The ladder laced boots add complexity to the message by harking to the late 1960s British skinhead subculture. The adorned toecaps hint at mystical and secret society symbology, adding a fraternal message to the working-class aesthetic of the boot. This look amalgamates and recodes a number of subcultural fashion practices, on the one hand, for the sake of novelty, which is still an essential impetus for the fashion cycle. On the other, Michele's unorthodox and absurdist pairing of cowboy, BDSM, skinhead and mysticism exemplifies the agglomeration of subcultures and class fractions into a series of signs available to the contemporary hyperconsumer. As Hebdige (1979) argues, the 'word "subculture" is loaded with mystery. It suggests secrecy, masonic oaths, an Underworld. It also invokes the larger and no less difficult concept "culture"' (4). Thinking of Jameson's notion of pastiche, the individual vestimentary signs cited by Michele can be read as 'a neutral practice of such mimicry without any of parody's ulterior motives' (1991: 17): in other words, a form of 'code surfing'. In the post-postmodern period, the absence of a critical slant in fashion marketing is reinforced by the consumer who now plays with identity, with the utter abandon of a child in a costume trunk, using formerly empowered or politicized style tribe codes as uncomplicated and equivalent commodities.

Lyotard asserts that the individual is no longer composed of a unified social identity.

> A *self* does not amount to much, but no self is an island; each exists in a fabric of relations that is now more complex and mobile than ever before. Young or old, man or woman, rich or poor, a person is always located at 'nodal points' of specific communication circuits, however tiny these may be. Or better: one is always located at a post through which various kinds of messages pass. (Lyotard, [1979] 1984: 15)

Individual identity, for Lyotard, is made up of numerous social positionings. However, this fragmentation of self has intensified in the current period of visual-based culture, as what were formerly dominant culture and subcultures have lost their normative force on the individual, as Hebdige argued. 'The fact remains that far from being locked up in a self-enclosed present, our age is the scene of a frenzy of commemorative activities based on our heritage and a growth in national, regional, ethnic, and religious identities' (Lipovetsky, 2005: 57). Michele's vestimentary praxis is able to take advantage of 'the disintegration of social aggregates', first theorized by Lyotard ([1979] 1984). Gucci's heterogeneous aesthetic responds to the waning normative power of dominant culture and the fragmentation of identity that has only intensified since Lyotard theorized the postmodern condition. Accordingly, contemporary consumption practices have moved away from Veblenian motivations. In the current society of hyperconsumption, the consumer is liberated from class struggle, operating in a mode of 'always more' ('toujours plus') and generalized 'channel surfing' ('zapping généralisé') (Lipovetsky, 2003: 81). The conspicuous consumer good, used to buttress class distinction, in fact, has been supplanted by what Lipovetsky calls the 'hypercommodity', from which all class agonism and conformism has been rooted out (Lipovetsky, 2003: 81), allowing the hyperconsumer to simply play with identity, respond to or highlight any of the number of messages that pass through the numerous 'nodal points' that form the social world. The aesthetic and cultural heterogeneity of Michele's 'The Alchemist's Garden' exemplifies this freeing of the fashion commodity from a teleological cultural and subcultural imperative. Hippy meets hip-hop; BDSM meets the Wild West; skinhead style gets spiritual; collective action goes corporate. Michele creates beyond all conformisms – citing from the formerly hegemonic and counterhegemonic to respond to a fashion hyperconsumer situated, as Lyotard asserts, 'at a post through which various kinds of messages pass'. Michele's Gucci exemplifies design that remixes former metanarratives to emit a composite code of heterogeneous (global) cultures and subcultures that expresses newness by erasing older, obsolete distinctions.

Consumer liberation is nevertheless mitigated. The vestigial power of habitus to guide and limit consumption has now transferred to the brand itself, which has gained greater dominance in constructing the world in which the hyperconsumer builds a supposed habitus-freed identity with some assurance. Lipovetsky cautions (2003) that as the fashion commodity becomes composite ('plurielle') and decentred and as the hegemony of cultural capital wanes, the brand is called upon to assume the role of arbiter. He asserts that in the period of hyperconsumption, the economic success of brands depends on the individual's increasing anxiety in the face of consumption's liberation from social agonism and the plethora of consumer choices now divested of political force.

On the one hand, Michele's Gucci hybridizes style tribe and cultural codes, creating a new space where the individual can consume in uncoordinated, eclectic and asymmetrical ways, adopting and adapting a heterogeneous set of vestimentary practices. Michele's praxis at Gucci exemplifies this intensification of fashion aesthetic through his play with style codes. On the other, this aesthetic freedom is gained in post-postmodernity at the cost of a guiding social structure for consumption. Nealon (2012) proposes that the rise of finance capitalism is one of the key aspects of the intensification of experience inherent to post-postmodernism. 'In the move from Fordism to post-Fordism and beyond, capital has become increasingly deterritorialized, floating free from production processes and coming to rest more centrally in the orbit of symbolic exchange and information technologies' (Nealon, 2012: 20). By 'post-Fordism', Nealon suggests, like Lyotard before him, that capitalism is no longer tied to industrial production. Nevertheless, capital – like scientific knowledge for Lyotard – is abstracted so that its movement and stratifying functions become more amorphous; late capitalism's effects are now all-encompassing, while the source is harder to detect for the individual.[2] 'The Alchemist's Garden' is fashion's equivalent to this deterritorialization. Consuming Michele's Gucci, bordering as it does on the frenetic, runs the risk of expressing a diffuse 'noise'. Gucci's aesthetic no longer responds to overarching narratives that structure the social world. However, in a very real sense, the consumer still works, lives and plays in the social context. Adopting Gucci's code surfing aesthetic can imperil the coherence of the clothed self on which social interaction still depends. It is through the distillation of brand identity that this potential 'noise' is refined into a coherent message.

The logos of the logo

With the loosening of habitus-based practices and the greater importance given to the individual to ensure his or her own happiness, contemporary consumers have come to rely on the brand and, importantly, its logo to structure the subjectivity-creation of fashion consumption. At one level the logo is a sign that emits a brand's message and represents its equity. Louis Vuitton, Dior, Prada, Balenciaga and Gucci, among other high-fashion brands, use logos on entry-level and signature pieces to incite cathexis and consumption for entry-level consumers looking to brands and their equity to experience the 'affective relations between brands and consumers, which typically include some degree of trust, respect, and loyalty but may also include playfulness, scepticism, and dislike' (Lury, 2004: 9). In the society of hyperconsumption, the logo's value has shifted from purveyor of status to purveyor of subjectivity and personal experience. Nealon, citing Hardt and Negri, points to the advent of the 'prosumer' (Nealon, 2012: 64) to explain the new function of post-postmodern consumption in which the consumer *produces* an idiosyncratic identity through consumption, as opposed to earlier modes, in particular the modernist fashion system that imposed a certain alienation on the consumer.

Geczy and Karaminas (2019) invoke Dior's 'New Look' as the pivotal moment when fashion 'ends' (Geczy and Karaminas, 2019: 3) as a mode of consumption governed mainly by status-based concerns. This eschatological perspective on the fashion system is tied to the shift from modernity to postmodernity and post-postmodernity thereafter, as hegemonic fashion norms were increasingly countered from and inspired by less elite class fractions and subcultures. Valerie Steele rightly determines that 'no longer can a single designer like Dior create a collection that women everywhere adopt. Already by the 1960s, the empire of fashion had begun to break up into multiple style tribes' (Steele, 2019: 8). Jameson asserts that the fragmentation of the bourgeois subject into a number of heterogeneous 'appearances' is part of the impact of late capitalism on the cultural sphere. 'If the ideas of a ruling class were once the dominant (or hegemonic) ideology of bourgeois society, the advanced capitalist countries today are now a field of stylistic and discursive heterogeneity without a norm' (Jameson, 1991: 17). The breakup of the 'empire of fashion's' hegemony led first to the rise in autonomy of various 'style tribes', which were free to perform group identity through fashion practices, as Polhemus (1994: 14) establishes. The same movement has now freed the individual to play with various style tribe identities.

In order to mitigate the anormativity that risks loss of self or simple bewilderment before the confusion of style subjectivities, consumers look to brands that harness the artificially constructive power of the logo to assuage consumer anxiety. Lury (2004) argues that the brand 'is a platform for patterning of activity, a mode of organising activities in time and space' (1). The current period of so-called 'democratization of luxury', that is to say, the commercial impetus to expand a putative consumerist inclusivity to all economic levels of society, has in fact rendered the market more opaque for the consumer, as Linda Turunen highlights in her innovative brand management study, *Interpretations of Luxury. Exploring the Consumer Perspective* (2018). She suggests that the current luxury market incites greater confusion: 'do these apparent "luxurious" brands make us more "luxury-like" consumers or is it just a way for brands to sell us more with higher price tags? Is democratization a dead-end after all?' (92). In the current moment, brands like Gucci, Vetement, Saint Laurent and Burberry have focused on brand image and the logo as a means of instigating 'a set of relations between products in time' (Lury, 2004: 2). The logo signifies continuity, linking a heterogeneous grouping of commodities produced, services offered and spaces built; conversely, the logo also signifies difference, when brands graphically or etymologically alter the logo to signify an aesthetic break, as is the case when Yves Saint Laurent was rebranded as Saint Laurent under Hedi Slimane or Burberry, which only recently changed the house logo, under Riccardo Tisci, invoking the founder's identity, Thomas Burberry, to foreground a more storied history. A luxury fashion logo focuses the message of the house so that consumers can connect at a personal level with the brand's supposed 'human' qualities and thereby build its equity. 'The brand, then is a conjunction of the sensuous and the intelligible, a classification of commoditized elements and the immaterial qualities (reputation, affective resonance, characterological traits, etc.) that such material objects are felt to uniquely share and actualize in the world' (Nakassis, 2013: 112). Brand equity – its value in the market – is condensed in the logo and encompasses both the affective and the empirical traits of the commodity attached to it. The process of building brand equity entails incorporating information about and practices of consumers as an essential aspect of brand-making. The brand, then, is equally dependent on consumers' use to generate meaning (Nakassis, 2013). Lury uses the example of the 'loop' in computer programming to explain the brand as a 'mechanized circuit of control' for product differentiation and brand integration (7). In Michele's use of the logo, the 'loop', theorized by Lury, is twisted into a Möbius strip – a loop having the appearance of two sides but that is in fact in a continuous one-dimensional plane. By drawing from and appropriating historically illicit uses of the brand, Michele effectively flattens the constructive relationship linking the subcultural misuses – the surfeit, in Nakassis's (2013) terms – and the bona fide uses of brand identity. In his convincing analysis, 'Brands and Their Surfeits', Nakassis unpacks the dependent relationship between the brand and its counterfeit: 'the surfeit is not simply constitutive of the brand through its externalized transgressions (i.e., material "counterfeits") and the risk they pose, but ... contemporary brand marketing internalizes that very transition in order to exploit it' (122).

Michele mines the Gucci archive to resurrect or reinvent defunct logos and, remarkably, to introduce the counterfeit as a new original. From a brand marketing perspective, Elyette Roux (2009) explains, in her study 'Le Luxe aux temps des marques', that the contemporary consumer now attaches importance to assured values and the perceived authenticity of the offering. At one level, Michele's 2018 collaboration with Dapper Dan, the formerly infamous – and now famous – Harlem couturier-counterfeiter of 1980s hip-hop culture, is a very interesting case in Michele's brandishing of the post-postmodernist power of the logo. The Gucci–Dapper Dan collaboration began from what could have been a scandal of cultural appropriation, launched on Instagram, in response to a look from his 2018 Resort collection[3] shown in May 2017. Michele showed a now well-discussed fur bomber jacket with ballooned and emblazoned sleeves that bore a more than passing resemblance to a late 1980s Louis Vuitton counterfeit jacket designed by Dapper Dan for the African American Olympic sprinter Diane Dixon.[4] Since its early days, hip-hop has historically adapted luxury brand fashion, particularly their logos, in ways that create a slippage in the emitted message of naturalized and racialized class dominance, highlighting instead the arbitrariness of luxury as a sign of elite cultural habitus.[5] Through the Dapper Dan collaboration, Gucci revisits an aesthetic praxis and, ironically, challenges the logo's pre-eminence in luxury brand fashion. Much like in 'The Alchemist's Garden', Michele and Dapper Dan look to a subcultural practice to structure the collection. However, for this collaboration, the aesthetic codes originate from one historical subcultural mode of expression. The iconic Guccissima logo of facing G's, one right side up and the other upside down, linked in a diamond pattern formed with dots diagonally connecting each pairing, covers bomber jackets, sweat suits and footwear, enlarged as if by a photocopier. Gucci's interlocking insignia of two mirrored G's in gold is also emblazoned on patch pockets, the sleeves or the breast of leather jackets, velvet sweat tops and sports jerseys. The oversized red–green–red Gucci stripe – called the Gucci web – lines track top necklines, sleeves and the length of track pants. Through the excessive aesthetic of this collection, Michele and Dapper Dan (who famously called his counterfeiting practice 'knocking up') repurpose hip-hop's counterfeiting codes. Michele's use of the surfeit aesthetic reintegrates the 'immaterial excess of social meaning' (Nakassis, 2013: 112) into the brand, generated by the authentic brand and materialized in the counterfeit styling, as a mode of speculation to increase value and shift meaning in the brand – *intensification* at its best.

Gucci's adoption of the hip-hop aesthetic does not constitute a pure historicism, blindly citing the past. The cultural conditions of existence of Dapper Dan's original aesthetic, on which this collection is based, are not homologous to the contemporary moment. The economic oppression of the 1970s and 1980s, based on a practice of privatization that created the conditions of racialized marginalization, birthed an aesthetics of subversion that is altogether different than late, financial capitalism's diffuse domination of the coalesced economic and cultural sphere.

> Under an economic logic that is in fact dedicated to the unleashing of multifarious individual desires and floating values (broadly speaking, a corporate-nation-state model), rather than desire's dampening or repressive territorialisation on a gold standard of univocal value (broadly speaking, the traditional nation-state model), the role of social 'normalization' (previously the purview of the state's Ideological Apparatuses) needs to be rethought from the ground up. Put simply, a repressive notion of 'normalization' is not the primary danger lurking within contemporary capitalism. (Nealon, 2012: 21)

In Dapper Dan's heyday, economic capital and cultural hegemony functioned in concert to buttress power and those in the elite classes. Hip-hop's remixing of dominant cultural capital served a counterhegemonic function. In its original iteration, Dapper Dan's fashion aesthetic did not seek to toe the line of normalization, but sought to bypass the norm entirely, that is, 'knock up' luxury fashion. Michele's Gucci uses this cultural and racialized history as *intertext*. Michele and Dapper Dan cite the subversive style of hip-hop culture – once considered bad taste – and go as far as remaking classic pieces from this earlier period. For example, jackets originally designed with counterfeit Gucci appliqués for the rap duo Eric B. and Rakim's album *Follow the Leader* (1988) are repurposed for Michele's Gucci (see Figure 4.4).

Jameson considers intertextuality an essential component of the postmodern aesthetic for which the use of earlier aesthetics functions neither as homage nor as parody. With the explosion of meaning in the present, following the

Figure 4.4 Eric B. and Rakim's *Follow the Leader* album cover, © Drew Carolan 1988.

breakdown of the master narratives of modernity (in the case of the fashion system, the shrinking of class concerns as a controlling function of consumption and identity creation), fashion harnesses a pastiche historicism to fill in the gap left by a waning dominant culture. Gucci's aesthetic look backwards offers, in Jameson's description of 'intertextuality', 'a new connotation of "pastness" and pseudohistorical depth, in which the history of aesthetic styles displaces "real" history' (Jameson, 1991: 20). The Michele–Dapper Dan collaboration, inspired by the Harlem designer's 1980s fashion counterfeiting practices, attempts to recode Gucci's history *as if* the brand itself were the source of hip-hop's counterculture aesthetic.

The images from the advertising campaign for this collection reproduce original aspects of Dapper Dan's history, such as 1980s-style wood panelling, seen in the original Diane Dixon image, among others, or rewrite it entirely. For example, an image of a model sitting in the open doorway of a brown car, beside a spare tire, wrapped in a gold and brown signature diamante patterned cover, emblazoned with 'Dapper Dan' and the double-G logo updates an image of a young Dapper Dan sitting in a 'Guccified' brown Mercedes Benz beside a similarly adorned tire.[6] This collaborative collection reinterprets history via the logo-centric aesthetic of 1980s hip-hop culture, visually inferring that the brand currently represents a counterhegemonic aesthetic embodied in the erstwhile practices of hip-hop culture. This historical counterfeiting foregrounds the ever-widening gap separating value from commodity, characteristic of finance capitalism and the ensuing abstraction of brand-meaning attached to a given commodity. 'The brand's fragility and openness to novel (re)signification creates surplus value because it makes the brand a possible site, a medium, for sociality and affective attachment' (Nakassis, 2013: 122). By repurposing Dapper Dan's practices in this collaboration, Michele's Gucci revisits the past as a mode of hyperconsumption. 'This come-back of the past comprises one of the facets of the cosmos of the hyperconsumption of experience: it is no longer just a matter of gaining access to material comfort, but of buying and selling reminiscences, emotions that evoke the past, and memories of days deemed to have been more glamorous' (Lipovetsky, 2005: 60). Michele's adoption of the formerly subcultural codes of hip-hop creates the potential for the brand to inspire an *intensification* of affect in the consuming public and to continue building the authentic brand's equity by annexing previous surfeit uses.

Much like hip-hop culture's repurposing of luxury signifiers, Michele consciously plays with the brand's history through manipulation of the logo, which, in his hands, is divested of its classifying function (see Figure 4.5). As well as invoking an aesthetic pseudohistory altering the perception of the brand's own history, Michele has also marshalled the simulacrum as a representation of the real. The same Resort 2018 collection featured a revised 'Guccy' logo that underscores the artificiality of authenticity differently than the Dapper Dan collaboration. Ironically, the 'Guccy' logo exemplifies the reduced legitimacy of the logo in and of itself to attenuate the anxiety of habitus-liberated hyperconsumption. Lipovetsky (2003) asserts that in the contemporary period, the buying act can no longer solely be considered a form of canalized desire or consolation. Consumption, under late capitalism, is also a self-referential act that creates its own value. 'Guccy', in earlier times, was a valueless ersatz-commodity, a bad knock-off, valuable only to the consumer with insufficient cultural capital to either be able to distinguish fake from real or understand that there was in fact an original to be counterfeited. However, under Michele's hand, the 'Guccy' logo is granted value as an original piece based on an ersatz copy; value is given to what should be without value, demonstrating that at the apogee of deregulated and globalized capitalism, the contemporary moment gives way to a consumption that no longer heeds conventions of legitimacy or authenticity, inasmuch as it no longer abides by normative restrictions.

Figure 4.5 Resort 2018 Collection, Look 83, © Getty Images Europe/Pietro S. D'Aprano.

Consider, for example, the function of the logo as equivalent to knowledge in Lyotard's thinking.

> What we have here is a process of delegitimation fuelled by the demand for legitimation itself. The 'crisis' of scientific knowledge, signs of which have been accumulating since the end of the nineteenth century, is not born of a chance proliferation of sciences, itself an effect of the progress in technology and the expansion of capitalism. It represents rather, an internal erosion of the legitimacy principle of knowledge. (Lyotard, [1979] 1984: 39)

Michele's legitimation of the illegitimate finds its conditions of possibility at the end of the fashion system whose gears were oiled with class antagonism and habitus-based practices. 'Guccy' is the logo of the new fashion system, one that is only possible in a fragmented and polycentred society (cf. Lipovetsky, 2003: 91) in which fractured hegemonic structures have left room for a new individualism and a more diffuse domination. To return for a moment to the example of Dapper Dan, it is illustrative to recall that, at the height of his success in the 1980s, clients would pay the same price for a counterfeit as if it were an authentic piece. One of Dapper Dan's clients from this period, Azie Faison, a former drug dealer, explains it thusly: 'You had to pay on the same level as if it was from Gucci. So it *is* Gucci, to us.'[7] Michele's 'Guccy' logo demonstrates an isomorphic value structure, exemplifying the contemporary schism of style from distinction (in Bourdieu's sense of the term). In the society of hyperconsumption, the logo and its brand can no longer be treated as a fixed value or assurance of distinction. Nealon looks to Las Vegas as the contemporary economic expression of the post-postmodern condition as a locus of intensification. Accordingly, the city's individualism is the new mode in which value is determined. 'The heroes of Atlantis, Troy, Greece, and Rome did not die in vain; they persisted to help create this new empire of "freedom" – which, as we know, means subjective empowerment as consumer choice, the only water fit to satisfy our thirsts' (2012: 30). Gucci or, more precisely, 'Guccy' shatters the hegemony of the logo, leaving in its wake a multiplicity of signs that relate randomly to the Gucci commodity and incite a feeling of liberation from the domination of 'brand authenticity' and its controlling influence: Gucci or 'Guccy', the choice now belongs to the consumer.

Conclusion: Michele's hyperaesthetic

Michele's 'deregulated' fashion aesthetic cites and interpolates disparate style codes, thereby blurring traditional classifications and opening up new modes of fashionable self-expression. While his work at Gucci draws from the brand's archives and codes, as well as global fashion history and style tribe practices, it is the juxtaposition and intercalation of these codes that deregulate the social meaning of the commodity, in an analogous way to capital's deregulation through the financialization of the economy. This post-postmodern instrumentalization and abstraction of brand meaning institutes a veritable break with the brand's previous aesthetics and, importantly, materializes the new contemporary practice of hyperconsumption. Michele's carnivalesque collections and their ensuing cultural and economic success signal that the fashion system has undergone another paradigm shift, since the move from a Bourdieusian top-down structure and the later postmodern double focus on the classic, timeless aesthetic as a materialization of scepticism for progress and – at the opposite end of the spectrum – on the plurality of aesthetic possibilities open to the consumer of the 'supermarket of style' (Polhemus, 1994: 130). This is only part of the conditions of existence for Michele's aesthetic. The post-postmodern period has granted greater autonomy to the hyperconsumer to play with subcultural identities not only freed from an overarching dominant cultural aesthetic but also evacuated of their political impact.

Lyotard explains that the efficiencies of computer logic have further liberated the individual from the confines of meta-narratives but have also imposed their own systems of control. Nealon (2012) glosses this evolution through the Foucaldian programme of surveillance and discipline.

> Discipline has been taken to the limit of what it can do; and in this intensive movement, discipline's limit has become a threshold, inexorably transforming this form of power into a different mode, a 'lighter' and even more effective style of surveillance that can only accelerate the already lightning-fast spread of that monstrous form of power/knowledge known as globalization. (40)

For Nealon, economic globalization and financialization provide the context for the post-postmodern experience of *intensification*, which is, fundamentally, an aesthetic experience. Michele's Gucci responds to this post-postmodern intensity with aesthetic choices that highlight consumer freedom to construct a mobile and amorphous identity but that refuse to mute the anxiety of trying to 'make sense' in a period when the meaning imbued in signs – from the vestimentary to the social to the corporate – has been liquidated. Credit has killed class distinction and the 'democratization of luxury' means that everyone has a right to conspicuous and so-called luxury consumption. Michele's aesthetic at Gucci plays with the new arbitrariness, remixing styles and signs to dress the consumer who now has a freedom – despite economic determination – to create a self that is neither predetermined nor confined. Evacuated of their former meaning, style tribe aesthetics, as interpreted by Michele at Gucci, are free to express new possibilities of social existence.

Notes

1   This is not to ignore Vivienne Westwood and Malcolm McLaren's marshalling of punk subculture since their beginnings in the 1970s. Westwood's aesthetic, however, represents the reversal of fashion's traditional trajectory by asserting autonomy from dominant forms of fashion expression and gradually shifting to a dominant position in the field.

2   The November 2018 General Motors' announcement of the decision to close five North American plants, placing 14,000 workers and related automobile sector jobs in economic precarity, was met by an 7.9 per cent increase in GM stock price (cf. https://www.bloomberg.com/news/articles/2018-11-26/gm-to-cut-10-000-jobs-targets-5-factories-for-closing-next-year). It is easy to imagine Nealon interpreting this downward move for labour with the ensuing rise in stock value illustrative of the intensification of effects under post-industrial capitalism: 'the upward distribution of wealth to CEOs and shareholders while management and workers are ground under finance's heel is the real agenda and effect of '80s-style corporate privatization' (Nealon, 2012: 19).

3 Cf. Darío Dixon, 'Fashion Does Not Need Appropriation', Business of Fashion, 6 June 2017, https://www.businessoffashion.com/articles/opinion/op-ed-fashion-does-not-need-cultural-appropriation.

4 Cf. Dixon's Instagram post, dated 30 May 2017, https://www.instagram.com/p/BUuXDUbjueP/.

5 For an in-depth discussion of hip-hop's transformation of the codes of dominant cultural capital, see Nigel Lezama, 'Mo' Money, Mo' Problems: Hip Hop and Luxury's Uneasy Partnership', in *The Oxford Handbook of Hip Hop Music Studies*, Justin D. Burton and Jason Oakes (eds), Oxford: Oxford University Press, 2018 and 'Status, Votive Luxury, Labour: The Female Rapper's Delight', *Fashion Studies*, 1 (2): 1–23, 2019.

6 Cf. Dapper Dan's Instagram post, dated 11 February 2013, https://www.instagram.com/p/VnYa1FjMC7/.

7 Kalefa Sanneh, 'Harlem Chic', *New Yorker*, 23 March 2013, https://www.newyorker.com/magazine/2013/03/25/harlem-chic.

References

Baudrillard, J. (1970), *La Société de consommation*, Paris: Éditions Gallimard.

Bourdieu, P. (2010), *Distinction*, London: Routledge.

Delsaut, Y. (1975), 'Le Couturier et sa griffe: contribution à une théorie de la magie', *Actes de la recherche en sciences sociales*, 1 (1): 7–36.

Geczy, A., and V. Karaminas (2019), 'Introduction', in A. Geczy and V. Karaminas (eds), *The End of Fashion: Clothing and Dress in the Age of Globalization*, 1–4, London: Bloomsbury Visual Arts.

Harvey, D. (2010), *The Enigma of Capital and the Crises of Capitalism*, New York: Oxford University Press.

Hebdige, D. (1979), *Subculture: The Meaning of Style*, London: Routledge.

Jameson, F. (1991), *Postmodernism or, the Cultural Logic of Late Capitalism*, Durham: Duke University Press.

Lipovetsky, G. (2003), 'La Société d'hyperconsommation', *Le Débat*, 2 (124): 74–98.

Lipovetsky, G. (2005), *Hypermodern Times*, Cambridge: Polity Press.

Lury, C. (2004), *Brands: The Logos of the Global Economy*, London: Routledge.

Lyotard, J. F. ([1979] 1984), *The Postmodern Condition: A Report on Knowledge*, trans. G. Bennington, Minneapolis: Minnesota Press.

Morgado, M. (2014), 'Fashion Phenomena and the Post-Postmodern Condition: Enquiry and Speculation', *Fashion, Style & Popular Culture*, 1 (3): 313–39.

Nakassis, C. (2013), 'Brands and Their Surfeits', *Cultural Anthropology*, 28 (1): 111–26.

Nealon, J. (2012), *Post-Postmodernism or the Cultural Logic of Just-in-Time Capitalism*, Stanford, CA: Stanford University Press.

Polhemus, T. (1994), *Street Style*, London: Thames and Hudson.

Rocamora, A. (2016), 'Pierre Bourdieu. The Field of Fashion', in A. Rocamora and A. Smelik (eds), *Thinking through Fashion: A Guide to Key Theorists*, 233–59, London: I.B. Tauris.

Roux, E. (2009), 'Le luxe au temps des marques', *Géoéconomie*, 2 (49): 19–36.

Simmel, G. ([1905] 2013), *Philosophie de la mode*, trans. Arthur Lochmann, Paris: Éditions Allia.

Steele, V. (2019), 'Fashion Futures', in A. Geczy and V. Karaminas (eds), *The End of Fashion: Clothing and Dress in the Age of Globalization*, 5–18, London: Bloomsbury Visual Arts.

Thomas, D. (2007), *How Luxury Lost Its Lustre*, New York: Penguin Press.

Turunen, L. (2018), *Interpretations of Luxury: Exploring the Consumer Perspective*, Switzerland: Palgrave MacMillan.

Wallenberg, L., and A. Kollnitz (2019), 'Introduction', in L. Wallenberg and A. Kollnitz (eds), *Fashion and Modernism*, 1–15, London: Bloomsbury Visual Arts.

5

HYPERMODERN BRANDING: THE CASE OF UNIQLO

Myles Ethan Lascity

Fashion branding is often chalked up to a postmodern undertaking where clothing is given an extra layer of meaning (Hancock, 2016: 20–7) or otherwise provided with intangible signification (Wigley, Nobbs and Larsen, 2013). This structuring of meaning is generally diffused across various actors, networks and practices (Entwistle and Slater, 2012), but the most successful brands are able to become culturally significant icons (Holt, 2004), where they tell stories (Hancock, 2016) or develop an associated lifestyle (Saviolo and Marazza, 2013).

And then, there's Uniqlo.

The Japanese firm, which dubs itself a specialty store retailer of private label apparel (Uniqlo, n.d.b), has been growing around the globe since it opened its first international location in 2001 in London. Known for its abundance of brightly coloured and purportedly high-quality basics at relatively cheap prices, the store was heralded as the hottest retailer in New York (Urstadt, 2010) as it began a period of growth across the United States. During its 2014 expansion into Los Angeles, Philadelphia and Boston, Uniqlo utilized social media-based hashtag campaigns, where Twitter users were encouraged to post messages using city-specific slang along with a specific hashtag, and sponsored articles on BuzzFeed to announce its arrival in each city. Since then, other brand promotions have included The Selfless Selfie Project, where the brand used 3D printing to replicate an image of the consumers who support good causes, and UTme!, where users designed their own graphic T-shirts. Overall, the brand has not cultivated a clear message but remains ambiguous and multidimensional.

This chapter takes a case study approach to argue that Uniqlo's efforts are uniquely designed for hypermodernity, as outlined by Lipovetsky (2005). Hypermodernism, one of the proposed post-postmodern theories, notes that consumer culture did not result in the feared 'social homogenization' (Charles, 2005: 19) but rather prioritized individuality above all else. The result is that social distinctions, like class, have begun to fall away and instead the self-expression of individuals is coming to the forefront. At the same time, there is a deep anxiety embedded in the liberation of the individual, leading to fear of what comes next (Lipovetsky, 2005: 40; Morgado, 2014: 319–20). Uniqlo's branding efforts answer these anxieties and build a brand that is open and malleable for hypermodern consumers.

Branding in brief

While trademarks predate the concept of a brand (Mercer, 2010: 21), contemporary use of branding dates to the early 1900s (Stern, 2006: 217; Bastos and Levy, 2012: 353). During the early twentieth century, brands were largely seen as markers of quality that 'showed pride' in the product being sold (Bastos and Levy, 2012: 354). The advent of mass media helped to propel branding forward by allowing 'greater richness and complexity' in advertisements and messaging (Moore and Reid, 2008: 429).

Today, brands are largely understood to be complex semiotic systems (Danesi, 2013; Conejo and Wooliscroft, 2015) where tangible communications are pulled together into intangible meaning structures (Wigley, Nobbs and Larsen, 2013). These structures have been described in various forms, like 'image' and 'personality', but are largely understood as intangible constructs that add symbolic and financial value to products. These elements can provide meanings that bridge cultural contradictions (Holt, 2004: 6–8) or proscribe a particular lifestyle that goes along with related products (Saviolo and Marazza, 2013: 48–9). As Hancock (2016) notes, brand storytelling, in which consumers can see themselves using the products, has been especially useful for fashion brands (28–35).

Regardless of how these meanings are created and/or discussed, the idea that brands lend an extra layer of meaning has long roots (Gardner and Levy, 1955; Levy, 1959). As brands moved beyond simply being markers of quality, they also had to distinguish themselves from one another, leading brands to become more symbolic and meaningful (Bastos and Levy, 2012: 357–8). Baudrillard places these intangible constructs within the postmodern paradigm, suggesting that brands help to develop a 'hyperreality', or something that seems more real than the real (1981: 143–63).

Modernity, postmodernity and beyond

Exploring the idea of postmodernity or the postmodern condition has always been a sticky undertaking since both the causes and outcomes vary depending on the 'postmodern' theorist (Charles, 2009: 390–1). For example, Lyotard (2003) suggests that postmodernity was an 'incredulity toward metanarratives' (260), while Jameson (1991) focuses on researchers turning their attention towards theorizing modernism and the effects on representation (iv). Baudrillard positions communication as key to postmodernity, through mass media production and alteration of meaning (2003: 426). For Baudrillard, mass media erases the original references and meanings, creating something new in its place.

Specifically within fashion, Baudrillard suggests that earlier theorists, like Veblen, describe a situation where the meaning was embedded within garments and that the materiality denotes 'prestige, status and social differentiation' (2003: 427). However, the mass media, including fashion advertising and other types of communication, work to subdue the original meanings and instead replace them with a simulation of what has an altered or non-existent meaning (Baudrillard, 1994: 6–7; Tseëlon, 2016: 222–3). This later stage manages to blur the boundaries of reality as a way to create a 'hyperreality' and seduce consumers into purchasing the products (Baudrillard, 2003: 430–1; Hancock, 2016: 21).

Tseëlon (2016) builds on Baudrillard's arguments to suggest signification chains have varied between pre-modern, modern and postmodern societies. In pre-modernity, there was a direct link between signifiers and what they signified. In modernity, signifiers included an indirect signification – in the vein of Veblen, above – and in postmodernity signifiers only referenced other signifiers, as Baudrillard suggests (Tseëlon, 2016: 221). The final stage, where the signifiers may have no reference to reality, is what brand managers and advertisers have picked up on in order to make their products seem desirable to various target markets (Hancock, 2016: 20–4). Hancock (2016) uses a Maidenform ad as an example of postmodern advertising. While the advertisement is for Maidenform bras, it tells a story where women are successful because of their undergarments (22–3). From a postmodern standpoint, the advertisement no longer reflects reality: the Maidenform advertisement references winning or success; however, neither the brand nor its product can actually deliver on that promise.

The digital turn and creation of the internet has upended mass media – including advertising and branding processes. Poster (2001) argues that the internet promotes a culture of underdetermination, where there are no clear pathways of meaning creation or interpretation (13). While print media promoted stable meaning and social categories, and broadcasting multiplied and fragmented these ideas, the internet does not offer one specific way for it to be used and, as such, cannot determine meanings in the same way (Poster, 2001: 14–17). As Levinson notes,

If the digital age is characterized by people personalizing their selection of information via Windows and Web browsers, we can expect to find similar vehicles for expression of choice in the age that follows the digital, used in different ways, for different purposes, and with different results. (1999: 197)

Contemporary consumers are heavily situated within corporate algorithms, both through social network sites and through the internet at large. Some of these algorithms are unknown (Beer, 2013: 91–7; Turow, 2011: 88–110), while others are controlled by users, including the social media accounts we follow. Returning this to Tseëlon's signification order, it can be argued that the internet has offered a new signification construction. Instead of the postmodern construction where a given signifier references some other signified, there is a situation where multiple signifiers can reference the same signified. Using Hancock's example with Maidenform, advertising algorithms may present one user with an impression of success, while another user may be presented with the ideas of wealth, or even sportiness. As with the postmodern construction, Maidenform is unable to deliver on these promises, but now consumers are unsure whether they are even receiving the same messages.

At first blush, the diversity of messages may not seem like a major issue; however, accepting that postmodern brand constructs are useful communicative tools, how should consumers understand images and meaning that are not universally or at least culturally shared? The tenets of cultural branding and the postmodern brand constructions assume consumers purchase and use goods to express themselves (Featherstone, 1987: 59). Therefore, if consumers are not guaranteed that the messages presented in advertisements (e.g. Maidenform means success) transfer to the social realm, the postmodern branding schema falls apart. While individuality during postmodern times ran the risk of being incoherent (Featherstone, 1987: 60), the dawn of the internet and social media has made the incoherence more prominent.

The internet and hypermodernity

The internet's underdetermination and the influence of social media algorithms both speak to recent developments in which people communicate and understand the world around them. Given the variety and flexibility, this appears as a different moment than postmodernity and something akin to hypermodernity (Arnould and Tissier-Desbordes, 2005; Lipovetsky, 2005; Morgado, 2014; Martineau, 2017). Largely, the idea of hypermodernity can be traced back to Lipovetsky's foundational work, *Hypermodern Times* (2005), where he sees 'hypermodernity' coming in the wake of postmodernity (33). Postmodernity, according to Lipovetsky, liberated individuals from 'social roles and institutional authorities' and group membership (39–40) and, in doing so, prioritized the individual above all else, making novelty and ephemerality prized qualities (36).

Charles (2009) suggests that despite postmodern arguments to the contrary, some overarching narratives and values have remained intact. Specifically, human rights, scientific invention, capitalistic production and the triumph of individualism all remain after postmodernity (391). Instead, Charles asserts that modernism had actually been hindered in the past by various social structures, like royal families and religious institutions, and as those structures give way modernism has only expanded its reach and influence (392). Charles writes,

> Hypermodernity thus amounts to a *radical* modernity characterized by the exacerbation and intensification of that modern logic by which human rights and democracy have been made into mandatory values, by the market having become a global economic reference system reaching the remotest places on the planet and invading every sphere of our existence, and by science as an only partly controllable instrument that now throws even the notion of humanity itself into question by opening the possibility of human cloning. (392)

While the liberation of individuals to freely enter consumer societies may be positive, this change has brought with it significant downsides as well. Excessiveness now reigns supreme in everything from fashion to tourism to technological developments (Lipovetsky, 2005: 32). There has been a retreat from prioritizing the present, and individuals now worry about and fear the future (Lipovetsky, 2005: 45–8). In hypermodernity, meaning resides in oscillation: discourses struggle to give consumers' lives meaning because they, too, fall in and out of fashion (Charles, 2005: 15). This oscillation, however, has not resulted in the feared social homogenization and, instead, has created greater diversity as individuals have fewer social bonds (Charles, 2005: 19–20).

If modernity sought metanarratives and collective action, and postmodernity tore down the structures, our current condition as a 'society of fashion' that relies on 'technologies of ephemerality, novelty and permanent seduction' can be chalked up as hypermodern (Lipovetsky, 2005: 36). The ephemerality of the society of fashion has the potential to lead to hyperconsumption and accelerated obsolescence (Morgado, 2014: 319). However, despite the increased consumption and its environmental effects, there is also a paradox within hypermodernism where individuals are 'fraught with fear, anxiety, worry and insecurity' about things like 'pollution, the environment [and] climate change' (Morgado, 2014: 319). Additionally, people are no longer attempting to live out media projections, but rather are constantly in search of something new and something more 'real' (Lipovetsky, 2005: 52–5). Charles attributes the hypermodern condition, in part, to society becoming immune to the effects of media, which provided some form of authority and transcendent meaning (Charles, 2005: 22–7). Likewise, as the mass media gives way to the internet and social media, the multitude of ways people use these newer technologies has made it even harder to find concrete or shared meaning structures.

Idiosyncratic brand meanings and hypermodernity

While theorists largely understand brands as having a shared identifiable meaning, MacInnis, Park and Prister point out that individuals can 'impart unique and idiosyncratic meaning to brands through their brand relationships and personal experiences' (2009: x). Even though this is a dialectic process with brand managers, once multiple people hold the same 'idiosyncratic' interpretations we can begin to discuss them as intangible elements such as image and brand. In this way, brands are similar to what Boje calls an 'antenarrative': a postmodern form of storytelling without closure (2001: 1). Antenarratives remain open in their structure and audience interpretations and are 'collective memory before it becomes reified into the story, the consensual narrative' (Boje, 2001: 3–4).

Boje suggests that an antenarrative is akin to a bet – a wager on how the story will be assembled. Brands follow this logic by offering various messages and 'betting' on which messages are received and how consumers put together the brand image. Consumers take in Uniqlo's store experience, advertisements, social media promotions and other activities, but there is no guarantee they make sense of the brand in one prescribed manner. In this vein, Boje suggests individuals are key to antenarratives. Like the play *Tamara* – which is acted out on several different stages where the audience must choose which actions to follow (Boje, 1995; 2001: 4–5) – individuals are presented with more information than they can reasonably obtain and interpret. People see the brand and attribute meaning through a unique – and at times selective – interface. Individual brand understandings are based on the tangible messages people have experienced and interpreted as part of the brand. Grow (2008) adds that advertisements can work as antenarratives by looking at Nike's advertising to women in the 1990s and points out that female-specific advertisements worked in conjunction with the dominant Nike brand to provide unique meanings (2008: 325–36). The advertisements led to a strong intertextuality for a niche consumer market, as the advertisements were only released within the 'female media' (Grow, 2008: 326). Grow's work demonstrates that consumers interpret brands from the messages they receive and each can experience a brand differently.

While this process has long been at work, the internet has expanded the variety of interpretations that can be made about any brand. Social media users have been resistant to branded content (Fournier and Avery, 2011), and these platforms have allowed consumers to break into smaller and smaller subcultures, which, in turn, allows for even more fragmented brand messaging (Holt, 2016). Similarly, in hypermodernity, hyperindividualism and hyper-recognition reign (Lipovetsky, 2005: 65), where people consume in hyperindividualistic manners (Charles, 2005: 19–20) but also want to be recognized for their consumption choices. Taste cultures, lifestyles or other demarcated structures are submersed and, instead, individuals want to break away from the crowd and to be recognized for their 'unique' consumption.

Meanwhile, Holt (2004) suggests that the most successful brands are those that are able to address contradictions for consumers (6–8). For example, while masculine identities were in crisis due to changes in the labour market threatening their 'breadwinner' status, Mountain Dew created a 'slacker' myth that suggested work itself is a joke (Holt, 2004: 51–6). This myth provided a different meaning which helped allay the threats to men's identities. Elsewhere, these contradictions have been answered by 'associating the brand with aspirational figures: the good-looking, wealthy and charming guy who happens to drink Heineken, wear Tommy Bahama, or drive a Mercedes' (Holt, 2004: 7). This view of branding is largely symbolic and rather postmodern in its creation of immaterial meaning; however, holding onto the belief that consumers will seek to alleviate contradictions through consumption is useful for understanding a hypermodern brand; contradictions abound within hypermodernity.

Arnould and Tissier-Desbordes (2005) argue that 'scientific discourse' remains a powerful tool at marketers' disposal during hypermodernity, as science was one of the overarching themes not disrupted by postmodernism (239–40). In comparison, Morgado (2014) suggests that hypermodernity would require something that is constantly in flux and supportive of overconsumption (319–21). While both of these themes may be true, they do not seem to fully address the fundamental issue of hypermodernity which prioritizes the individual (Arnould and Tissier-Desbordes, 2006: 238; Charles, 2005: 23; Lipovetsky, 2005: 50, 65) and the logic of fashion (Lipovetsky, 2005: 36–8; Charles, 2009: 390; Morgado, 2014: 319), while also causing instability, uncertainty and anxiety over the environment and financial conditions (Morgado, 2014: 320; Charles, 2009: 396–7; Lipovetsky, 2005: 41–5). In all, there are several qualities a brand could develop which would alleviate some of the contradictions of hypermodernity; potentially, they are as follows:

Simplicity

Theories of hypermodernism suggest that people are purchasing more out of anxiety and fear of the future and that consumers have a 'throw-away' mentality (Lipovetsky, 2005: 36; Morgado, 2014: 319–20). Something along the lines of 'fast fashion' might generally fall into this category. However, eventually fast fashion will not be able to offer changes quickly enough and consumers will need a different way to quickly change their consumption. Rather than purchasing garments that directly play into trends, a move towards more simplistic clothing that can be altered as needed would provide more flexibility and have the added benefit of allowing consumers to style their garments and use them towards individualistic intentions.

Quality

Hypermodernity brings fear and uncertainty within the economic realm and rather than throwing away the garments, consumers might aim to throw away the look, while reusing the garment. If products are cheap, too, even better, but having garments that can be used multiple times might help alleviate some of the anxiety of hypermodernism since they can last. If these products are well-made there may be less need for new products during financial difficulties or other times of distress.

Comfort, ease and protection

If consumers are afraid of the future due to economic and environmental conditions, it seems likely they would respond to products that offer comfort, ease and protection. Garments that can help consumers survive in unpredictable elements and can be transported easily would appear to be more appealing than something that is limited in its use or transportability. If there is a fear of what comes next, flexible and protective garments would be more useful for hypermodern consumers.

Following these ideas, Uniqlo has clearly positioned itself as a *hypermodern brand*. Known for its basic garments with few distinguishing characteristics, Uniqlo's clothing can be consumed in a variety of manners and circumstances. Moreover, through its branding processes, Uniqlo has made it easy for consumers to read a variety of meanings into the brand as it remains flexible and open to interpretation. All of Uniqlo's garments are offered in abundance while, paradoxically, consumers can attribute individual meanings to the brand and its goods.

Uniqlo's branding efforts

The Fast Retailing company opened the first Uniqlo store in Hiroshima, Japan, in 1984. The chain grew within Japan until 2001 when it launched an international expansion that first brought stores to the UK, and later to China and South Korea (Fast Retailing, 2010a, 2010b). The first US stores opened in 2005 as mall-based locations before they were shuttered as the brand moved towards a flagship entry strategy (see Moore, Doherty and Doyle, 2010). This resulted in a New York City flagship store opening in 2006 (Fast Retailing, 2010c) and later large-scale stores opening in the city in 2011 (Fast Retailing, 2012). Uniqlo's initial goals for its US expansion expected two hundred locations by 2020 (Wahba, 2011); however, the brand underperformed expectations (Wahba, 2015) and, as of 2020, only operates fifty stores (Fast Retailing 2020).

Still, since the brand's 2014 push into Philadelphia, Boston and Los Angeles, it has relied on a series of unique strategies seemingly custom-made for hypermodernity. Specifically, Uniqlo's social media has targeted specific markets, while its products are created using technologically enhanced fibres and some offerings can be customized. Taken together, Uniqlo presents a brand that is not bogged down with specific, consumable meanings, but that remains flexible enough to be used by a variety of consumers in a variety of contexts.

In-store experience

Uniqlo's stores are generally large and eye-catching, offering an abundance of clothing choices and highlighting the brand's close connection to technology. Within New York City, this included stores in SoHo, on Fifth Avenue and in Herald Square that ranged from 29,000 to 89,000 square feet. As Uniqlo expanded into other metropolitan areas, flagships opened in San Francisco's Herald Square, in

Figure 5.1 Initially called the 'Heattech Tunnel', this area of the Fifth Avenue flagship store features Ultra Light Down products in October 2018. Credit: Myles Ethan Lascity.

Center City Philadelphia and along Michigan Avenue in Chicago. These large-scale stores were accompanied by the opening of smaller mall-based locations in the surrounding areas and in other metro areas like Los Angeles, Boston and Washington, DC.

These stores have remained highly experiential, inviting customers into a bright, technologically pervasive environment full of choice and abundance. In the Fifth Avenue store, customers ride an escalator up from the smaller first floor, up past the second floor to end up at the third floor. The third floor contains clothing for men, women and children, as well as a 'Heattech Tunnel' that originally promoted the brand's line of warmth-creating garments (Figure 5.1). The second floor of the store includes a Starbucks location and promotes the brand's SPRZ NY (referred to as 'Surprise New York') line of T-shirts and products through a series of display cases. The store is also dotted with technological elements, including large screens showing in-store promotions both near the clothing displays and at the check-out and a red-light ticker giving messages to customers. The

Figure 5.2 A digital advertising screen stands in front of the staircase in the Herald Square store in October 2018. In the bottom right of the photo, a dressed mannequin can be seen hanging from a pulley system. Credit: Myles Ethan Lascity.

outside of the Fifth Avenue location is equally as eye-catching: mannequins turn along one display window while the backs of elevators carry colourfully dressed mannequins up and down the three levels of the store casting a rainbow display onto the street.

These ideas are also brought into its other locations. The Herald Square store has mannequins that rise and fall on mechanical pulleys (Figure 5.2). A red promotional ticker can be seen in the various locations and the Philadelphia flagship also boasts a display area for the SPRZ NY line-up. A new element that has appeared in the New York Herald Square location is a large, touchscreen portal that allows customers to use the Uniqlo app while in the store. And in the locations big and small, the store is stocked with its signature basics in a plethora of colours in large displays.

Product development and design

The clothing sold in Uniqlo is promoted not only as a product of Japanese simplicity but also products of technological advancement that promote better quality and adaptability. These products help support a hypermodern brand by allowing flexibility of use and meaning, as well as allowing advertisements of scientific discourses and the promise of adaptability in extreme or uncertain conditions. For example, Uniqlo promotes its clothing as 'LifeWear', which they explain as

> Who you are, what you believe in: that's what you wear every day. And that is what we make clothing for. Welcome to a new way of apparel.
>
> Apparel that comes from our Japanese values of simplicity, quality, and longevity. Designed to be of the time and for the time. Made with such modern elegance that it becomes the building blocks of your style.
>
> A perfect shirt that is always being made more perfect. The simplest design hiding the most thoughtful and modern details. The best in fit and fabrics made to be affordable and accessible to all. (Uniqlo, n.d.d.)

This description works on several levels, including attaching the clothing to ideas of Japan, which is associated with technological advancements (Anholt, 2007: 47–8). Moreover, as fashion has been used as a form of Japanese soft power (Kimura, 2018), it makes sense that this clothing would be seen as technologically advanced. Uniqlo's LifeWear largely consists of the brand's Airism, Heattech and Ultra Light Down lines, which according to marketing materials have all been specially developed. Designers created Heattech with four fibres 'specifically engineered … to provide the body with warmth and comfort' (Lewis, 2015: 44). Meanwhile, Airism was designed as a breathable base layer (Uniqlo, n.d.a) and the Ultra Light Down was designed to be warm yet thin and easy to back (Uniqlo, n.d.c).

Beyond these lines, Uniqlo's clothing seems to be an almost endless collaboration with brands and other pop culture products or initiatives. One of their most prominent collaborations is the SPRZ NY line, which was developed in conjunction with New York City's Museum of Modern Art. The initial line-up featured works by seven artists – Andy Warhol, Jean-Michel Basquiat, Keith Haring, Jack Pierson, Jackson Pollock, Laurence Weiner and Ryan McGinness (Sarah Morris was added soon after). As of 2019 there are thirty different artists featured in the line-up.

In a similar way, the UT T-shirt line was described by the brand's marketing materials as including 'a wide range of content from current pop culture – from art and music to movies and anime – and produced a huge range of T-shirts as tools for free self-expression'. The UT line-up has featured designs by Pharrell, Jonathan Adler and Vera Bradley, as well as diverse pop culture references from cartoons like Toy Story and Hello Kitty to movies like *Edward Scissorhands* and *The Nightmare Before Christmas* to brand images like Coca-Cola and Schwinn.

Beyond the array of graphic T-shirts Uniqlo launched a UTme! smartphone app in Japan, which allows users to design and purchase custom shirts, sweatshirts and tote bags. The customization was pitched to allow users to design 'one-of-a-kind' T-shirts (Uniqlo, n.d.f), although these shirts could also be sold on the Uniqlo marketplace. Users who submit and sell their designs at the marketplace are also eligible to receive money from Uniqlo. This customization is largely only available in the Japanese market (Byford, 2014); however, the UTme! name has been used selectively within the United States.

City-specific social media

During Uniqlo's roll-out into Philadelphia, Boston and Los Angeles, the brand attempted to target each city individually. This was largely done through the use of online videos and to a lesser extent through a hashtag campaign and a native advertising campaign on BuzzFeed. The initial social media campaigning seemed to be something of a glocalization campaign, whereby a global brand attempts to build unique, local connections or connotations (see Ritzer, 2004: 169–81). This campaign tried to imbrue Uniqlo with credibility within individual metro areas. This practice was repeated as the brand moved into more cities across the United States. The localization works to imbue Uniqlo with a more specific image for consumers living in a given city; however, this process also gives the overall brand more dimensions and unique appeals. Across various campaigns, Uniqlo created antenarrative communications that attempted to appeal to the populations of Philadelphia, Boston and Los Angeles. It is clear that their hope was for each city to embrace Uniqlo in its own way, providing a flexible brand image to all.

The 'Faces of Uniqlo' campaign in 2014 ran during the same time period that the brand was opening in Philadelphia, Boston and Los Angeles. The campaign featured videos of celebrities, categorizing them based on their connections to a specific city. These celebrities ranged from well-known actors and reality television competitors to professional surfers and tech CEOs. While few were household names, generally speaking, they all worked in industries that were forward thinking and required them to have a public persona.

Celebrities included actor Glenn Howerton and artist and Renaissance man Raheem Johnson for Philadelphia; RunKeeper CEO Jason Jacobs and reality show contestant and chef Kristen Kish for Boston; and surfer Warren Smith, musicians Francesco Yates, Amanda Sudano, Abner Ramirez and model Kenya Kinski for Los Angeles. The Uniqlo campaign tied the image of the individual to the city through a title card that read, 'From Tokyo to Philadelphia', 'From Tokyo to Boston' and 'From Tokyo to Los Angeles', and closing information on local store openings. However, the content of these videos varied, and it would be easy for consumers of each city to make different assumptions about the brand. For example, both Howerton and Johnson talked about Philadelphia and how the city is perceived by its residents and outsiders, while Jacobs and Kish mentioned their connections to Boston, but focused more on their careers. As such, consumers in different cities may see differing brand communications and thus come to alternative understandings of Uniqlo.

Similarly, Uniqlo-sponsored articles on BuzzFeed also aimed to be city-centric, with titles like '10 Things You'll Only Experience in Philadelphia', '10 Reasons Why Everyone Should Live in Philly at Least Once', '12 Best Things About Being from Boston' and '15 Most Boston Things Ever to Happen'. Additionally, Uniqlo's website promoted a social media contest description saying the brand was 'new in town' and 'fascinated' by the language of each city. It went on to ask, 'Will you show us your tweet style? The more your Twitter feed is jammed with local vocab, the more special discounts you can win up to $100 to shop at our online store' (Uniqlo, n.d.e). Users also needed to include hashtags such as #UniqloBoston and #UniqloPhilly along with the slang. Another effort sought out local social media influencers (as well as everyday users) to post Instagram photos with the #WhereUniqlo hashtag (Lascity, 2019). These posts were collected into a campaign website – whereuniqlo.com – that featured photos on a 'national level' and then by each metropolitan area where Uniqlo was located (Boston, Chicago, Los Angeles, Philadelphia, New York and San Francisco) or planned to locate (Toronto, Denver, Seattle, Washington, DC). Again, this process worked to localize the global Uniqlo brand and give it local flairs, thereby giving variation and the possibility to be interpreted differently by various local consumers.

Efforts in social consciousness

Other Uniqlo promotions speak towards the hypermodern fear of the future and increased individuality and recognition. The first is 'The Uniqlo Selfless Selfie' project, which used '3D printing technology to create unique 8-inch portraits of more than 600 customers in four different countries' (Uniqlo, n.d.g). Each portrait not only featured the customer in Uniqlo garb but also included a pledge of good deeds made by the customer. This included activities like teaching art and dance to poor children to fundraising and supporting disadvantaged communities. This is a conscious effort at corporate responsibility, but it can also be seen as a response to hypermodern conditions that have left people financially vulnerable.

A less pronounced, but also important brand effort is Uniqlo Sustainability, which is tagged with the slogan 'Making the World a Better Place' and the related booklet, 'The Power of Clothing' (Uniqlo, n.d.h). These efforts include a global partnership with the United Nations High Commissioner for Refugees, which led to Uniqlo hiring refugees worldwide and helping refugees become independent. Other efforts seek to tackle both human rights and environmental issues, including empowering factory workers, donating clothing to those in need and promoting the repair and recycling of clothing. In this vein, Uniqlo has supported disaster victims, such as those affected by the 2011 Great East Japan Earthquake and Tsunami. Altogether, Uniqlo seems to push their social consciousness in a world increasingly disrupted by many hypermodern fears.

Conclusion: A hypermodern fashion brand

Given the various branding activities, Uniqlo can be seen as – if not *the* first – a prominent hypermodern fashion brand. Returning to Holt's suggestion that the way to become an iconic brand is to offer answers to a pressing social contradiction (2004: 6–8), in the case of hypermodernity, brands contend with two intertwining contradictions. First, individual consumption is assigned more meaning as goods are mass produced and sold at a breakneck pace. Second, consumption is expected to continue and even increase as resources diminish and as economic and environmental conditions deteriorate. Uniqlo answers both contradictions.

In order to bridge the difference of individual consumption while in an ever-increasing mass-produced world, Uniqlo has dialled back the explicit, logo-centric efforts that have long been pursued by mass market fashion brands and instead has focused on producing non-descript clothing with a modest brand image. By using social media promotions and glocalization within its advertising, Uniqlo has produced a flexible brand image that may not look the same to consumers in Boston, Philadelphia and Los Angeles, or can even appear differently to consumers within the same city. Between the lack of strong brand meanings and intangible constructions, Uniqlo's products can be used by individuals in a variety of ways and to a variety of ends. By not creating a monolithic brand image, consumers can stylize the products differently (think different accessories

Figure 5.3 A promotional display for Ultra Light Down products in the Fifth Avenue flagship store advertises the product's ability to withstand wind gusts. Credit: Myles Ethan Lascity.

or different ensembles), thereby showing their own flair and tastes – important factors for hypermodern consumers who prize individuality.

Likewise, this flexibility helps answer the second source of contradiction. While there is a fear and anxiety in what comes next, Uniqlo's simple garments can be used in a variety of situations. As such, the garments can be dressed up for an office job or dressed down for retail work. Beyond that, Uniqlo's emphasis on quality means that despite the abundance consumers can choose from, products can be expected to last, even in the cases of tough environmental conditions. Moreover, the promotion of Uniqlo's new technological developments emphasizes the new fabrics and designs that will help consumers in extreme conditions, like those caused by climate change and likely await hypermodern consumers (Figure 5.3). Showing the brand takes environmental concerns seriously, Uniqlo's sustainability programme also combats a variety of social and environmental problems, and the company is clearly helping individuals prepare for an uncertain future.

For its part, Uniqlo's promotions acutely address the concerns of the hypermodern consumer. By doing away with the strong brand constructions that were lauded and common within postmodernity, Uniqlo products can be assigned meanings by consumers and used in a variety of ways. And, when consumers are afraid of what the future brings, flexibility might be the best selling proposition there can be.

References

Anholt, S. (2007), *Competitive Identity: The New Brand Management for Nations, Cities and Regions*, New York: Palgrave Macmillan.

Arnould, E. J., and E. Tissier-Desbordes (2005), 'Hypermodernity and the New Millennium: Scientific Language as a Tool for Marketing Communications', in A. J. Kimmel (ed.), *Marketing Communication: New Approaches, Technologies and Styles*, 236–55, Oxford: Oxford University Press.

Bastos, W., and S. J. Levy (2012), 'A History of the Concept of Branding: Practice and Theory', *Journal of Historical Research in Marketing*, 4 (3): 347–68. doi:10.1108/17557501211252934.

Baudrillard, J. (1981), *For a Critique of the Political Economy of the Sign*, St. Louis: Telos Press.

Baudrillard, J. (1994), *Simulacra and Simulation*, Ann Arbor: University of Michigan Press.

Baudrillard, J. (2003), 'From *Symbolic Exchange and Death*', in L. Cahoone (ed.), *From Modernism to Postmodernism: An Anthology*, 421–34, Malden, MA: Blackwell.

Beer, D. (2013), *Popular Culture and New Media: The Politics of Circulation*, New York: Palgrave Macmillan.

Boje, D. M. (1995), 'Stories of the Storytelling Organization: A Postmodern Analysis of Disney as "Tamara-Land"', *Academy of Management Journal*, 38 (4): 997–1035.

Boje, D. M. (2001), *Narrative Methods for Organization and Communication Research*, Thousand Oaks, CA: Sage.

Byford, S. (2014), 'I Designed a Uniqlo T-shirt with My Phone', *The Verge*, 10 July. Available online https://www.theverge.com/2014/7/10/5886635/uniqlo-utme-app-lets-you-design-your-own-t-shirt (accessed 22 December 2018).

Charles, S. (2005), 'Paradoxical Individualism', in G. Lipovetsky (ed.), *Hypermodern Times*, 1–28, Malden, MA: Polity Press.

Charles, S. (2009), 'For a Humanism Amid Hypermodernity: From a Society of Knowledge to a Critical Knowledge of Society', *Axiomathes*, 19: 389–400. doi:10.1007/s10516-009-9090-3.

Conejo, F., and B. Wooliscroft (2015), 'Brands Defined as Semiotic Marketing Systems', *Journal of Macromarketing*, 35 (3): 287–301. doi:10.1177/0276146714531147.

Danesi, M. (2013), 'Semiotizing a Product into a Brand', *Social Semiotics*, 23 (4): 464–76. doi:10.1080/10350330.2013.799003.

Entwistle, J., and D. Slater (2012), 'Models and Brands: Critical Thinking about Bodies and Images', in J. Entwistle and E. Wissinger (eds), *Fashioning Models: Image, Text and Industry*, 15–33, New York: Berg.

Fast Retailing (2010a), 'History: 1949–2003', 20 December. Available online https://www.fastretailing.com/eng/about/history/ (accessed 26 December 2018).

Fast Retailing (2010b), 'History: 2005', 20 December. Available online https://www.fastretailing.com/eng/about/history/2005.html (accessed 26 December 2018).

Fast Retailing (2010c), 'History: 2006', 20 December. Available online https://www.fastretailing.com/eng/about/history/2006.html (accessed 26 December 2018).

Fast Retailing (2012), 'History: 2011', 7 February. Available online https://www.fastretailing.com/eng/about/history/2011.html (accessed 26 December 2018).

Fast Retailing (2020), 'North America', 2 September. Available online https://www.fastretailing.com/eng/group/strategy/northamerica.html (accessed 20 September 2020).

Featherstone, M. (1987), 'Lifestyle and Consumer Culture', *Theory, Culture and Society*, 4 (1): 55–70.

Fournier, S., and J. Avery (2011), 'The Uninvited Brand', *Business Horizons*, 54 (3): 193–207. doi:10.1016/j.bushor.2011.01.001.

Gardner, B. B., and S. J. Levy (1955), 'The Product and the Brand', *Harvard Business Review*, 33 (2): 33–9.

Grow, J. M. (2008), 'The Gender of Branding: Early Nike Women's Advertising a Feminist Antenarrative', *Women's Studies in Communication*, 31 (3): 312–43.

Hancock, J. H. (2016), *Brand/Story: Cases and Explorations in Fashion Branding*, New York: Bloomsbury.

Holt, D. B. (2004), *How Brands Become Icons: The Principles of Cultural Branding*, Boston: Harvard Business School Press.

Holt, D. B. (2016), 'Branding in the Age of Social Media', *Harvard Business Review*, 94 (3). Available online https://hbr.org/2016/03/branding-in-the-age-of-social-media (accessed 27 December 2018).

Jameson, F. (1991), *Postmodernism or, the Cultural Logic of Late Capitalism*, Durham, NC: Duke University Press.

Kimura, T. (2018), 'Cool Japan: Fashion as a Vehicle of Soft Power', in A. Peirson-Smith and J. H. Hancock (eds), *Transglobal Fashion Narratives: Clothing Communication, Style Statements and Brand Storytelling*, 341–58, Chicago: Intellect.

Lascity, M. E. (2019), 'Stores, Shoppers and Mediated Images: The Relational Space of Uniqlo', in J. H. Hancock and A. Peirson-Smith (eds), *The Fashion Business Reader*, 147–53, New York: Bloomsbury.

Levinson, P. (1999), *Digital McLuhan: A Guide to the Information Millennium*, New York: Routledge.

Levy, S. J. (1959), 'Symbols for Sale', *Harvard Business Review*, 37 (4): 117–24.

Lewis, J. (2015), 'Powers of Warmth', *The LifeWear Book*, Fall/Winter, 42–7, Uniqlo.

Lipovetsky, G. (2005), *Hypermodern Times*, Malden, MA: Polity Press.

Lyotard, J. (2003), 'From *The Postmodern Condition: A Report on Knowledge*', in L. Cahoone (ed.), *From Modernism to Postmodernism: An Anthology*, 259–77, Malden, MA: Blackwell.

MacInnis, D. J., C. W. Park and J. R. Prister, eds (2009), *Advertising and Consumer Psychology: Handbook of Brand Relationships*, Armonk, NY: M.E. Sharp.

Martineau, J. (2017), 'Culture in the Age of Acceleration, Hypermodernity, and Globalized Temporalities', *Journal of Arts Management, Law, and Society*, 47 (4): 218–29. doi:10.1080/10632921.2017.1369482.

Mercer, J. (2010), 'A Mark of Distinction: Branding and Trade Mark Law in the UK from the 1860s', *Business History*, 52 (1): 17–42. doi:10.1080/00076790903281033.

Moore, C. M., A. M. Doherty and S. A. Doyle (2010), 'Flagship Stores as a Market Entry Method: The Perspective of Luxury Fashion Retailing', *European Journal of Marketing*, 44 (1): 139–61. doi:10.1108/03090561011008646.

Moore, K., and S. Reid (2008), 'The Birth of Brand: 4000 Years of Branding', *Business History*, 50 (4): 419–32. doi:10.1080/00076790802106299.

Morgado, M. A. (2014), 'Fashion Phenomena and the Post-Postmodern Condition: Enquiry and Speculation', *Fashion, Style & Popular Culture*, 1 (3): 313–39. doi:10.1386/fspc.1.3.313_1.

Poster, M. (2001), *What's the Matter with the Internet?*, Minneapolis: University of Minnesota Press.

Ritzer, G. (2004), *The McDonaldization of Society: Revised New Century Edition*, Thousand Oaks, CA: Pine Forge Press.

Saviolo, S., and A. Marazza. (2013), *Lifestyle Brands: A Guide to Aspirational Marketing*, New York: Palgrave Macmillan.

Stern, B. B. (2006), 'What Does *Brand* Mean? Historical-Analysis Method and Construct Definition', *Journal of the Academy of Marketing Science*, 34 (2): 216–23. doi:10.1177/0092070305284991.

Tseëlon, E. (2016), 'Jean Baudrillard: Postmodern Fashion as the End of Meaning', in A. Rocamora and A. Smelik (eds), *Thinking through Fashion: A Guide to Key Theorists*, 215–32, London: I.B. Tauris.

Turow, J. (2011), *The Daily You: How the New Advertising Industry is Defining Your Identity and Your Worth*, New Haven, CT: Yale University Press.

Uniqlo (n.d.a), 'Airism Collection'. Available online https://www.uniqlo.com/us/en/men/airism-collection (accessed 26 December 2018).

Uniqlo (n.d.b), 'Corporate Information'. Available online https://www.uniqlo.com/us/en/company/corporate-information.html (accessed 23 May 2019).

Uniqlo (n.d.c), 'Featured: ULD'. Available online https://www.uniqlo.com/us/en/page/uld-featured-m.html (accessed 26 December 2018).

Uniqlo (n.d.d), 'This If LifeWear'. Available online https://web.archive.org/web/20190301013624/https://www.uniqlo.com/lifewear/us/en/ (accessed 26 December 2018).

Uniqlo (n.d.e), 'Uniqlo Philadelphia'. Available online https://web.archive.org/web/20141205123650/http://www.uniqlo.com/us/uniqlophilly.html (accessed 26 December 2018).

Uniqlo (n.d.f), 'UTme!' Available online http://utme.uniqlo.com/about_en.php (accessed 26 December 2018).

Uniqlo (n.d.g), 'The Uniqlo Selfless Selfie Project'. Available online http://www.theselflessselfieproject.com/ (accessed 26 December 2018).

Uniqlo (n.d.h), 'UNIQLO Sustainability'. Available online https://www.uniqlo.com/us/en/special/sustainability/ (accessed 26 December 2018).

Urstadt, B. (2010), 'Uniqlones' *New York*, 9 May. Available online http://nymag.com/fashion/features/65898 (accessed 26 December 2018).

Wahba, P. (2011), 'Uniqlo Starts U.S. Expansion, Eyes 200 Stores', *Reuters*, 13 October. Available online http://www.reuters.com/article/2011/ 10/13/us-fastretailing-idUSTRE79C7IG20111013 (accessed 26 December 2018).

Wahba, P. (2015), 'Uniqlo's Big American Mistake? Betting on Suburban Malls', *Fortune*, 8 October. Available online http://fortune.com/2015/10/08/uniqlo-united-states/ (accessed 26 December 2018).

Wigley, S. M., K. Nobbs and E. Larsen (2013), 'Making the Marque: Tangible Branding in Fashion Product and Retail Design', *Fashion Practice*, 5 (2): 245–64. doi:10.2752/17 5693813X13705243201577.

6

POST-POSTMODERNITY AND SOUTH ASIAN MUSLIM WOMEN'S FASHION

Iqra Shagufta Cheema

Diverse religious, cultural, global, industrial and colonial factors amalgamate into making South Asian fashion an intriguing subject of study. Despite exponential growth of its fashion market during the last few decades, the arresting nuance of South Asian Muslim female fashion remains neglected. In this chapter, I discuss fashion trends among Muslim South Asian women in the post-postmodern era. I argue that Muslim women have gained more agency in their fashion choices in post-postmodernity. Their choices are more politically charged in visual and global post-postmodern culture because these choices translate into significant statements about their sociocultural and religio-political location. Moreover, the global rise of Islamophobia and the preconceived notion of women's oppression in Islam also complicate and politicize Muslim women's fashion more than that of their male counterparts, particularly in patriarchal societies like India and Pakistan.

In arguing that, this chapter examines and explores the following questions: what challenges does post-postmodernity pose for Muslim women's fashion choices in South Asia?[1] How do these women represent their religious, cultural, regional, national and global identities through their fashion? How do political and feminist movements like #MeToo affect these choices? How does global or Western fashion affect the South Asian Muslim fashion?

I deploy the words 'dress' and 'fashion' synonymously in this chapter to mean anything that is used to cover or adorn the body (Eicher and Roach, 1965). The reason this chapter solely focuses on Muslim female fashion is because, traditionally, they are held responsible for representation, preservation and transfer of religious identity and cultural traditions across generations. Additionally, considering the chapter limitation, I use South Asia to refer to India and Pakistan only. I choose these countries because centuries-old shared history between both countries makes their fashion, culture and arts similar in more ways than not.

Though there has been a wide adoption and appropriation of Hindu cultural and religious rituals and objects, development of Muslim fashion has not gained much attention. Hence, this chapter will enable cross-cultural fashion connections as well as enhance readers' comprehension of post-postmodern Muslim women's identity as expressed through fashion choices. Readers might find it ironic that I, in this chapter, deploy Western theories to discuss the ramifications of Muslim women's fashion and representation of their religio-political and sociocultural identities via fashion. This irony highlights the significance of the discussion of non-Western subjects by a non-Western subject on a global platform in this chapter. It also displays the increasing post-postmodern impossibility of drawing hard lines between different cultural and religious factors.

Historical overview of South Asian fashion

Geoclimatic and ethnoreligious diversity inspires versatility in fabric, style and cuts in South Asian fashion. Draped and wrapped dresses have always been popular in some form among Muslims and non-Muslims alike to this day. Some examples include *sari* (five- to nine-yard-long fabric draped on body with a blouse), *dhoti* (a rectangle garment tied around the waist to cover legs), *sarong/lungi* (printed un/ sewn fabric worn in a tube shape on lower body), *dupatta* (head cover), *chaadar* (broader piece of clothing that coves head and upper half of body) and *choli* (skirt-like bottoms). In Indian culture, Islamic sartorial traditions blended with the prevalent Hindu religious influence (along with others) – so much so that they gradually became indistinguishable.

A Harappan sculpture in the Indus valley (2000–3000 bce) shows a priest draped in an unstitched garment with an embroidered motif, while women wrapped scanty garments around their hips. The Vedas (1200–1000 bce) deploy onomatology like *antariya* (lower garment), *uttariya* (upper garment), *pesas* (skirts) and *pratidi* (breast covering) to describe glossy garments with gold threaded embroidery. The Ramayana and Mahabharata (500–300 bce) also mention garments in vague form.[2] Chandra Gupta Maurya, emperor of Maurya Empire in South Asia (320–297 bce), who married a Greek princess, had ties with Greece and China; these connections strongly influenced South Asian dresses and launched the ancestral form of the *sari*. Later, the Satavahana Empire (200 bce–200 ce) developed trade with Arabia and the Roman Empire – resulting in traces of tunics and stitched and unstitched garments in that period. When the

Kushans (130 bce–185 ce) invaded Punjab in the Indian subcontinent, a blend of Greek, Roman and Kushan trends diversified local sartorial fashion. Sculptures from that era show the amalgamation of these influences in coats, jackets, tunics, blouses, pants, scarves, caps and other pieces. Royalty wore unstitched luxuriously long and flowy fabrics, while the masses wore stitched garments during Gupta's period (4–8 ce). Lexicon continuity of clothing terminology (7 ce) to contemporary terms is also evidenced in ancient languages like Sanskrit and Prakrit (Dhamija, n.d.).

While Islam forbids flamboyance and ostentatiousness, it recommends that dress shows its wearer's social status. Historically, Muslim rulers wore dresses with intricately calligraphed Quranic *ayat* (scripture) to ward off evil, rewarded their servants with embroidered silk *khalat* (gowns) and used dresses and their colours to express or withdraw allegiance to the rulers (Baker, n.d.; Janaki, 2018). South Asian clothing style transformed significantly when Mahmud Ghaznavi invaded India in the eleventh century. Records from that era, along with Ibn-e-Batuta's travel narratives, mention an advanced stitching style with multiple fabrics for lining, edging and so on. This new clothing style, with its fabric, originally came from the textile workshops in Baghdad. Over time, however, rulers throughout the Muslim Caliphate set up their own textile workshops.

In the Muslim Caliphate, sartorial designs, styles and techniques were shared because of strong cross-regional trade between Syria, Egypt and Baghdad – along with South Asia. Consolidation of the Mughal Empire (sixteenth to seventeenth century) also inspired changes in the regional courts and fashion therein. Humayun (sixteenth century) founded textile workshops in Agra and Lahore and introduced a more urbane Mughal style that was inspired by the Persian court. This style was later elevated by Emperor Akbar, who designed some of his own costumes that were more suitable for the geoclimatic conditions. He also replaced foreign sartorial terms with indigenous vocabulary which resulted in wider cultural acceptability and adoption of these dresses by the masses (Dhamija, n.d.) (Sandhu, 2015). The dresses – that included *chokdar pajama*, coats with pointy corners and head covering – were similar for men and women in Akbar's reign, but women's style was altered when Jahangir took over the rule; henceforth women started wearing floating brocade tunics and gossamer veils. More regional, indigenous styles emerged with the Mughal Empire's decline.

The arrival of Europeans (eighteenth to nineteenth century), however, changed these indigenous styles. The colonial government expected people in bureaucracy, military and academia to adopt formal European dress codes. Gradually, the elite adopted Western clothing styles, while the middle class amalgamated European style with their own fashion. Female blouses copied the European neckline, puffed sleeves, and collars (Dhamija, n.d.), (Sandhu, 2015). Men also, more frequently, opted for pantaloons and Western suits.

Since the European colonization, Western fashion has maintained its influence on South Asia. In neoliberal cultural imperialism and speculative global economy, South Asia's geopolitical and ethnoreligious history has problematized these fashion choices. This is visible in post-postmodern sartorial confusion and fusion between Western trends and local traditions. Fashion and its politics particularly affect Muslim female subjects and their identity. Via easy internet access, they have awareness of post-postmodern global fashion and culture, but the same remains politically, economically and geographically inaccessible to them. Muslim female fashion in South Asia is affected and altered by this post-postmodern neoliberal condition.

Post-postmodernism and South Asian dress

The dominant notion that fashion theorization originated in the West has persisted for centuries. But it is in 'need of review and revision' (Niessen, 2018: 105). The above-described concise historical context of the evolution of Muslim fashion in South Asia highlights the complex connection between fashion, politics and power. As South Asian interregional and global politics changed over time, so did culture and fashion – even more so particularly for women under the cultural logic of late capitalism, that is, postmodernism. The following facets of post-postmodernity facilitate and contemporize our comprehension of Muslim women's fashion.

Gilles Lipovetsky contends that we have entered the phase of *hyper* after that of *post* – hence hypermodernism instead of postmodernism. Hypermodern society experiences time as a 'major preoccupation' where now clashes are not 'class against class' but rather 'time against time' (2015: 161). Highlighting hypermodernity's 'inseparable' link to 'traditional and institutional frameworks' (2015: 163), Lipovetsky argues that 'globalization occurs along with mobilization of myths, foundation stories, symbolic inheritance, and traditional values' (2015: 165). Particularly, the older generation frequently reminisce about the cultural traditions and religious celebrations of the past. They search for authenticity, an ideal time, a fixed point in history. South Asian women, due to gender, communal and ethnoreligious issues, have relatively less interregional geographical mobility. Even those who are more geographically and culturally mobile yearn for a revival of past traditions – and they make an active effort in that regard. This yearning is often expressed through fusion of contemporary and traditional fashion. This newer and post-postmodern fashion is a fusion of past and present traditions, as are contemporary South Asian Muslim women. Hypermodernity, argues Lipovetsky, assigns 'new dignity' to older traditions by 'invoking the duties of memory, remobilizing religious traditions' in a present that constantly 'exhumes and rediscovers the past' (2015).

Among the younger generation of women, this memory also shows up in vintage fashion trends. Any nostalgic yearning for the past already announces that the past is irretrievable. We can only retrieve or mimic objects from the past. We can blend that past memory and its objects (like traditional accessories and embroidery) via mix, collage, cut and paste with the contemporary tradition (jeans, dress, capris). Vintage made a comeback in South Asian fashion in the form of *ghararas* (wide legged pants with dramatically exaggerated flare down the knees) and golden frill-laced dupattas in 2018. *Gharara* was traditionally worn by Muslim women – as an item of clothing it bridges the generation gap between Muslim women that was widened by globalization and multiculturalism. Because of its separate legs, *gharara* is also feasible for day-to-day physical activities, but it can be easily elevated and accessorized for multiple events and occasions. South Asian women, through this hypermodern mobilization of symbolic inheritance and tradition in the form of *gharara*, are able to add longevity to this symbol's life and contemporize the past.

Fashion designers, in their vintage collections, render Barthes's mythic status to fashion articles as a sign of the past. They select *gharara* as a sign, empty some of the meaning that it carried in the past and assign it a second level of significance (Barthes, 1975). Hence, *gharara*, which was in the past a casual dress for Muslim women in South Asia, now indicates their appreciation for cultural lineage on a second level of significance. Fashion becomes more prevalent as human beings start experimenting with multiple ways of being and delve into complex modes of existence. Dress is a means to express that multiplicity of being – particularly in South Asia where multiple religious and cultural factors have amalgamated in inseparable ways over centuries. Gilles Lipovetsky argues that Europe started experimenting with individualism, aesthetics and hedonism in the fourteenth century when the rest of the world pursued their traditional clothing style as an expression of their reverence for the past. Hypermodernity is defined by 'revisionary memory, remobilization of traditional beliefs, and individualist hybridization of past and modernity' (2015: 169).

Hypermodern revivals of centuries-old fashion items such as *gharara* invalidate claims about Europe as the sole centre for aesthetic activities. Fashion decisions for Muslim women in South Asia are even more charged in the age of neoliberal globalization and social media. Their choices of appearance represent their societal status as well as religious beliefs. *Gharara*, like most other South Asian clothing items, is modifiable and can be accessorized and accommodated for different levels of price and modesty. These choices of accessories, along with style, also reflect women's sociocultural and religious preferences. Under the pressure of representing multiple identities, hypermodern fusion of past and present, tradition and invention expands Muslim women's sartorial options and complicates the politics of these choices and representation.

In weaker democracies, like Pakistan, hypermodern fashion provides Muslim women the means of transforming and playing with traditions of institutional patriarchy. Pakistan, with a literally and politically Muslim national identity, complicates the expression of religio-cultural elements of womanhood. In stronger democracies, like India, secularization has resulted in a more subjective and de-institutionalized form of religion. This alternative religious system invokes a reflexive ideology – one's daily life reflects their politics and their system of belief because they do not perform any ritual under institutional or governmental pressure (2015: 167). I propose, however, that this ideology is reflective as well as reflexive. Despite the absence of governmental interference, sociocultural norms require their subjects to constantly question, rediscover and refigure the foundations of their identity. This reflection enables Muslim women to comprehend, embrace and express diverse political, religious and cultural constituents of their identity and personhood via fashion.

This political deployment of fashion goes way back in South Asian history. One example of this is the choice of wearing *khaddi* as a social equalizer during the freedom struggle from the British; Jinnah cap (named after Pakistani leader Mohammad Ali Jinnah), Gandhi *topi* (named after Gandhi), Jawahar jacket (named after Jawaharlal Nehru) and *Kaptaan's chappal* (named after former Pakistani cricket captain and now Prime Minister Imran Khan) are all examples of explicit expression of politics in sartorial choices. The same can be said for former Indian prime minister Indira Gandhi's *sari* and for progressive socialist Pakistani leader Benazir Bhutto who wore a particular style of *shalwar kamiz* and *dupatta*. Hence, *sari* and *dupatta* assumed the significance of a political announcement of patriotic values – where *dupatta* also indicates Muslim religious affiliation in the Pakistani context.

Though *shalwar kamiz* with *dupatta* is worn widely as everyday dress by Muslim women in South Asia, the cuts and styles differ widely according to geoclimatic and religio-cultural factors across regions. In urban areas, more Western cuts or more glocal (global + local) style of *shalwar kamiz* is prevalent. Just like in colonial times, the elite deployed the whole Western dress code while the middle class mixed it with their own indigenous and familial fashion. Modern usually means Westernization of style, which usually means shedding of *dupatta*, sleeveless *kamiz*, higher-than-ankles *shalwar*/bottoms – all of which is considered against the strict religious dictate. Western inspiration and local values are hard to weave together smoothly – that is where the challenge lies for the post-postmodern female subject. Western fashion styles are considered contemporary or modern (in this case post-postmodern), whereas local style is archaic or traditional. This misperception prevails both in local and global contexts.

Sandra Niessen speculates that in the sixteenth century, the British admired Indian textiles for their fineness and technological brilliance as a means of creativity and individuality, but in the twentieth century when the South Asian expatriate population grew in Britain, their clothing became a symbol of foreignness and otherness (2018). Jennifer Craik also affirms that non-Westerners' adoption of their local or indigenous styles is considered 'traditional' not fashionable, but adoption/appropriation of the same by Western designers is deemed fashionable (2018). Globalization and increased immigration have made Muslim women hyper-aware of this cross-cultural adoption/appropriation of their fashion and style.

Lipovetsky points to the hyper-ization of everything in hypermodernity: this includes hyper-power, hyper-class and hyper-capitalism that lead to 'galloping commercialization' and 'hyper consumption' (2015). Mass production and industrial mechanization in a neoliberal speculative global economy have only accelerated the above-described hyper-suffixes. But this hyper-capitalism eventually results in hyperindividualism. Hyper-modernity and hyperindividualism, along with alternative religious practices in countries like Pakistan, lead to a search for 'hyper-recognition' (2015: 168). These hypermodern sociocultural changes are more acute for Muslim women in an institutional patriarchy like Pakistan. Clothing is the most convenient way for women to express their individuality and even their political position. Additionally, post-postmodernism has amplified the postmodern focus on micronarratives. In this hyper-recognition and hyperindividualism, South Asian Muslim women want their micro-identities to be acknowledged and accepted.

Post-postmodern hyperindividualism, I argue, results in hyper-fashion practices for Muslim women who can express their non-monolithic micro-identities this way. *Burqa* (also referred to as abaya, hijab, niqab, etc.) is an example to explain the relation of hypermodernity and hyper-fashion. South Asian women wear hijab or cover their faces for cultural reasons more than religious reasons. Growing up, I was encouraged to cover my head while going out of the house or in the presence of elders as a cultural tradition and sign of reverence – never because it was a Quranic dictate or Allah's command. Undoubtedly, the practice has its roots in a religious narrative of honourable women staying in *pardah* (cover), but it is mostly practised like a religious ritual under cultural pressure.

There are as many styles of burqas as sets of beliefs and religio-cultural contexts: it can range from plain fabric burqas to heavily embellished and embroidered ones; from a tube-shaped dress to multilayered expensive fabric; from just a body covering garment to burqas concealing the entire body with only the eyes exposed or a net over the eyes. They can cost from 500 rupees up to 50,000 rupees. Women from more tribal or rural families wear it to avoid *na-mehram* men (men who a woman could legally marry) as well as men from other tribes/families; working women opt for a burqa for safer public travel, to avoid street harassment or because of the pressure from a conservative or traditional family.

Like *gharara* and *shalwar kamiz*, women can still express their personal style in a burqa through unique cuts, design and embroidery. More rigid women might opt for solid coloured and completely plain burqas. Some women choose not to wear burqa as a protest and some women wear a burqa as a protest. The fabric, style and embroidery can also show the social and financial status of a woman. *Burka* is also tied to women's financial independence; some women who wear burqa under family pressure shed it when they take up a career and become financially independent – economic pressures in neoliberal globalization have affected this sociocultural shift in South Asia. These are only a few among numerous variations in burqa styles that Muslim women in South Asia use to express their micro-identities. *Burqa* serves as a good example of the ways in which Muslim women aim for hyper-recognition and hyperindividualism through hyper-fashion. These diverse religio-cultural stylistic choices in South Asian women's fashion also glimpse Nicolas Bourriaud's post-postmodern theory, altermodernism.

Altermodernism brings cross-cultural collaborations, connections, negotiations and experimentation together for productive compromises. Bourriaud defines altermodernism as the possibility of envisioning 'human history as constituted of multiple temporalities' to produce something from an assumed heterochrony from 'exploring all dimensions of present' (2015: 257). Any work of art, he argues, combines multiple 'interrelationships' that decentralize singular authority to form a 'collective authorship' (2015: 258). Through this 'fragmentation of work of art', altermodernism not only elevates the work of art but also problematizes it by thinning the line between original creation and copyright infringement. Fashion, as art, reflects the same theory.

Cultural appropriation of fashion, sometimes veiled as inspiration, can be understood and analysed using altermodernism as a departure point. In 2017, Forever 21 and Urban Outfitters used *Ajrak*, a traditional Sindhi print that goes back to the Mohenjo-daro tradition, for bikinis and skirts. Similarly, Paul Smith, an English fashion designer, 'introduced' *Peshawari Chappal*, traditional footwear from the Khyber Pakhtunkhwa and Gandhara region, to international markets.[3] The audacious adoption – which is more akin to cultural appropriation – of this traditional fashion equates to cultural erasure of the previously colonized region. Almost three centuries of British colonization blur the distinction between genuine recognition, cultural appropriation or mere Western capitalization of the South Asian market in neoliberal speculative global economy. Besides that, art and fashion travels across spaces and temporalities. It goes not only across countries but also across histories. Contemporaneous hyper-fashion, according to altermodernism, creates more room for expression of diverse identities through 'voluntary confusion of eras and genres' (Bourriaud, 2015: 260), but this confusion does not bode well for under-represented South Asian Muslim fashion. Weak and ambiguous fashion copyright laws further aggravate these issues, leaving expansive room for exploitation of the South Asian market. Additionally, altermodernism results in hyper-capitalism and hyper-commercialization by expanding the reach of global or Western fashion.

Neoliberal globalization and mass production have also attracted Western brands to South Asian markets. These brands outsource human labour, which can be exploitative of gender and workplace discrimination. Under the veneer of respect for religio-cultural traditions where women lack safe access to public spaces, they provide South Asian women opportunities to work from home. Hence, they exploit women workforce with meagre financial incentive and without affecting any real sociocultural change – and, sometimes, end up strengthening institutional patriarchy. Working from home hinders women from interacting with other women. Therefore, it keeps them from forming feminist or unionist alliances for access to better work rights, human rights and safety in work and public places. Hence, capitalist interests of foreign investors and international brands blind them to the ways in which they contribute to sociocultural injustice and religio-political misogyny in South Asia. Along with that, South Asia has also witnessed an increase in Western fashion retail stores.

High-end European brands that have catered to the oil-rich Arab Muslim women for decades are monetizing the speedily growing South Asian consumer market. Globally, Muslim market is worth US$ 2.1 tn with an annual increase of US$500 bn, according to a 2016 market analysis (Sherwood, 2016). With more women joining the workforce in most globalized Muslim economies, women's purchasing power has increased. Western brands are capitalizing on that. For example, Dolce & Gabbana launched their hijab collection targeting Middle Eastern and Muslim women in 2016. More than being an appreciable accommodation of religious diversity, this furthers global domination of Western fashion brands. Ignorance or insensitivity of the religious rituals also leads to controversies. For example, MAC stirred quite a controversy and invited ridicule for launching a Ramadan-themed make-up tutorial in 2018. It would be unfair, however, to not talk about the positive impact that these brands make on Muslim women's fashion. For example, Nike's hijab sports gear has definitely helped women assert their Muslim identity. It also fights the stereotypical assumption that hijab bars women from living an active and ambitious life (Davids, 2018). Increasingly, it is becoming harder to distinguish whether a fashion designer takes a cultural artefact as a point of initiation and inspiration or as capitalistic exploitation. But now Muslim women entrepreneurs from South Asia are joining the fashion market to resolve these post-postmodern/altermodern issues of representation and collaboration.

These entrepreneurs – called 'Gummies', acronym for global young urban Muslims – belong to the new glocal South Asian Muslim identity categories. They have more exposure to a global fashion market and have started their initiatives to cater to the Muslim consumers (Sherwood, 2016). They are 'hyper-diverse', 'transnational', more 'spiritual rather than religious' and may originally belong to South Asia but their families are spread in the West too (Sherwood, 2016). Even when located in small communities and producing locally, most of these new start-ups cater to a global Muslim diasporic consumer base in a globalized world.

Gummies' diversity and multiculturalism reflect post-postmodern theory of automodernism. Robert Samuels, in automodernism, announces the end of postmodernism by declaring the contemporary global world a cyberspace (2007). He enumerates four versions of post-postmodernity: multiculturalism, social constructivism, combination of diverse elements and academic critique or deconstruction (2007). The post-postmodern focus on multiculturalism is usually equated with erasure of micro-identities, but Samuels claims that multiculturalism helps us ascertain our identities. When surrounded by a multitude of identities, human subjects tend to question the foundation of their most fundamental beliefs and the formation of their subjectivities. Thus, multiculturalism becomes a socially constructive force for non-monolithic marginalized identities like Muslim women. This might also be one of the reasons for the upsurge in Muslim fashion and its market. In automodernism, women have a wide range of sartorial temporalities, histories and accessories to fuse and collaborate for a better expression of their gender and geographical, religio-political and sociocultural identities. They have multiple styles of head covers, shirts/tops and bottoms along with other accessories. The Gummies are one example as they combine and customize South Asian, Western and Muslim constituents of their subjectivities. They use South Asian accessories as well as introduce new styles in traditional dress. Use of statement jewellery like *jhumka*s and bangles, *khussa*s (embroidered flat leather footwear) and traditional embroidery are a few of the things that the Gummies use in their daily life to embrace tradition. Hence, Muslim women bridge spatial and ideological boundaries through altermodern collaboration and negotiation of fashion in globalization.

Globalization becomes viatorization where the fashion designer turns into a 'homo viator' or a nomad by residing in multiple worlds and bringing them together through art and fashion. Bourriaud contends that globalization has far exceeded Jameson's and Lyotard's anticipations. Any artist working in this multicultural global sphere is a 'homo viator' and/or 'nomad', he argues. He describes three types of nomadism: space, time and signs – all mutually inclusive. Fashion designers, as artists, bring multiple signs, spaces and temporalities together. Postmodern and postcolonial schools of thought that started in the 1970s are no longer well equipped to describe the changes wrought by an increasingly global culture. Altermodern fashion creates possibilities of bringing these diverse and insufficient theories together in hopes of something more nuanced and comprehensive. Bourriaud has been accused of recycling ideas such as the

Deleuzian nomad, the Lyotardian archipelago, the Derridean archive, postcolonial hybridization and Robert Samuels's theories of cyberspace (2007: 252). But recycling is historicizing and a creative force in the post-postmodern age of creative exhaustion: vintage fashion, fusion of old and contemporary trends, blending sartorial tradition and innovation are all different forms of recycling. This accusation of recycling these terms from different theorists verifies post-postmodern collaboration, multiple authorship, haphazardness, openness, evanescence and multiculturalism in altermodernity.

In post-postmodernity, according to Bourriaud (2015), 'creolization' has taken over multiculturalism. Alter-globalization seeks to find and propose singular solutions within models of sustainable development instead of neoliberal, economic globalization. Creolization facilitates that by enabling the blend of new and inherited cultures and blends – the new creole trends contain elements that are dearest to the consumers or wearers. The 'Gummies' are identifiable because of the same creolization, viatorization and nomadism. They collage their different glocal identities – the chosen expatriate identity and the inherited old identity – together via fashion in a globalized space.

Platforms like Instagram and YouTube have further inspired, accelerated and promoted altermodern fashion elements like collaboration, creolization and online viatorization. This online presence and visibility is particularly critical for South Asian Muslim women who – along with frequent harassment – have restricted access to most public spaces. Religious and sociocultural constraints in institutionalized patriarchies pose challenges. These platforms give 'the Othered' Muslim women designers and consumers an increased sense of political and personal agency and expressive freedom in their sartorial designs. These platforms have also made Muslim women more aware of the subtle and impractical misogynistic cuts and styles: the absence of pockets in female clothing, as well as heavy burqas that are unsuitable for South Asian geoclimatic conditions are examples of that. This awareness has inspired some practical changes to traditional style.

For example, recently *sari-pants* emerged as a new trend for women's fashion in South Asia. Traditional styles of *sari* – seven feet long silk fabric that is wrapped around the body in multiple layers – have become somewhat impractical for working women. But in *sari-pants*, women can wear regular bottoms/pants – with the *sari pallu* (end of the sari) hanging loose over the shoulder as it does in a regular *sari*. This innovation in style contemporizes a tradition and makes it practical for daily wear. With easy access to fashion trends via TV, film and social media, women can easily reimagine and customize their dresses according to their personal preference. Post-postmodern theories of digimodernism and automodernism also facilitate a discussion of fashion customization and autonomy.

Alan Kirby, in Digimodernism (2009), discusses the influence of digital technology on culture and cultural artefacts using examples from film, TV and popular cultural movements. Whereas Robert Samuels, in Automodernism (2007), rejects the oppositional human versus machines binary, Kirby claims that digimodern texts are characterized by 'haphazardness, evanescence' and 'multiple authorship' (2009: 273), some of which I have explained above as applied to Muslim women's altermodern fashion. While traits of digimodernism are 'infantilism, earnestness, and endlessness, and apparent reality' (2009: 273), Samuels contends that automatization awards humans tameable autonomy. Samuels exemplifies this autonomy through his nephew writing a paper for a school project. His nephew uses interactive chat groups and online guides, simultaneously working on the paper switching between multiple tabs. This forces Samuels, who is observing the nephew, to rethink and reform his own perceptions of plagiarism, multitasking, and human and machine collaboration. In my opinion, the same writing model is applicable to fashion stylists, bloggers and fashion consumers. Samuels's automodernism is more positive than Kirby's digimodernism. While postmodernism had only changed traditional perception of autonomy and agency, post-postmodern automodernism and digimodernism further transform these ideas. This necessitates further discussion of the critical role of social media in Muslim women's agency, visibility and creativity in fashion.

Blogs, vlogs, websites and social platforms like Instagram, Facebook and Snapchat –with their built-in templates – have transformed the way we perceive and practice agency, autonomy and creative freedom. Creating any text, be it an essay or a fashion design, involves 'technical automation' with 'human autonomy' to express the creative freedom via that text (Samuels, 2007: 175). This, ultimately, brings human subjects and their machine expertise together – which can be both liberating and limiting. Since there is already a given template on Instagram, designers have limited choice in Instagram video lengths or the styles of their profiles. In print fashion, Pakistan has some established fashion magazines like *She*, *Good Times*, *Fashion Central*, *Pakistan in Vogue*; while Indian magazines include *GQ India*, *Femina*, *Elle*, *Vogue India*, *Open* and *Stardust*. But with a disappearing printing industry, social media platforms like Instagram are becoming the only feasible medium for Muslim women to access the latest fashion. They can see show business people's outfits daily via their ootd (outfit of the day) updates, their style guides and make-up routines. This online engagement inspires these women's cuts and styles too – they can use that inspiration in accordance with their own micro-identity.

For example, I, as a South Asian Muslim woman, scroll through an international or Western fashion blogger's Instagram post or watch a YouTube tutorial. Let us assume that I like the style of sleeves on her dress in the post. Next time, I would direct my *darzi* (tailor) to add those sleeves to my traditional *shalwar kamiz*. My *darzi* might suggest a different fabric or embroidery thread for that dress – from their personal taste, another client's dress or may be another online video. Eventually, I would have a *kamiz* that has unique, non-traditional sleeves but still complies with the religious and cultural sartorial dictates and norms that I prefer or find comfortable. This *shalwar kamiz* has multiple authorship (designed, perceived, stitched by different people), haphazardness (fusion of local and global styles might appear mismatched or unusual to some) and openness (I could cut the *kamiz* shorter, wear it with jeans to Westernize it or wear a *dupatta* with it to make it more traditional). I might comment on that blogger's post to express my appreciation of that sleeve style. In response, I would receive replies from people located all around the world who might (dis)agree with me. The process of inspiration, imitation and collaboration has substantially accelerated due to accelerated digital access to fashion in post-postmodernity. Women can access top global fashion shows as they are happening, which has increased the fashion transfer rate significantly. It enables cross-religious and cross-cultural connections.

This style of sleeves on a traditional *kamiz shalwar*, which is now a multiauthored text in digimodernism, expresses my willingness to explore and adopt other cultures, while preserving my own. I might accessorize this dress by choosing from numerous options like bangles, *khussa*, *jhumkas*. I might add something new when a new fashion trend or accessory emerges and is mass produced by cheaper brands. This is a long, complex process that was initiated via mere scrolling through a screen and staring at a picture for a few seconds. So, in post-postmodernity, my dress becomes the digimodernist multi-authored endless text that expresses the automodern autonomy and agency through this creative freedom – all of which would have been impossible without expeditious post-postmodern digital access to personal gadgets like smart phones, computers and satellite TV.

Samuels (2007) equates this experience of personal computer to 'personal culture'. Personal culture is synonymous with micro-identities. In post-postmodernism, access to gadgets means easy access to other cultures and fashions. The virtual life has diminished temporal and spatial differences and enabled Muslim women to express their micro-identities. Women can just sit at their home and watch the latest fashion trends in 'autonomous passivity'. Furthermore, personalization and customization of these trends creates the illusion that the wearers have created the fashion object themselves. Mass-produced and affordable copies of the high-end clothing items become available in the market within days after the launch of those designs. Hence, along with facilitating nuanced personal/micro-culture and individual expression of micro-identities for Muslim women, the digital age also poses challenges for fashion designers and consumers.

Due to the inseparable interlinkage of real and online life, the internet is not beyond the influence of economic and political forces. Doris Teske (2003) describes the internet as a space that started beyond any geographical and economic terrain, but gradually economic control caught up with it, with 'commercialization and state control breaking its earlier "anarcho-libertarian" bubble' (108). Most fashion designers prioritize instant monetary gratification over human labour or ecological concerns. This makes it hard to ensure the maintenance and accountability of copyright infringement and the protection of humans against exploitation in fashion markets. It is even harder in countries with wide class stratification and weaker sociopolitical and legal infrastructure – like India and Pakistan. In 2017, *Khaadi*, one of the top Pakistani clothing brands, was accused of not even giving bathroom breaks to their workers, most of whom were women. Fashion, by its very nature, is class specific. In a neoliberal global economy, fashion market complicity often partakes in sociopolitical inequity. But post-postmodern ecological and sociopolitical challenges have also made fashion consumers and producers, particularly women, more aware of the repercussions of their choices.

Marginalized consumers, like South Asian Muslim women, tend to engage with fashion more cautiously because fashion is more politically charged for them. Gilles Lipovetsky describes fashion as a 'form of social change without any particular object' (1994). Emma Tarlo also highlights the protest potential of sartorial decisions and states that the British 'acted out' their domination through imposition of dress but the nationalist leaders 'contested it' through their sartorial choices too (n.d.). Though national politics and women's fashion have historically mutually affected and altered each other in South Asia, this was not as visible when feminist movements were subtler, but contemporary fashion designers and artists are taking a stronger and clearer stance on these issues. For example, in Zia ul Haq's Islamized Pakistani regime (September 1978–August 1988), female TV anchors and actors could not appear on screen without their *dupattas*. This was a sudden change from a previously progressive tradition. As a protest against this law, many women refused to perform on screen. Most of these protests did not surface publicly and did not become part of the popular narrative. But in the post-postmodern global village, there is a stronger international accountability.

Powerful political bodies or corporations are forced to devise better strategies to stand up for women's rights and implement the laws. The recent #MeToo movement took the form of #MeinBhi (a literal Urdu translation of #MeToo) in Pakistan. This grants women the expressive freedom via fashion since they can choose what to wear more comfortably. Besides #MeinBhi, this movement also inspired #InkaarKaro (say no) and #KhanaKhudGaramKaro (warm your own food) hashtag movements. Women demanded equity and freedom of choice through these movements. These movements also spurred a plethora of fashion shows where designers recorded their protest and spread awareness through the dresses they wore and catwalks. Sartorial protests came alive in Pakistan Fashion Week 2018, where, for the first time, the runway was walked by real-life plus-sized, elderly, differently abled models, instead of zero-sized youngsters. These models and their clothing aimed to raise awareness about romanticizing women's ideal age and unreal body and beauty standards for them. Along with that, these fashion shows also highlighted social issues like Jinnah's Pakistan, child labour, #MeinBhi, net neutrality and the water crises (Pakistan Fashion Design Council, 2006). Maheen Khan's brand *Gulabo* stood out with their Fashion for Change and Liberation collections in 2018. The *Gulabo* collection deployed ramps to shed light on child abuse, women's rights, street harassment, ecological crisis and national politics. In a fusion of Western and Eastern trends, Khan used graphic statements like #MeinBhi, Save the Earth, *Number phenk, tamasha dekh* (try sliding me your phone number and watch the shit show) and *Naya Pakistan* (slogan of Pakistan Party for Justice (PTI) that is popular among the youth). Cheena Chappra also showcased her collection Revivalist on older and plus-sized working women as models (Figure 6.1). Previously in 2016 FPW, designer Rozina Munib chose Mukhtaran Mai – a gang-rape survivor – as her showstopper to raise voice against women's rape. When accused of using Mai as a gimmick, Munib responded that she, as a woman, has the 'ethical responsibility' of portraying these issues in a booming fashion industry (Rehman,

Figure 6.1 Photo from Cheena Chappra's collection *Revivalist* at Fashion Pakistan Week 2018.

Figure 6.2 Women wearing *Lahori Ink*.

2016). This has also led to some brands capitalizing on the market potential of feminism: for example, a Lahore-based brand *Lahori Ink* primarily sells clothing items that mix pop culture with feminist and political slogans and graphics (Figure 6.2).

The same relationship between fashion and social change is also visible in androgynous clothing. Designers – by adding feminine prints, embroidery and cuts to male clothing and vice versa – tried to make gender boundaries more fluid. Men wearing *cholis* and heavily embroidered *chaadar* (previously embroidered *chaadar* was reserved for women, while men wore plain shawls) are accepted more easily and widely now. Instead of being considered effeminizing, they are perceived as style statements. This fluidity of gender boundaries in fashion gradually seeps into daily life practices and affects real, albeit slow and small, change towards gender equity (Figure 6.3).

Younger South Asian Muslim women more flexibly tend to explore and adapt to a more global Muslim identity. In opting for a dominantly cosmopolitan and global Muslim identity, they relegate the regional factors to a secondary status. Emma Tarlo (2013) highlights this intergenerational conflict about religious and cultural adaptation and sartorial choice and observes that Bollywood-esque

Figure 6.3 Photo from Pakistan Fashion Design Council's Fashion Week 2018.

female objectification contrasts with Islamic modesty or covering of body to evade the male gaze. Younger Muslim women are a cultural blend of global, South Asian, regional and religious influences. That is why a modest mix and match of loud and subtle cuts, colours and trends is more popular among them. This is truer for professional and expatriate South Asian women. This trend is particularly visible in blogs and vlogs run by Muslim South Asian women.

One more post-postmodern phenomenon is the emergence of fashion bloggers and vloggers. This is a complex paradox of monetary inequality, more than geopolitical and sociocultural factors. Most female fashion bloggers and vloggers hail either from upper middle class or the film and fashion industry, neither of which are relatable for the majority of South Asia Muslim women. Most middle-class or poor Muslim women can neither afford nor relate to the style or cost of the fashion in these blogs and vlogs. Economically disadvantaged Muslim women face different challenges in fashion. Usually knock-out copies of international, as well as local brands are easily available in *bazaars* (local markets) both in India and Pakistan. But the variety of machine-produced fashion products in the market help these women choose, modify and customize their style and fashion. There is a rising need for fashion bloggers and vloggers who cater to different socioeconomic classes. This is particularly significant in the Muslim context in institutionalized patriarchies like India and Pakistan where honour killings are still a frequent occurrence. These women's fashion choices are more significant because they have material consequences for them. Some of these practices like recycling of older styles and trends have been recurrent in fashion but post-postmodernism provides us with the theoretical lens to critically understand different approaches towards customization and personalization of fashion according to micro-identities of Muslim female subjects.

Conclusion

South Asian Muslim women have wider options to represent their personal, sociopolitical and religio-cultural location in post-postmodernity. Fashion and dress as the most common aspects of everyday life carry radical potential for the expression of Muslim women's subjectivity. They can use that as a tool to express their personal and socio-political micro-identities. Post-postmodernism also provides women the digital means of access to online spaces. This occupation of online spaces is critical in institutional patriarchies where public spaces are not safe for women. Bourriaud's viatorization in altermodernity facilitates intercultural collaboration, while Lipovetsky's hypermodernist revisionary memory reimagines ways of reviving the past and integrating that in current trends. Kirby's digimodernism expands the online spaces and occupation of those spaces like Instagram and YouTube by women, whereas Samuels explores the ways we create fashion and showcase it on online mediums. Collectively, all of these post-postmodern theories provide newer and nuanced ways to approach and understand Muslim women's subjectivity and its placement within post-postmodern culture.

Notes

1   I use the word 'female' or 'woman' to refer to the persons who identify with this gender category, feel closer to it than any other gender identity or prefer to wear traditionally female fashion.

2   Vedas are religious texts in Sanskrit in ancient India; similarly, Ramayana and Mahabharata are Sanskrit epics in India.

3   Khyber Pakhtunkhwa is a Pakistani province which was originally known as North West Frontier Province and was changed to Khyber Pakhtunkhwa in 2010.

References

Baker, P. L. (n.d.), 'Middle East: History of Islamic Dress', *lovetoknow*. Available online https://fashion-history.lovetoknow.com/clothing-around-world/middle-east-history-islamic-dress (accessed 20 December 2018).

Barthes, R. (1975), *Mythologies*, New York; Hill and Wang.

Bourriaud, N. (2015), 'Altermodernism', in D. Radrum and N. Stavris (eds), *Supplanting the Postmodern: An Anthology of Writings on the Arts and Culture of the Early 21st Century*, 251–71, New York: Bloomsbury.

Davids, N. (2018), 'How Nike's Hijab Sports Gear Is Taking on Islamophobia and patriarchy', *IOL*, 10 August. Available online https://www.iol.co.za/capetimes/opinion/how-nikes-hijab-sports-gear-is-taking-on-islamophobia-and-patriarchy-16491097 (accessed 10 November 2018).

Dhamija, J. (2006), *Fashion Pakista*. Available online http://www.fashionpakistan.com.pk/fpw-ss-2018/ (accessed 2 December 2018).

Dhamija, J. (n.d.), 'South Asia: History of Dress', *lovetoknow*. Available online https://fashion-history.lovetoknow.com/clothing-around-world/south-asia-history-dress (accessed 15 November 2018).

Gani, A. (2016), 'Dolce & Gabbana Launches Luxury Hijab Collection', *The Guardian*, 7 January. Available online https://www.theguardian.com/world/2016/jan/07/dolce-gabbana-debuts-luxury-hijab-collection (accessed 10 November 2018).

Janaki, T. (2018), 'Being Fashionable in the Globalization Era in India: Holy Writing in Garments', in M. A. Jansen and J. Craik (eds), *Modern Fashion Traditions: Negotiating Tradition and Modernity through Fashion*, 73–97, London: Bloomsbury.

Kirby, A. (2009), 'Digimodernism: How New Technologies Dismantle the Postmodern and Reconfigure Our Culture', in D. Radrum and N. Stavris (eds), (2015), *Supplanting the Postmodern: An Anthology of Writings on the Arts and Culture of the Early 21st Century*, New York: Bloomsbury.

Lipovetsky, G. (1994), *The Empire of Fashion: Dressing and Modern Democracy*, Princeton, NJ: Princeton University Press.

Lipovetsky, G. (2015), 'Hypermodernism: Time against Time, or the Hypermodern Society', in D. Radrum and N. Stavris (eds), *Supplanting the Postmodern: An Anthology of Writings on the Arts and Culture of the Early 21st Century*, 153–73, New York: Bloomsbury.

Niessen, S. (2018), 'Afterword: Fashion's Fallacy', in J. Craik and M. A. Janesen (eds), *Modern Fashion Traditions: Negotiating Tradition and Modernity through Fashion*, 209–219, London: Bloomsbury Publishing.

Niessen, S. (2018), 'Pakistan Fashion Week 2018: From #MeToo to Jinnah's Pakistan', *Indian Express*, 12 April. Available online https://indianexpress.com/photos/lifestyle-gallery/pakistan-fashion-week-2018-day-1-metoo-movement-jinnahs-pakistan-highlights-5134733/ (accessed 12 November 2018).

Rehman, M. (2016), 'Mukhtaran Mai Will Make Her Fashion Week Debut Today', *Dawn Images*, 1 November. Available online https://images.dawn.com/news/1176510/mukhtaran-mai-will-make-her-fashion-week-debut-today (accessed 10 December 2018).

Roach, M. E., & Eicher, J. B. (1965). *Dress, Adornment, and the Social Order*. New York: John Wiley.

Samuels, R. (2007), 'Automodernism: Auto-modernity after Postmodernism: Autonomy and Education in Culture, Technology, and Education', in D. Radrum and N. Stavris (eds), (2015), *Supplanting the Postmodern: An Anthology of Writings on the Arts and Culture of the Early 21st Century*, New York: Bloomsbury.

Sandhu, A. (2015), *Indian Fashion: Tradition, Innovation, Style*, London: Bloomsbury.

Sherwood, H. (2016), 'Muslim Lifestyle Expo in London Highlights Largely Untapped Market', *The Guardian*, 7 April. Available online https://www.theguardian.com/world/2016/apr/07/muslim-lifestyle-expo-london-global-brands-spending-power (accessed 10 November 2018).

Tarlo, E. (2013), 'Landscapes of Attraction and Rejection: South Asian Aesthetics in Islamic Fashion in London', in E. Tarlo and A. Moors (eds), *Islamic Fashion and Anti-Fashion: New Perspectives from Europe and North America*, 73–93, London: Bloomsbury.

Teske, D. (2003), 'Beyond Postmodernist Third Space: The Internet in a Post-Postmodern World', in K. Stierstorfer (eds), *Beyond Postmodernism*, 101–10, Berlin: Walter de Gruyter.

7

LIGHTS, CAMERA, FASHION: FROM DESIGNER TO DIRECTOR IN TOM FORD'S *A SINGLE MAN* AND *NOCTURNAL ANIMALS*

Grant Klarich Johnson

This chapter argues that Tom Ford's feature films, *A Single Man* (2009) and *Nocturnal Animals* (2016), recognized film as a novel medium for the expression of fashion, particularly for the self-fashioning of the designer as author. While designers have certainly appeared in documentary and fictional features, for example, Isaac Mizrahi in *Unzipped* (1995) or the fictional Tracy Chambers of *Mahogany* (1975), Tom Ford became the first to direct his own feature film. By working not only as screenwriter but director too for both films, Ford performed and condensed the roles most associated with filmic authorship. By turning its attention to Ford's film-making, this chapter offers a critique of the films' internal content while also considering how the film-making they index redefines the role of the designer and concretizes a sociological author function apparently external to their fictions (Foucault and Hurley, 1998). By taking on the role of a film director, Ford demonstrates the degree to which both this vocation and that of the fashion designer have distanced themselves from the conditions of anonymity previously more typical for both.

Before he expanded into movie-making, Tom Ford had already distinguished himself as a distinct kind of fashion designer, a man who authored a brand more so than any particular collection of clothing, pioneering the role of the 'creative director' – a phrase that both borrows from the field of film production and anticipates Ford's particular move into film direction.

Ford's reputation as a fashion titan was secured by his extremely successful revival of the Italian luxury brand Gucci. Hired as Gucci's chief women's ready-to-wear designer in 1990 (at the age of 29) at a moment when the company was on the brink of bankruptcy, he ultimately assumed the role of creative director in 1994. When Gucci acquired Yves Saint Laurent in 1999, Ford's directorial role expanded to oversee it as well. Ford exited the Gucci group in 2004, at a moment when the company was valued at around 8 billion dollars. He launched his film production company, Fade to Black, shortly thereafter in 2005 and his own successful namesake label in 2006 (Pulver, 2010).

Though the term 'designer' is often still used in casual and media descriptions of Ford, it may be more precise to recognize his work for Gucci and later Yves Saint Laurent, and now Tom Ford, as exemplary of that of the 'creative director'. An historically novel phrase (basically unused before 1950), the demarcation of 'creative director' was increasingly employed towards the end of the twentieth century, alongside Ford's rise as an influential fashion figurehead, to define the most senior creative at any one fashion brand. As the most superior creative at Gucci, and later YSL, Ford established an aura for either brand via his unique orchestration of decisive styling and a consistent and particularly evocative symbolic language. To this day, Tom Ford is known not for creating any particularly innovative style but rather for espousing and visualizing a branded lifestyle. As demonstrated by Ford, the designer as author, as 'creative director', supersedes any individual item of clothing to design life itself.

This transition from designer to creative director distinguished Ford as working in a mode unique from the more modernist model of the designer, understood as an innovator in garment design and construction (as typified by a persona such as Cristobal Balenciaga). Ford conjured an always sexy, at times pointedly risqué, air around Gucci that insisted on revealing cuts often defined by thoroughly unbuttoned shirts, plunging necklines, or decisively placed cut-outs to reveal a frisson of skin. Ford's often curve-conscious, sinuous silhouettes were heightened by thin, slick fabrics, and his slinky dresses often left little of the wearer's form to the viewer's imagination. That said, few of Ford's garments demonstrated anything stylistically 'new'. In fact, wildly profitable, they reinforced the old truism that sex sells. More important and iconic than Ford's garments in generating Gucci's sex appeal were its advertisements, an orchestration of models, lighting, implied narrative and costuming that anticipate his moody broody film work. Advertising produced under his direction typically featured provocatively nude and exposed women, most famously a woman with her pubic hair monogramed into a 'G' (for Gucci).

As such, Ford's earliest successes at Gucci resulted as much if not more upon the production of a seductive 'image', an observed synthesis of actor, styling and environment over any particularly novel or autonomous garment. In this, his stance as more of a creative director than classical designer anticipated his later work as a director, not of fashion but of film. That said, to speak in terms of creative director and director, as opposed to designer/director risks not only confusion at the level of language but also fails to mark the real difference that remains still today between the work of fashion and the work of film. As such, in this chapter I will follow common parlance and primarily use the term 'designer' (as opposed to creative director) to designate Ford's work in fashion and 'director' in relation to film work.

After postmodernism

Rehearsing the modernist trope developed by *Ulysses* and *Mrs. Dalloway*, Tom Ford's *A Single Man* submerges viewers in an extremely stylized stream-of-consciousness narrative, employing the same lifetime in a single day condensation by punctuating the experience of Professor George Falconer (played by Colin Firth) with informative flashbacks that especially enrich our understanding of his relationship with his late partner, Jim, beginning with his death and, towards the film's conclusion, their meeting. *Nocturnal Animals* likewise employs a framed narrative, with flashbacks, doubling and other interpenetrations that capture its protagonist's (Amy Adams's Susan Morrow) interior life and blur fiction with reality. Here too, Ford draws a parallel with *Mrs. Dalloway*, where the protagonist Clarissa Dalloway feels oddly connected to the suicidal Septimus Smith, to the point that he begins to act like a kind of doppelganger throughout the narrative. Likewise, *Nocturnal Animals* leads us to confuse Susan's identity with others in the film. Meanwhile, Jake Gyllenhaal plays both her ex-husband Edward and the fictional protagonist of his novel, Tony. While Tony sits in a bathtub, Susan does too, and then later they occupy showers at the same time. As Gyllenhaal (as Tony) seeks revenge, we see the word 'revenge' appear in a painting done in the style of Christopher Wool in Susan's world (interestingly, the painting is not a real Christopher Wool but rather one created specifically for the film). We are led to see Susan echoed too in the fictional Tony's murdered wife and daughter; all three are red-headed.

In concert with the greater theoretical inquiry of this volume, these local, aesthetic conceits, as well as Ford's film career as a whole, demonstrate patterns symptomatic of cultural logics understood as typically post-postmodern, especially those articulated by Raoul Eshelman and his concept of 'performatism' in particular (Eshelman, 2008). Both the aforementioned stream-of-consciousness, the framing and double-framing, and the recognition of the designer as an author evidence Eshelman's 'theist' plots and narratives. By framing George Falconer's last quotidian day in *A Single Man* with the most significant moments in his life, we are led away from postmodern irony towards belief in a new sincerity. Likewise, Susan's otherwise banal daily life in *Nocturnal Animals* becomes cinematic, charged with the stakes of life and death, when intercut with the nested fictions she reads alongside her own life. Notably, Eshelman develops many of these ideas in response to *American Beauty* (1999). Beyond this, as a director, of both fashion and film, Ford performs the role of godlike, or 'monist', author Eshelman describes as typical of performatism's impetus to believe.

A Single Man, based on the 1964 novel of the same name by Christopher Isherwood, and *Nocturnal Animals*, based on the 1993 novel *Tony & Susan* by Austin Wright, are both works of adaptation. While Ford received the sole writing credit on *Nocturnal Animals, A Single Man* was co-written with David Scearce, who had already been working on a version of the screenplay before intersecting with Ford (Lederman, 2009). By adapting novels, rather than starting from scratch, Ford could focus on the creation of a distinct visual experience, assuming plot as something always already determined, an assumed readymade of secondary importance, a blueprint for the production of compelling imagery. This occupation and adaptation of an existing mythology mirrors what Ford perfected in his work for Gucci, YSL and ultimately his own namesake brand. Like Eshelman's theist author, Ford's 'authorial posture as a director is a commercial "breakthrough"' because 'unlike the apparent vulgarity detected by critics in [Baz] Luhrmann's literary adaptation of *Gatsby*, Ford's ultra-tasteful film takes a mood board approach in which narrative drama, however deftly deployed, is ultimately subordinate to the stylistic coding and value system of branded communication' (Rees-Roberts, 2018: 63). As defined by *A Single Man* and *Nocturnal Animals*, notably distinct within a greater continuum of approaches to film-making, dialogue often feels secondary to image. How characters look delivers more for the viewer than what they say, which is straightforward, at times flirting with cliché. Likewise the settings, meticulously chosen and designed, subsume any action performed within them. In *A Single Man*, Falconer either matches exactly or is deterministically swallowed by the sublime affect and carefully calibrated architecture of his house or the luscious blue of the ocean with which the film begins. Likewise in *Nocturnal Animals*, Susan's work as a gallerist feels important not because of what we see her do (which is either nothing or very dull) but because of the elaborate spaces in which it occurs, or because of the dramatic stakes of the fiction she reads. Similarly, Gyllenhaal's Tony's perversely violent suffering is underscored, maybe made inevitable by the endless desert and blackness, the hopeless highway he travels down.

That said, Ford's adaptations were not without important alterations. Notably, in *A Single Man*, Falconer is made intentionally and explicitly suicidal, clearly preparing to kill himself across the course of the day. As such, Ford gave the singular day a sense of gravity, a figuratively ticking clock (reproduced by literal ticking sound effects throughout the movie) which accords with Eshelman's sense of performatism and is otherwise absent from or more lightly implied in Isherwood's novel. More so, both books are adapted to serve Ford's requisite taste for hyper-glamour. As Pamela Church Gibson has excoriatingly summarized, Isherwood's George Falconer shifts from a more stereotypically curmudgeonly English expatriate to a swanky modernist, besuited and wearing Creed aftershave, Frank Sinatra's preferred brand. And Julianne Moore's beautiful, slim and elaborately coifed Charley is a sharp departure from the bohemian, with 'her sagging figure, flowing grey hair, and fondness for antiquated ethnic garments', in a 'hilltop bungalow' filled with Japanese paper lanterns imagined by Isherwood (Gibson, 2017: 630). Similarly, Amy Adams's Susan shifts from a part-time teacher and mother of three in Chicago to a gallerist in Los Angeles, from middle class to 1 per cent. Reiterating his approach to design as creative direction, Ford's most significant adaptations are not restructurings of plot but rather of persona, editing people into more glamorous images, the perfect career, with the perfect house, all perfectly dressed and accessorized.

The scenes and sequences of both films are primarily psychologically rather than causally related, strung together by the experience and perspective of their main characters (Colin Firth's George Falconer and Amy Adams's Susan and Jake Gyllenhaal's Edward and Tony). This bias, for affect and psychology over plot, again draws from important precedents of modernist literature, like *Mrs. Dalloway* (a source Ford has acknowledged in relation to *A Single Man*; Black, 2013: 106). Like an extremely extended advertisement (in the vein of fashion films, longer than usual, more narrative or conceptually anchored commercials created as luxury advertisements in recent years), both films supply a series of visual scenarios and vistas for Ford's red carpet avatars to pass through, fleshing out the ideal performance of a 'Tom Ford' lifestyle (Fig. 7.1). A new kind of advertising, these films shape our notion of Tom Ford, informing our understanding of its clothing and accessories, the brand at large, as well as the man himself.

What is a designer?

The elevation of film directors as omnipotent authors depends upon the long legacy and elaboration of auteur theory, an implicit touchstone of film criticism that in fact surfaced explicitly in some of the more deconstructive criticism surrounding *A Single Man* (Wollen, 1972). Rather than breaking with them entirely, Eshelman's 'performatism' builds upon the work of earlier postmodern theorists, an intellectual history evidenced by Eshelman's explicit references to Foucault (if not explicitly to Wollen, though he does indulge in the use of the term auteur from time to time). Ford's pursuit of these two distinct fields as occupations that can be logically and synthetically connected demonstrates that we are increasingly comfortable with recognizing both fashion designers and film directors as creative authors, akin to how novelists were understood at an earlier historical moment.

In 'What is an Author?', Michel Foucault probes, 'the singular relationship that holds between an author and a text, the manner in which a text apparently points to this figure who is outside and precedes it' (Foucault and Bouchard, 1977: 115). Along with other queries, Foucault asks,

> What, in short is the strange unit designated by the term, work? … If we wish to publish the complete work of Nietzsche, for example, where do we draw the line? Certainly everything must be published, but can we agree on what 'everything' means? … what if, in a notebook filled with aphorism, we find a reference, a reminder of an appointment, an address, or a laundry bill, should this be included in his works? Why not? These practical considerations are endless once we consider how a work can be extracted from the millions of traces left by an individual after his death.

To answer Foucault's questions fully, it is fruitful to turn one's attention to fashion, but particularly to designers like Ford creating 'work' beyond fashion's usual or assumed medium of clothing. As such, one can meaningfully expand Foucault's prompt to theorize authorship in media distinct from writing.

Relevant to this discussion of fashion and film, Foucault underscores that the same or similar types of texts (such as fairy tales, epic poems or folk songs) have not always required or assumed an author in order to signify properly, in fact their authenticity often depended particularly on the anonymity or mystery of their origin. Whereas the history of literature has increasingly depended on reference to an author, film and fashion have increasingly incorporated this literary necessity within their own history as well, so that both enter the world now according to the logic of authorship, an assumption that they are 'authored', generally by the proper name nominated as their director or designer, respectively. As such, Ford's excursions into film-making doubly dramatize Foucault's inquiry. First, they expand the 'work' of the fashion designer, his texts, into narrative film-making. Second, they invite the viewer to read the film in relation to Ford's existing persona as an author, to 'Tom Ford' the proper name, a fashion brand apparently external to the movie's self-contained world but, I argue, one that is essential to its significance.

In her application of Raoul Eshelman's theory of performatism to fashion after postmodernism, Marcia A. Morgado has underscored 'simple-minded subjects who have authorial power; theistic plotlines; transcendence; double framing, and locked frames', as especially symptomatic of performative aesthetics. Confronted by Ford's films, I see the double or locked frame first and most obviously in the framed narrative of *Nocturnal Animals*, where Susan reads Edward's manuscript, nesting a fiction within a fiction. The framed narrative dramatizes the play between fiction and fact, as Susan uses fiction to escape from the disappointments of her real life, a vehicle to transcend her every day, her cheating husband, and a marriage which has become its own kind of fiction. Likewise, Tony is overwhelmed by the task of vigilante detective work, filled with disbelief at the murder of his daughter and wife. At turns he seems tempted to reject this turn of events as fiction, and if not, he is forced to track down the evidence, the facts that will prove these crimes are real. Susan even experiences her life as distinct from the real world, as she is told, 'our world is a lot less painful than the real world'. Of course, Susan's 'reality' is also a fiction, pointing out from the filmic universe, first to the novels *Nocturnal Animals* and *A Single Man* are based upon, and then one remove further to Ford's role beyond this frame as the god-like author Morgado indicates via Eshelman's performatism, a reader and editor of these telescoping levels of nested fictions. We see this play between narratives too, distinct presents intermingling, in the flashbacks that punctuate *A Single Man*, especially in how they serve to enrich the meaning of George's quotidian day for both him and the naïve viewer, imbuing it with the significance of an epic narrative that synthesizes an entire life, a potency of feeling and consequence it otherwise would not have. The flashbacks are proof both for George and the viewer that his relationship and depression are valid and real.

More provocatively, Ford blurs the distinction between the fields of fashion and film by acting as author of both. As such, he constructs, 'the double frame', Morgado identifies as an 'attempt to manipulate viewer response through erasure of interpretive categories'. Viewers and interpretation are confused by this categorical collapse. Is it better to understand Ford as a designer who makes movies, or a director who designs clothing? Both or neither? Both questions risk sounding ridiculous. The desire to understand *A Single Man* and *Nocturnal Animals* through a modernist, medium-specific lens or a more postmodern gambit dramatizes at the very least the provocation of performatism. What happens if we understand Ford as the 'simple-minded subject' with 'authorial power' in this scenario, self-endowed with the power to confuse genres and collapse fields and narratives into one another? (Morgado, 2014: 321–5). Especially in *Nocturnal Animals*, Susan, Edward and Tony, each in their own way (as reader, writer and confused victim turned vengeful vigilante) also trace a version of the 'simple-minded subject' with 'authorial power', condensing facets of Ford's own authority into the filmic text. As fashion erases its categorical distinction from film, by assuming the role of director, Ford models a definition of authorship not only beyond actual garments but also normal advertising, from still images to the ephemeral performance of the fashion show. As Church Gibson notes, between work on his feature films, Ford became significantly involved, both financially and sartorially, in the production of the latest James Bond films, dressing the namesake protagonist in his designs and investing his money in the franchise. Building on this impulse, with *A Single Man* and *Nocturnal Animals*, he pioneered a foothold for fashion within the landscape of transmedia world building, an ascendant strategy most often grounded in filmic production and thinking but also a logical development of his previous mastery of lifestyle branding (fashion's version of and nomenclature for this gambit) to create alternate realities for the ideal existence of his luxury commodities branded with his own identity (e.g. Gibson 2017: 631).

Quite literally me

Like most of Isherwood's writing (including several works with a fictional character named Christopher Isherwood) *A Single Man* is taken to be at least partly autobiographical, informed by Isherwood's life as a gay, British man in Los Angeles, particularly his thirty-three-year relationship with Don Bacardi, thirty years Isherwood's junior, and 18 at their meeting (Geherin and Isherwood, 1972: 143). Like Falconer, Isherwood taught as a professor, at California State University Los Angeles. As such, *A Single Man* (as novel) already instigates the Foucaultian questions introduced above, setting Ford up to only further them via adaptation, echoing the play between author and text, internal/external, fake/real by inserting himself as another suspect in the quest for an author. Isherwood's autobiographical dynamic of older/younger gay desire echoes throughout the movie, most prominently in the partnership of Jim and George, whom Jim affectionately calls 'old man', but also in the flirtation between Falconer and Kenny Potter, his undergrad student, and Carlos the parking lot hustler who looks like James Dean. Witnessing all this confident, unwavering attraction of the young for the old, we begin to believe that Firth's George Falconer is desired by all men (and women) of all ages, a dream of gay (or simply any) male wish-fulfilment par excellence. This May-December pattern points outward to Ford's own well-publicized, more than thirty-year relationship with Richard Buckley, thirteen years his senior (*Out* magazine, 2016). It also recalls the familiar psychological tactics employed for his explicitly sexual Gucci advertising and later his own namesake brand, perennially charged with youthful figures erotically offering themselves to the voyeuristic and likely largely older viewers of these images.

Indeed, Falconer, as played by Firth, becomes a proxy for Ford internal to the movie. To begin, all three men carry surnames that begin with F: Falconer, Firth, Ford. Like Ford, Falconer is gay and perpetually impeccably styled and dressed. They both own iconic property and live on the west side of Los Angeles. Admittedly, Falconer's John Lautner home, fictionally sited in Santa Monica (the structure is actually located in Glendale), is more modest in scale than Ford's stately Betsy Bloomingdale mansion (Kudler, 2012; Dangremond, 2016). And yet its selection becomes decisive. In a flashback towards the beginning of the film, George and Jim banter about the advantages and disadvantages of life in a 'glass house', especially in light of their sexuality. Jim suggests the transparency of their house matters little, reminding George, jokingly, 'You're the one that's always saying we're invisible', a loving jab at George's comparative discomfort at being known as gay to his neighbours.

The film makes significant use of the home's fully transparent moments, especially to portray George's isolation and vulnerability laid bare by walls constructed entirely of clear glass. Just as our perception of inside and outside is confused by the panes of the house, George struggles to match his 'drowning' inner temperament to his pristine gentlemanly façade, to similarly reconcile inside with outside. Ford also makes use of the home's cosier and sheltering counterpoints, such as the scene of George and Jim curled up on the couch, surrounded by opaque redwood woodwork and shelving lined with books (Figure 7.1).

For those in the know (including Jim and George, living in their own modernist icon), the phrase 'glass house' alludes to *The Glass House* (1949), the iconic home of architect Philip Johnson and his partner David Whitney, a notably out mid-century gay couple. Like George, Jim, Tom and Richard, Johnson and Whitney were also dramatically separated by age. They met when Whitney was an undergraduate at the Rhode Island School of Design and Johnson, thirty-three years his senior, came to lecture. They remained together for forty-five years until Johnson's death (Kennedy, 2005). As such, the selection of the Lautner house parlays the aforementioned play of old and young (as well as questions of the

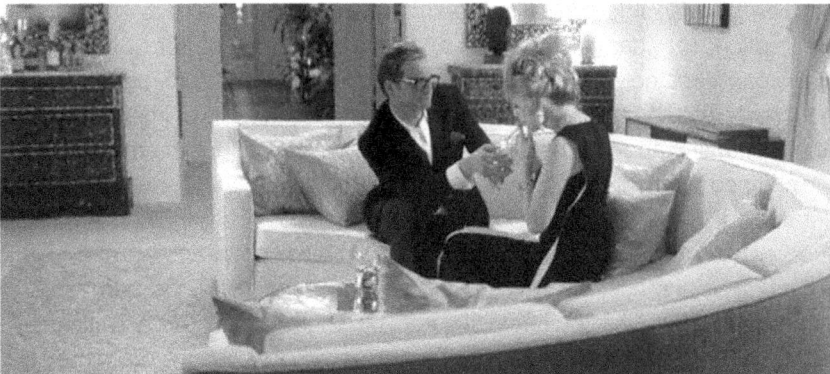

Figure 7.1 Colin Firth as George Falconer and Julianne Moore as Charley share a stylish evening in Charley's lavish living room (*A Single Man*; Tom Ford, Andrew Miano, Robert Salerno, Chris Weitz; dir. Tom Ford).

closet discussed below) through the prism of architectural history, especially as it shaped the lifestyles of its inhabitants.

The parallels continue. Ford and Falconer are both around the same age, Falconer is 52, while Ford was 48 when the film debuted. On the occasion of *A Single Man*, they are both seemingly undergoing a midlife crisis. Following the death of his partner Jim, Falconer has decided to kill himself. Less dramatically, *A Single Man* emerged from Ford's film production company, Fade to Black, founded in 2005, founded a year after departing from Gucci, and a year before his namesake brand launched. Ford himself has deemed this period a 'midlife crisis', when, like Falconer, he drank a bit too much and sorted out a new identity ('Tom Ford', 2011). Entirely funded by his own money (after other investors withdrew), Ford's decision to produce *A Single Man* was met with confusion and regarded as quixotic by both the fashion and film world (as well as their attendant critics) (Pulver, 2010). At the time, Ford was likewise an expatriate, an American in Britain, a neat inversion of Falconer's trajectory.

Falconer appears in every scene in the film, stressing the film's nature as a psychological portrait with no reality other than the one he observes, no plot or driving propulsion other than the pulse and development of his day from waking up to his final breath, dying of a heart attack at its conclusion. As such, the film apparently exists because George does; the film begins when George wakes up, and concludes when he dies. To draw a parallel to Eshelman's definition of performatism, Falconer's meditative anticipation of his own death recalls the 'tranquillity' he finds in Lester Burnham, the protagonist of *American Beauty*, a key example for Eshelman of filmic performatism. Eshelman's diagnosis of *American Beauty* applies too to *A Single Man*, namely, 'that Lester's tranquillity is made possible by the holism of the narrative framework, which is oblivious to the ontological difference between implicit author and character–and hence to death itself' (Eshelman, 2001).

A Single Man's novelistic first-person perspective, tied always to Falconer's perception, provides an extended analogy for the role of Ford as the film's director. Repeatedly, Ford plays with film as a pliable medium, slowing down the frame rate and saturating the picture to create intensely pigmented images that contrast with the otherwise washed out, bluer cast of the movie. These heightened moments suggest Falconer's perception of the world has similarly intensified. In this, he echoes possibly the most famous passage from *American Beauty*, film-maker Ricky Fitts and his sublime white plastic bag and how it informs Lester's perception of a real bag afterwards. As Eshelman notes of *American Beauty*, the protagonist's framing death anticipated and ultimately achieved in *A Single Man* ordains the entire movie, as well as the many ordinary, everyday moments that fill it with religious or sublime significance. Beyond this, these moments remind us of the film's materiality and Ford's control (like Fitts) over it, his ability to adjust the speed, saturation and colour of film. As such, it is more correct to say that moments when film's ability to slow time or enhance perception bring attention not to Falconer's consciousness but to Ford's aestheticizing direction, executing formal decisions that shape the viewer's experience. Ford reminds the viewer that his perception reigns greater than Falconer's as well as the filmic viewer's, possibly more so because of its apparent invisibility or omnipotence. This authorship of perception itself parallels similar pursuits by Ford's contemporaries, such as Marc Jacobs, whose stance as an author not simply of objects but of experience itself I have explored previously (Johnson, 2015: 315–30) and Alessandro Michele at Gucci as discussed by Nigel Lezama in this book.

Nowhere is the analogy between Falconer and Ford more clearly discussed than in the short featurette that accompanied the film. As the cast discusses how well-dressed and put-together Ford always appeared on set, they draw the obvious connection to Falconer's own fastidious self-presentation, his defining feature introduced potently in the getting ready sequence at the film's beginning. To drive the point home, the featurette quotes the image of Falconer's dresser drawer, stacked with seemingly endless, crisp white shirts, several wrapped in blue tissue paper bands (which seem to await a christening with a Tom Ford logo). And yet, even identifying this conscious connection forged between Falconer and Ford made by his own cast, if we agree with Foucault's articulation of authorship, no such smoking gun is required. As Foucault establishes, the text eternally points back to its author, whether that author announces itself explicitly in the text or not. Indeed, it is hard to imagine that many viewers sought out or even casually experienced *A Single Man* without some awareness of Ford's career as a highly profitable designer.

This autobiographical sense would inform *Nocturnal Animals* as well, with Ford referring to Amy Adams's Susan as 'quite literally me' and identifying her unsatisfying life of ostentatious wealth as his world too. Like Falconer and Ford, Susan too lives in LA, in a glamorous mansion decorated with conspicuous luxury baubles left for the knowing eye by the knowing director. She is surrounded by references to blue chip art. Naked women that introduce the film resemble Lucian Freud's *Benefits Supervisor Sleeping* (1995), and she lives with a Jeff Koons balloon sculpture and a Sterling Ruby painting. If Susan is 'quite literally' Ford, these allusions may be taken as evidence of Ford's own aesthetic preferences. Freud, Koons and Ruby are united not by a similar style or thematic concern but rather by the exemplary price point of their work, at the top of the market. 'She's someone who has material things but realizes – maybe this happened to me seven or eight years ago – those aren't the things that are important', Ford claimed of Susan. 'She is struggling with the world that I live in: the world of absurd rich [people], the hollowness and emptiness I perceive in our culture.' The moment Ford identifies, 'seven or eight years ago', would have coincided with the release of *A Single Man*, encouraging one to wonder whether

Ford's investment in film was an escape or the defining trauma that revealed the emptiness of a culture predicated on celebrity and wealth (Galloway, 2016).

Nostalgia of the closet

A Single Man and *Nocturnal Animals* drip with a gay, 'high camp' sensibility. As defined by Isherwood himself in a fictional conversation between two 'queer' men in his 1954 novel *The World in the Evening*, 'High Camp is the whole emotional basis of the ballet, for example, and of course baroque art … High Camp always has an underlying seriousness … expressing what's basically serious to you in terms of fun and artifice and elegance'. Isherwood's 1954 definition anticipated Susan Sontag's much better known 'Notes on Camp' of 1964 which also diagnosed a love for 'the unnatural: of artifice and exaggeration' as key. In keeping with Isherwood's remarks, both *A Single Man* and *Nocturnal Animals*, sombre and deadly serious, and likewise obsessed with a perfect presentation of artifice and elegance, are manifestations of a contemporary baroque, high camp aesthetic. From the perfect bodies and costumes of their characters to the rich decoration of their homes and the world through which they travel, both films also rehearse Sontag's camp, cherishing, 'a certain mode of aestheticism … of seeing the world as an aesthetic phenomenon … in terms of the degree of artifice, of stylization'. As I have said, Ford's films use plot as an excuse to produce images, as Sontag says, 'To emphasize style is to slight content.' If an association between a camp and a gay male sensibility is implicit in Sontag ('These notes are for Oscar Wilde'), Isherwood's articulation of it via a Socratic flirtation between two men makes it more explicit, aligning high camp aesthetics with a white, cis gay male sensibility and subjectivity.

Recycling and in part helping to concretize cues symptomatic of a high camp aesthetic for the twenty-first century, *A Single Man* and *Nocturnal Animals* evoke not only Ford's sensibility but capture the tastes and fascinations of increasingly socially mobile and economically privileged gay men. The legibility and palpable thickness of a gay, high camp aura in both films demonstrates Ford's ability to commodify and materialize a queer aesthetic consensus, an aspirational fantasy appealing to a diverse cross section of viewers queer and otherwise that recalls his earlier prowess as a creative director.

Ford's high camp sensibility is possibly most explicit and easily discussed when one considers his casting decisions, which construct intertextual echoes out into a larger field of queer film (an arena defined both by its producers and consumers). The most blatant and flagrantly camp example is Ford's delicious but absurd decision to cast Laura Linney (in reality only 10 years older than Amy Adams) as Susan's elite Southern mother for a brief cameo in *Nocturnal Animals*. The pairing requires a significant suspension of disbelief, recalling Sontag's diagnosis that 'to perceive Camp in objects and persons is to understand Being-as-Playing-a-Role'. More subtly, George's late partner is played by Matthew Goode, who had just appeared in 2008's *Brideshead Revisited* as Charles Ryder, a man tempted by the explicit homosexuality and Wildean aestheticism espoused by his upper-class peers at 1920s Oxford.

Called a 'queer icon' by *Out* magazine, Moore's inclusion in *A Single Man* points backward to the queer cinema of Todd Haynes and her roles in his *Far from Heaven* (2002) about a wife confronted by her closeted husband, and *Safe* (1995), a film with allegorical nods to the HIV/AIDS crisis (Smith, 2015). One year after *A Single Man*, Moore portrayed a lesbian mother with her own identity crisis in *The Kids Are Alright* (2010). The getting ready sequence with which *A Single Man* begins recalls *The Hours* (2002; based on Michael Cunningham's novel of the same name) where Moore appears as a severely depressed (potentially due to her repressed attraction to women) housewife and mother to a gay son. Just as *The Hours* had, *A Single Man* glamorizes suicide not only as a way to escape life's suffering but also as a way of expressing autobiographical meaning for queer subjects. To style suicide as an act of authorship underscores death's power to shape our experience of narrative significance. As Caroline Evans has argued, this 'deathliness' also informed the increasingly dark tenor of fashion as it pivoted into this century alongside Ford's success at Gucci (Evans, 2003: 4). *A Single Man* aestheticizes death, neatens and tidies it, lined up and condensed in the keys, paperwork and legal documents assembled on George's desk. In *Nocturnal Animals* the red of blood is luxurious and tactilely seductive like the red velvet of the sofa upon which the two women's murdered bodies rest. As such Ford's films offer an act of transference, a processing of the trauma inflicted by the AIDS epidemic upon the unconscious of a generation, those who saw their friends and lovers die and for whom queer life seemed intrinsically inflected by the deathly. Via either murder or suicide, Ford's characters reclaim agency over death's random meaninglessness, likewise recouping the authorial power it may occasion.

Moore's red-headed presence in *A Single Man* sublimates and extends into the image of Amy Adams in *Nocturnal Animals*. In *Nocturnal Animals*, Adams's hair echoes touches of red throughout the film, really the only pronounced colour used throughout. It appears in the blood associated with the central murders and rapes, the aforementioned couch upon which the murdered bodies rest, the walls of Susan's lavish office, her daughter's collegiate sheets below her ideally nude body, another sofa, an electric guitar, the threatening neon of Texas and so forth. Red condenses a sense of danger and death as well as an erotic charge. Moore's and Adams's iconic red hair might be taken as a metaphor for the outlier or minority status associated with queer identity, as red heads are statistically rare (if not also a site of sexual fascination) (Box, 2018). Like members of the queer community, red heads are also a target for social stigma.

Echoing this identification and transference, Susan is haunted by her husband's infidelity, likened by a female friend to her own sexless marriage to a gay man. In contrast, hypermasculine homosocial encounters plague Jake Gyllenhaal's Tony Hastings, surrounding him with repressed homosexual desire that tempts the viewer (and maybe the reading Susan) into homoerotic fantasy although sex is never realized. Instead, it sublimates into more violence, encouraging the viewer to read *Nocturnal Animals* as a parable about what repression or the confusion of desire may beget.

Like *A Single Man*, *Nocturnal Animals* also stands as an intertextual node in a history of queer film, inheriting Gyllenhaal's significant performance, in *Brokeback Mountain* (2005) and Armie Hammer's (Morrow's husband) future in *Call Me by Your Name* (2017). In a flashback to their first date, when Edward admits his teenage desire for Susan, she reveals and discusses her brother's desire for Edward well before admitting her own. As such, Susan and Edward are bound by this unfulfilled homoerotic desire, predicating the origin of their relationship on Edward's inability to recognize and realize male intimacy. As Tony's quest for vindication intensifies and turns increasingly vigilante and violent, the film's homoerotic gaze becomes especially pronounced.

Tony confronts one of the killers while the man sits fully naked (slim, muscled, abs tensed, torso toned) on a toilet beside his camper. The pose recalls Gyllenhaal's earlier in the film, made to sit fully naked on the rim of his motel tub, an oddly presentational and unlikely posture especially when one considers his supposed devastation and panic over his missing wife and daughter. Returning us to this confused moment of both pain (for the character) and voyeuristic pleasure (for the viewer), the pose's echo later not only eroticizes the criminal's status as a murderer and rapist but also draws our attention to the anality of defecation and anal sex by proxy. From here, the sexual tension only intensifies as he is interrogated, asked, 'Get a little rough, would you like that?' This line recalls the notably rough, gruff presentation of sex to be found in *Brokeback Mountain*, when Heath Ledger's Ennis Del Mar wordlessly penetrates Gyllenhaal's Jack Twist with little overture or warning. An ambiguous conquering, *Brokeback* led one to associate gay pleasure if not definitively with pain and fear, at least as embedded in moments of mute force.

In *Nocturnal Animals*, the homoerotic tension constructed between Gyllenhaal, his cop collaborator (Michael Shannon) and the equally hunky criminals (Aaron Taylor-Johnson and Karl Glusman, from Gaspar Noé's *Love* (2015), notable here for its extensive depiction of unsimulated sex) culminates not in sex but rather sublimates it into a handgun fuelled pursuit, beating and interrogation where the phallic weapon punctuates the film's climax with ejaculatory shots and empowers Gyllenhaal, finally, as a dominating figure. Another trope of Eshelman's performatism, he claims that the phallic weapon returns as part of a greater 'return of the phallus as a positive enabling force in culture' (Eshelman, 2001).

Figure 7.2 Marketing for *A Single Man* promoted Firth and Moore as if they were the film's romantic leads. Critics argued that this presentation obscured the film's gay narrative (*A Single Man*; Tom Ford, Andrew Miano, Robert Salerno, Chris Weitz; dir. Tom Ford).

Troubling this dangerous idea, *Nocturnal Animals* presents toxic masculinity and its phallic tokens in full, terrible force. The daddy fantasies of *A Single Man* recur here in the contrast between the twenty-something criminals, the elder Shannon and Gyllenhaal's Tony, a literal father. And finally, as evidenced by the apparent failure and dissatisfaction that characterizes both of Susan's romantic relationships, heterosexual love too is doomed, and homosexuality cannot succeed it (Figure 7.2).

A Single Man and *Nocturnal Animals* are gay fantasies, but of what kind, and what anxieties lay embedded in them? 'Don't you ever miss this? What we could have been to each other, having a real relationship and kids?', asks Moore's Charley of Firth's George in *A Single Man*. 'I had Jim', he replies, while she insists, 'No, I mean a real relationship. Let's be honest what you and Jim had together was wonderful but wasn't it really a substitute for something else?' In the repressed homoeroticism of *Nocturnal Animals* and the closeted *A Single Man*, Ford dabbles in what I have come to think of as a nostalgia of the closet. This phrase plays upon Eve Kosofsky Sedgwick's *Epistemology of the Closet* (1990) but whereas Sedgwick revised our understanding of cultural history informed by more recent sexual liberations, Ford's nostalgia returns us to an era before homosexuality's normalization in order to romanticize its past in the shadows.

Ford's nostalgia appears to spring from doubt and self-consciousness, anxieties over the validity of queer intimacy and commitment (whether, as Charley asks, they are 'real relationships' on par with heterosexual marriage and reproduction). To compensate for this sense of lack, a repressed, frustrated or dormant homosexuality is fetishized and projected as an alluring fiction. Counterintuitively, Ford makes this nostalgia glamorous and desirable, much as he could a purse or sunglasses, although of course the seduction's stakes are hardly commensurate with this comparison. Eight months after the death of his partner, Colin Firth's Professor Falconer, in dark suits, white shirts and conservative glasses, models a heteronormative façade, albeit one that is more Madison Avenue than faculty club. His only real confidant (Julianne Moore's Charley) yearns for a sexual relationship with Falconer, again suggesting that he may be understood, 'pass' as straight even to his closest friends (Fig. 7.2). The film's marketing went all in on this fantasy of straight passing by exclusively featuring Firth and Moore on a variety of poster designs (with none picturing Matthew Goode, as George's late partner Jim), as if they were the film's romantic leads, and producing a trailer strategically edited to foreground female characters and 'de-gay' the film (Knegt, 2009; Vilensky, 2009). In an uncredited role, Jim's cousin on the phone is played by *Mad Men's* John Hamm, another icon of 1950s male standardization and a telling spectre of the pressure to normalize according to a stereotypical masculine norm (a force that hardly exists as a thing of the past). Indeed, *A Single Man* emerged as part of a generation of productions seduced by a nostalgia for the 1950s and employed *Mad Men* production designers to mimic its atmosphere. Ford's fetishization of this period evokes a conflicted sense of the demand to come out, effectively conjuring a nostalgia for a more closeted era, as well as for its Gothic seductions, charged with secrets and hidden identities that Ford works hard to glamourize and make lavish for the viewer.

While ostensibly set in the recent present, the design of *Nocturnal Animals* often cites the streamlined silhouettes, dark eyes and big jewels of the 1970s, a historic touchstone for Ford's aesthetic recycling both at Gucci and his own brand. We see touches of the 1970s too in the desert Tony inhabits, where they drive vintage cars (including a green GTO) and smoke Lucky Strikes, a brand at its height far earlier, in the 1940s, and entirely discontinued for sale in America in 2006. This period confusion continues with the proportions and palettes of the menswear of Tony's world, as well as the general cowboy inflections and indulgences that abound. From his careful attention to detail in *A Single Man*, we know that Ford can pinpoint period trappings with exactitude, making all this temporal play read as a decisive choice, a desire to go back in time to a moment when gay identity was configured and performed differently, either behind an encoded hypermasculine façade or completely in secret.

The black stain of ink on the bed beside which George wakes in *A Single Man* recalls the blood he imagines beautifully pooling around Jim's body in the snow, but also, recalling *Macbeth*, offers a symbol of Falconer's shame, a black spot that marks him, a stain of which he can't be rid, its shame at not being able to save his lover from death but also of the fact of their sexuality. The stain appears first erotically on his lower lip, as if left behind by the phallic pen in his mouth (and, pace Eshelman, of writing and narrative's capacity to create symbolic unity). The greater pool on the bed suggests the fluids, lubricating, ejaculatory or anal, often left behind by sex. When he apologizes for it to his housekeeper, we come to understand this shame is something George has become accustomed to, maybe even comforted by. One is led to assume that she would be uncomfortable and likely unaccustomed to Falconer's queer domesticity before becoming intimate with it. And yet, she is entrusted as the keeper of his lifestyle's secrets and their physical traces, the evidence, from dirty sheets to confessional letters to lavish dinner parties. She has performed this role (as he has too) for long enough that its signs seem banal and comfortable to them both, even as beyond the privacy of the house the open acknowledgement of this shared secret could garner shame for them both.

'Let's think of another minority, one that can go unnoticed if it needs to', George asks his students in *A Single Man*, a prompt Ford offers to the audience as well in what follows:

There are all sorts of minorities, blonds, for example, people with freckles. A minority is only thought of as one when it constitutes some kind of threat to the majority, a real threat or an imagined one. And therein lies the fear and if that minority is somehow invisible then the fear is much greater. That fear is why the minority is persecuted and so you see there always is a cause, the cause is fear.

Here, George flirts with outing himself and then steps back into the closet. At first, he positions minorities as a kind of non-event, like 'blondes' or 'people with freckles' (or, to return to an earlier discussion, red hair). Then they become threatening, fearsome and dangerous, especially when they can become invisible, a distinction that distinguishes sexual from, for example, racial minorities. But then, after suggesting that fear and thus persecution are inevitable timeless realities (and thus, due to this futility, not worthy of our concern?), he dials back his rhetoric completely again to the non-event, resolving, 'Minorities are just people, people like us.' With this, if he has begun to out himself, he slips right back into the pack here, playing between a diction of they, we and the ambiguous 'us' with which he ends.

Visually, this lecture is accompanied by the camera's specific attention to Nicholas Hoult's eyes, intercut with a more zoomed out view of two young male students looking a bit panicked by Falconer's speech. Although in this moment Hoult, as undergraduate Kenny Potter, is paired off with a perfectly coiffed Bridget Bardot-esque blonde, by the film's conclusion Potter will ultimately become the site of Falconer's last affection before death, tempting him into the ocean for a bit of skinny dipping and then back home for a bit of intimacy. If Hoult's Potter looks captivated and intrigued by George's lecture, the men seated beside him look stricken with fear, possibly because, unlike Kenny Potter, they do not have a glamorous female partner or the accompanying privilege of passing for straight.

The contrast occasioned by Ford's camerawork reminds that it would be harder for these young men to retreat from public scrutiny in moments of threat in the manner Falconer is simultaneously performing and in part advocating for in this moment. Unlike George and Kenny, they only have each other at their side, a position that will only ever reinforce the danger posed by their legibility as gay men.

While indulging in the comfort of Julianne Moore's Charley, and when he takes Potter home much later in the film, Falconer will reveal his own identification as distinct from these young men. Unlike them, his sees his identity as dependent upon both male and female companions from which a hybrid status arises. As he states at one point, 'I sleep with women but I fall in love with men.' Recalling Sedgwick's discouragement of imagining a strictly hetero- or homosexual binary, this stance allows Falconer to exist both in and out of the closet. On the one hand, he lectures about the persecution of minorities, while on the other he dresses and presents himself in ways that reinforce a heteronormative stereotype of the straight white man as a pillar of mid-century America whenever this identity might be to his advantage.

The increasingly flirtatious conversations with Hoult's Kenny Potter confirms this sense, when Kenny claims, 'You never really tell us everything you know about something.' 'It's not that I want to be cagey,' George defends. 'It's just that I can't really discuss things completely openly at school. Somebody would misunderstand.' Falconer's position makes sense for a man, a professor talking to a student in the 1950s, but it was an odd stance to rehearse in 2009.

To obsess over the historicism at hand here would be to fall for a red herring. For Falconer, his sexuality is just the tip of the iceberg of what he can't put into words, including the entire daunting mystery of life and the meaning or significance of his own particular experience. Both *A Single Man* and *Nocturnal Animals* indulge in not only dated but privileged and sheltered emotional climates, where desire, identity and psychological interiority can afford to remain shadowy, hidden and shot through with the frisson of danger. On the one hand, these are narratives of repression, and not just in the sense of sexuality, but they also evoke an environment of self-obsession and narcissistic indulgence, an echo of Falconer's aforementioned belief that his experience is in some way ineffable, that even if he could speak openly, the complexity of his experience could not be fully communicated. The narcissism at the base of both films likely draws from Ford's confidence that 'nobody ever writes about anyone but themselves' (Fleming, 2016). This egocentric self-fascination needs the closet in order to continue to indulge its decadent identity, to see itself as complexly and monumentally as it desires. Otherwise, were it to step out completely into the harsh, pragmatic and quotidian reality of a more socially real or emotionally banal world, the pressure to level out one's sense of self would overwhelm, ruining its elaborate fantasy.

Conclusion

In this chapter, I have examined Tom Ford's feature films, *A Single Man* and *Nocturnal Animals*, not as discordant breaks but as logical developments for his own career as a womenswear designer turned field-defining creative director. I analysed Ford's work as a film-maker not only to offer a critique of both films but also to address larger questions of how fashion evidences, constructs and complicates greater definitions of cultural authorship. Ford's example, and my analysis of it, expands beyond this particular case study as evidenced by the emergence of other fashion film-makers since his films debuted, including Agné's B's *My Name Is Hmmm...* (2013) and Kate and Laura Mulleavy of Rodarte's *Woodshock* (2017), both of which offer further opportunities for future analysis. Drawing on Eshelman's notion of performatism, I have examined Ford and his films as evidence of how culture has developed after postmodernism, particularly its attraction to theist narrators, overall narrative unity and a new, possibly indulgent and solipsistic sentimentality that represses the incoherence and crisis of our present. For Ford in particular, I argued that the fictional space of feature film allows for a nostalgia of the closet, an ironic romanticizing of a world before gay liberation encouraged by the narcissism indulged by the theist regard that has been normalized both for fashion's godlike creative directors and film's auteurs.

References

Black, P. (2013), 'Designed to Death: Tom Ford's A Single Man', *Film, Fashion & Consumption*, 2 (1): 105–14. doi:10.1386/ffc.2.1.105_1.

Box, B. (2018), 'Gay Men Fetishize My Red Hair and I'm Not Mad about It', *LOGO News*, 12 December. Available online http://www.newnownext.com/red-hair-ginger-gay-men/12/2018/ (accessed 15 December 2018).

Dangremond, S. (2016), 'Tom Ford Just Bought Betsy Bloomingdale's L.A. House for $39 Million', *Town & Country*, 11 April. Available online https://www.townandcountrymag.com/leisure/real-estate/g3145/tom-ford-betsy-bloomingdale-los-angeles-house/ (accessed 20 December 2018).

Eshelman, R. (2001), 'Performatism, or the End of Postmodernism', *Anthropoetics VI*, (2). doi:http://anthropoetics.ucla.edu/ap0602/perform/.

Eshelman, R. (2008), *Performatism, or the End of Postmodernism*, Aurora: Davies Group Publishers.

Evans, C. (2003), *Fashion at the Edge: Spectacle, Modernity and Deathliness*, New Haven: Yale University Press.

Fleming, M., Jr. (2016), 'How Tom Ford Wove "Nocturnal Animals" from an Austin Wright Novel & Own Personal Angst', *Deadline*, 30 December. Available online https://deadline.com/2016/12/tom-ford-nocturnal-animals-amy-adams-michael-shannon-jake-gyllenhaal-oscars-interview-1201869014/ (accessed 15 December 2018).

Foucault, M., and D. F. Bouchard (1977), *Language, Counter-Memory, Practice Selected Essays and Interviews*, Ithaca, NY: Cornell University Press.

Foucault, M., and R. Hurley (1998), *Aesthetics, Method, and Epistemology: Essential Works of Foucault, 1954–1984*, New York: New Press.

Galloway, S. (2016), 'Tom Ford's Inner Life: A Director's Turmoil, Depression Battles and Staggering Talent', *Hollywood Reporter*, 7 September. Available online https://www.hollywoodreporter.com/features/tom-ford-designer-turned-director-925601 (accessed 20 December 2018).

Geherin, D. J., and C. Isherwood (1972), 'An Interview with Christopher Isherwood', *Journal of Narrative Technique*, 2 (3): 143–58.

Gibson, P. C. (2017), 'The Fashion Narratives of Tom Ford: Nocturnal Animals and Contemporary Cinema', *Fashion Theory*, 21 (6): 629–46. doi:10.1080/13627 04x.2017.1357367.

Johnson, G. (2015), 'Citing the Sun: Marc Jacobs, Olafur Eliasson, and the Fashion Show', *Fashion Theory*, 19 (3): 315–30. doi:10.2752/175174115x14223685749322.

Kennedy, R. (2005), 'David Whitney, 66, Renowned Art Collector, Dies', *New York Times*. 14 June. Available online https://www.nytimes.com/2005/06/14/arts/design/david-whitney-66-renowned-art-collector-dies.html (accessed 15 December 2018).

Knegt, P. (2009), 'A Tale of Two Trailers: The De-Gaying of "A Single Man"', *IndieWire*, 9 November. Available online https://www.indiewire.com/2009/11/a-tale-of-two-trailers-the-de-gaying-of-a-single-man-246255 (accessed 20 December 2018).

Kudler, A. G. (2012), 'Touring John Lautner's Incredible Schaffer House and Talking about Why It Isn't Selling', *Curbed LA*, 6 November. Available online https://la.curbed.com/2012/11/5/10309814/touring-john-lautners-incredible-schaffer-house-and-talking-about-why (accessed 15 December 2018).

Lederman, M. (2009), 'The Canadian behind a Single Man', *Globe and Mail*, 14 September. Available online https://www.theglobeandmail.com/arts/awards-and-festivals/tiff/the-canadian-behind-a-single-man/article1202434.

Morgado, M. A. (2014), 'Fashion Phenomena and the Post-postmodern Condition: Enquiry and Speculation', *Fashion, Style & Popular Culture*, 1 (3): 313–39. doi:10.1386/fspc.1.3.313_1.

Out magazine (2016), 'Tom Ford and Richard Buckley Forever', *Out* magazine, 19 February. Available online https://www.out.com/fashion/2011/01/09/tom-ford-and-richard-buckley-forever (accessed 15 June 2018).

Pulver, A. (2010), 'Tom Ford: A Single Man and His Address Book', *The Guardian*, 28 January. Available online https://www.theguardian.com/film/2010/jan/28/tom-ford-a-single-man (accessed 15 June 2018).

Rees-Roberts, N. (2018), *Fashion Film: Art and Advertising in the Digital Age*, London: Bloomsbury Visual Arts.

Smith, N. (2015), 'Julianne Moore as Queer Icon of Cinema', *Out* magazine, 2 May. Available online https://www.out.com/movies/2015/2/17/julianne-moore-queer-icon-cinema (accessed 20 December 2018).

'Tom Ford: I am Really a Loner after All' (2011), *The Talks*, 11 February. Available online http://the-talks.com/interview/tom-ford (accessed 20 December 2018).

Vilensky, M. (2009), 'Harvey Weinstein Explains a Single Man's Marketing, Sort Of', *Vulture*, 23 November. Available online https://www.vulture.com/2009/11/harvey_weinstein_explains_a_si.html.

Wollen, P. (1972), *Signs and Meanings in the Cinema*, Bloomington: Indiana University Press.

8

SEEING SELVES: THE ABSENT BODY IN THE MUSEUM AND THE WORK OF EXHIBITION MAKER JUDITH CLARK

Caroline Bellios

We expect touch when we see a garment and feel distanced from it when touch is not permitted. Fashion curators have experimented with clever and innovative ways to display garments in exhibitions to overcome this sense of distance and circumvent the necessity of a live human to translate a garment.[1] Many have succeeded in amusing and inspiring awe in the viewer, whether through incorporating animated faces[2] or exaggerating peripheral elements,[3] approaches that by design or by coincidence also distract viewers from their limitations in accessing the garments. Perhaps though, none have delved quite as deeply into the connection between our methods of seeing and our intimate relationship with garments as a means of accessing their wholeness as the London-based exhibition maker, Judith Clark. Curators cannot put bodies in garments in museums,[4] and visitors cannot touch the garments on display, but rather than trying to replicate the human body or touch, Clark uses tools of vision, the mind and memory to bring us to understanding found by accessing other parts of our humanness. 'At the centre there is always the imagined body, a past real body for which the installation is a surrogate' (Clark, 2008: 160). Rather than relying solely on fiberglass, papier-mâché and acrylic to replicate absent bodies, Clark's exhibitions invite us to explore our archived knowledge of our bodies in conversations with garments, unearthing past experience of touch to know the garments on display.

In the timeline of fashion exhibition history, larger-than-life, fashion magazine editor Diana Vreeland could be credited with leading a postmodern direction in fashion exhibition (Clark et al., 2014: 6). She broke from the traditions of costume exhibition up to that time, eschewing fidelity to history and staid educational information for spectacle (Steele, 2008). During her tenure as special consultant, from 1972 until her death in1989, exhibitions at the Costume Institute of the Metropolitan Museum of Art unveiled new potential in garment display, she replaced a modernist ordered historical and chronological structure with playful combinations and dramatic tableau intended to capture the powerful emotions inherent in a relationship with fashion. 'What Vreeland very astutely identified was the importance of the exhibition visitor identifying in some way with the object, and the connection between someone finding something desirable and finding something interesting' (Clark, 2008: 159). Elizabeth Wilson discussing postmodernism in relation to fashion alternately describes its 'horror at the destructive excess of Western consumerist society, yet in aestheticizing this horror, we somehow convert it into a pleasurable object of consumption', its ambivalence, its fragmentation, its embrace of identities and its shift away from knowledge (Wilson, 1993). Each one of these attributes could be found in the irreverent displays of Vreeland. Succeeding Costume Institute curators Richard Martin and Harold Koda would say of her work, 'Seen or unseen, Vreeland insisted on the transfigured moment, the ordinary rendered extraordinary. ... a standard of her desire to extract feelings from clothing and its context, a regular practice to engage the viewer in an experience both reasoned and made magical by some exceptional presence' (Martin et al., 1993). In historian Stephen Greenblatt's (1991) dichotomy of resonance and wonder, Vreeland luxuriated fully in a pool of wonder. Her work made fashion in the museum fashionable and popular, and countless new interpretations and imitations sprung up in sites around the world.

Judith Clark's work confronting time, history, the archive, memory and the ways in which those haunt the present does not sit comfortably under any of the post-postmodern theories discussed in this book, but inhabits a structure alongside them; Clark's exhibitions demand diverse modes of engagement between the objects and the viewers. In doing so, Clark deconstructs the language of costume exhibition to push exhibition practice past the fractures of postmodernity, instead assembling post-postmodern spaces with focused slicing and splicing of memory and knowledge rather than the ambivalence of postmodernity, an open-ended intentionality replacing ironic informality. When I asked her if perhaps her work could be classified as installation art that uses garments as a medium, she replied,

> I think I'm nervous of that title as though it's sacred and that I didn't come to it that way, a lot of people have said well, you can just call yourself an installation artist. And I think, do I want to be an installation artist? or do I want to be somebody whose questioning one very particular, one very small field of inquiry? that is the fashion exhibition ... do I just chip away at this one

sentence? And I think that's quite interesting, it's like there's something about it that I feel justifies its own kind of insistence. (Clark, 2019)

Her work stimulates each viewer's personal associations and memories, their willingness to bring part of themselves to the story essential to creating a new multivalent language for fashion exhibitions. Reflecting on Judith Clark's definition of herself as an exhibition maker, this integration of the interiority of the viewer becomes clear as a post-postmodern act of building rather than splintering. And unlike modernity's quest for universal truth, her work contains individual truths, the integrity of the exhibition dependent on the personal experiences and memories of each viewer.

Clark's work appears similar to a curator's; she selects objects to place on display for the public, but her process is more akin to that of an author who rearranges the familiar elements of language to uncover meaning through unusual adjacencies and unexpected syntax. Elizabeth Wilson writes, 'Dress is the cultural metaphor for the body, it is the material with which we "write" or "draw" a representation of the body into our cultural context' (Wilson, 1993: 6). Garments and bodies are Clark's words and sentences; through their interaction with bodies and quotidian presence, garments have developed customary and readable structures of meaning. Through her 'writing', Clark breaks apart those relationships and then builds them back together in ways that are altogether new but retain shadows of familiarity. Throughout her career Clark makes many allusions to the writings of Argentinean author Jorge Luis Borges. Themes of labyrinths, libraries, archives, hidden meanings, infinite combination and patterns, and diverging paths of possibility are reflected in her practice. Clark's work is designed not just to be read but to be engaged with through revisiting the memories and experiences we each carry with us. Her exhibitions are spaces where objects and viewers unite – the viewer an active participant, as vital to her story construction as the objects and built environments. 'Absolutely the exhibition isn't complete without the viewer and their memories … a memory goes in all directions because it's the memory of an object within another object, it's the memory of that experience, it's the memory of another time, it's the memory of a kind of desire' (Clark, 2019). Just as the viewers are living a moment that blends their present experience with the memories that haunt them, Clark often references the history of fashion exhibition within her exhibitions, acknowledging the lineage of exhibition history as a body in itself with its own set of memories. She hints at installations from past fashion exhibitions that have become a part of the cultural consciousness and understanding of the medium (Clark, 2019). Through written language, the visual language of clothing and the properties of space, Clark maps exhibitions that investigate humanness and the means of communication we rely on to connect with each other and build our personal and cultural histories. Her exhibitions are not about the specific objects, those are her tools, like words for an author, each chosen carefully for its meaning, and most importantly for its contribution to the whole.

Strategies against absent bodies

How *can* we exhibit clothing to fully tell its story? The display of garments in a museum space offers unique challenges beyond the display of other types of objects and art. On her own experience curating fashion exhibitions, Alexandra Palmer wrote, 'The personal knowledge of wearing clothes makes museum visitors connoisseurs even before entering a dress exhibition. Viewers come with preconceived ideas, and tend to measure meaning and value in terms of their own life' (Palmer, 2008: 32). A museum visitor sees a painting on a wall in their home or in a gallery and the wall seems its natural environment, it is expected and the painting is understood in its proper habitat. A chair in a museum display, although designed to respond to bodies, does not need a body to be whole, because it doesn't need a body, one can appreciate the form as a designed sculpture even when not allowed to sit in it. Although our bodies do come in contact with chairs in spaces outside of the museum display, we view them at a distance from ourselves and leave them behind as we move throughout our day, they don't follow us from room to room, home to office, attached to our form. But garments inhabit a space in our understanding that is inexorably connected to touch and our bodies, we carry them with us, they cover us like skin, they move with us, we feel them. We clothe ourselves in a manner no other animals do, they are a marker of our humanity.

The museum exhibition of clothing is further complicated by this nature of garments; they are never just an object of looking, but an object of wearing. As our eyes feel the silhouette, colour and pattern of the exterior of a garment, our bodies see the texture of the weave, the constructed points of tension and weight of flow. Our understanding is twofold, our relationship symbiotic, but in a museum, how does one show the space inside of a garment? The space the human body inhabits? How do we perceive the garment's hidden interior surface when it rests on a mannequin, behind a vitrine? We cannot wear the garment, we cannot touch the interior, but we know the space exists, the next to skin, the hollow where our body once was. As we observe the dressed mannequin, we inhabit the interior of our own clothes, and see it through our touch, but how can we see that space in museum clothes, how can we know that story of body and garment? The pursuit of methods to replicate the human body or the idea of a body has long challenged costume curators even as they are defending the right of the garments to have equal consideration to traditional art objects in a museum space. Without access to touch, the viewer may still feel the missing parts of the whole and the artificiality of display.

Because we wear garments on our bodies, our bodies give them form and complete their integrity. Without the body, a garment could be seen as no more than an empty snake skin with an imprint of the past volume it enclosed or as a decorative object suggesting a form it might cover, but ultimately it is not whole. We understand them fully only when we can feel the material against our skin, or when we see them supported and animated by another's body, only when they are in their hybrid and complete form of material skin supported by the human frame. Museums and their objectives of edification and preservation offer unique challenges to exhibiting and understanding garments and fashion. When we enter a room full of garments in a museum, how should we understand their connection to one another and their connection to us without touch? Wilson, in describing the experience of an exhibition of garments populated by rigid white mannequins, bemoaned, 'without the living body, they could not be said to fully exist. Without movement, they became both oddly abstract and faintly uncanny. Nothing could have more immediately demonstrated the importance of the body in fashion' (Wilson, 1993: 15). In a museum exhibition of fashion where garments are mounted on artificial bodies, arranged in space for us to see but not touch, our understanding of the garments in their empty state is only partial, and we feel that imbalance.

The majority of fashion exhibitions rely on mannequin or museum bodies as authorized supports. But museum bodies are often hard, frozen in rigid poses, with faces erased in abstraction and bodies elongated to the alien proportions of a fashion illustration. A mannequin is clearly recognizable as inhuman and its stiff unyielding body, lacking in gesture and subtlety, removed from realities of breath and sweat, is a poor substitute to proper human stuffing. Mannequins are wanting in malleability, are both under- and over-detailed, and lack life. While they range from attempts at detailed copies of models' bodies, to stylized almost out of humanity, to sawn down to mimic the shapes achievable by pliable flesh, no one single approach can assure the viewer will see the garment in its wholeness. Visitors see still that hard, unforgiving body, so different from our own, and by extension the garment it displays also feels other-worldly. And perhaps it should. Perhaps in a museum setting among works that are considered Art (complete with a capital A), fashion must be presented as 'other' to our common wardrobe inhabitants to inspire awe and respect. But when a curator or exhibition-maker wishes to connect fashion to the daily lived experience of the visitor, to convey that deeper layer of familiarity beyond the impressive positioning, how can it happen? Faced with the challenge of institutional policies, garments in museum exhibitions seem doomed to be forever alien to our understanding born of touch and wear, decorative objects, but unknowable.

Fashion is also a memory of a moment – both clear and indistinct, an 'other-space' – tied to the now, haunted by the past and imagining the future – present in a dream state that we can observe but never re-enter, much like a glance in a mirror, visible yet inaccessible and impossible to hold on to. Fleeting, transitory and precarious, the moment in time fashion captures and preserves is what is rarely unlocked in the space of the museum.

In what way can something come back to life? is the question. If something is being repeated, what are the conditions for its repetition, and in fashion there's an ambiguity because it has its end date prescribed, you know that it's a very short lived phenomena, and you can never guarantee it will go away because when the fashion is superseded, it's in abeyance, but it will come back, we just don't know when, there are so many conditions for its reappearance that feel unplanned and I think that hauntings are unplanned return … you don't wish for a haunting, it happens to you. (Clark, 2019)

Our bodies/our selves

Exhibition maker Judith Clark 'is adamant that fashion displays should not simply be a matter of glamourisation, but that the curator has a duty to explain, to demonstrate the development of ideas' (Clark, 2004: 15). Historian and author Christopher Breward noted, in the introduction to Clark's exhibition catalogue for Spectres: When Fashion Turns Back, Clark creates exhibitions that distort our perceptions, puzzle us, focus on the hidden, 'freeing up room for objects to communicate with each other', and in doing so forces the viewer to look at the garments, the familiar, the idealized, the personal differently, to see differently. Visual culture historian Marius Kwint has written that not only are objects 'instrumental to the formation of consciousness' but 'objects stimulate remembering, not only through the deployment mnemonics of public monuments or mantlepiece souvenirs, but also by the serendipitous encounter, bringing back experiences which otherwise would have remained dormant, repressed or forgotten' (Kwint, 1999: 2). A viewer can no longer take the direct path to understanding a garment, touch is not an option and visuals without questions often lead to the postmodern 'glamourisation' – dramatic impact without a supporting focus on substance.

Clark chose to respond to this challenge by expanding the museum way of seeing to include knowing, pushing through the limits of the museum space into the recesses of our minds, exploring the potential of material and memory, and disorienting and reorienting vision to offer paths to understanding garments that are different from how one might view a garment on a runway, in a store, in their closet or on rows of mannequins in a museum gallery. She does this by accessing the *knowledge* of touch, the memory of skin and fabric. Clark develops her exhibitions with a contingent trust in the viewer's willingness to participate, an offer of an experience rather than completely defined statement. She doesn't rely only on the mannequin body, distorting or defining it, but connects to our subconscious and memories through distortions of space and unexpected visibilities, through the intimacy of gesture and the presence of absence. About her breakthrough international exhibition from 2004, Clark said 'Malign Muses is "a way of describing a relationship between fashion and its history. It is about quotation, about history as muse and the problematic relationship with repetition ...." Its imagery, like the clothing at its core, is intended to haunt the viewer' (Clark, 2004: 15). In reorienting us, Clark takes us down a pathway of visual understanding, one through texture, or shape, or detail and invites us to listen in on conversations among the garments out of time. 'The question might be: is curating about the clarity of connections, and if so how are they made visual or literal? How can objects be presented as a way into different stories?' (Clark, 2008: 160). Like Borges's and Foucault's labyrinths, these visual conversations between garments and between garments and ourselves are nonlinear, ever changing and infinite – they are avenues of discovery.

In response to the absence of the body in fashion exhibition, Clark has experimented with accessing other aspects of our relationship to garments beyond wearing and touching to bring us to a similar level of knowing. In considering museum restrictions and the multiple meanings of the word 'touch' scholar of research-creation Stephanie Springgay (2003: 5) offers, 'works of art are often said to touch or move us, thereby connecting the sensory experience to that of emotion'. Every act of touching is embedded within us. Susan Stewart, poet, professor and critic, reflects on the power of touch to change us:

> We may apprehend the world by means of our senses, but the senses themselves are shaped and modified by experience and the body bears a somatic memory of its encounters with what is outside of it. ... To be in contact with an object means to be moved by it – to have the pressure of its existence brought into relation with the pressure of our own bodily existence. And this pressure perceived by touch involves an actual change; we are changed and so is the object. (Stewart, 1999: 19, 25)

Clark's approaches push at memory to access stored thoughts and emotional associations, she employs resonant words and personal gestures to bring a wholeness to the clothes. As I will discuss specifically in relation to her exhibition making, she harnesses unexpected ways of seeing to create a new touchless version of touching; rather than trying to make the lifeless human, she finds other pathways through association and remembering to subvert the absent body and offers a unique view of fashion that employs thought as much as sight.

From 1997 to 2003 Clark produced shows in a small gallery space in Notting Hill. It served as a laboratory for experimentation and a space for conversation, both qualities she would build into her future practice (a thorough history of her innovation within this tiny space can be found in Pantouvaki and Barbieri's (2014) article). The *Malign Muses: When Fashion Turns Back* exhibition grew out of two years of discussion with fashion theorist Caroline Evans as she was working on a text defining the fashion impulses at the turn of the century, *Fashion at the Edge: Spectacle, Modernity and Deathliness* (Evans, 2003: VI). Clark's exhibition made corporeal a blend of both their musings on fashion relationships, labyrinths, telescopes and forking paths (Scaturro, 2010). Four years on, American fashion curator and editor Valerie Steele would praise *Malign Muses* as 'a paradigm-breaking show of great beauty and power' (Steele, 2008: 28). The show was developed as a joint venture shared between ModeMuseum in Antwerp and the Victoria and Albert in London, though notably the name of the exhibition changed to *Spectres* for the Victoria and Albert presentation. This change was based on the projection of a negative reaction of the British viewing public to the word 'Malign'. The British, however, have a long-standing affection for ghost stories and the title Spectres would both reference that history and already begin to activate memories of listening to stories told over winter fires. But the specificity in these titular words, Malign, Muse and Spectre, established the beginning of an evocative journey of the mind before the viewer had entered the venue. Their meanings of danger, divine inspiration and the other-worldly primed the expectations of the viewer for an exhibition about something human-like, but non-human, something ephemeral and difficult to look at directly. Indeed, the garment off of the body is a spectre of human past, a lifeless skin, an idea of new possibilities.

To suggest new ways of looking at garments in a museum exhibition, Clark employed tools and toys foundational in the development of contemporary visual culture from a time before the splintered understandings of postmodernism. From the distortion of scale and perception through lenses and mirrors, to magic lanterns' animation of the static and the familiar unfamiliarity of an exquisite corpse's segmented body, these visual tricks, teasing and toys reoriented the visitor's visual relationship to garments in the museum space. The body of the viewer was built into the space of the exhibition through limitations of distance, seduction of proximity and the challenge of fragmentation. Each section of the exhibition had mechanisms that entreated the visitor to pause and view the off-the-body garments through an unexpected lens or space, disrupting their comfortable relationship to it. Garments were presented as out of time and out of sorts.

Upon entering the exhibition, imposing magic lanterns towered over the visitors, projecting illuminated outlines of ghosts of fashion's past. The dark figures and their fashionable silhouettes glided along beside the visitor, bodies abstracted to shadows were separated from the viewer by thin screens, a veil between their pathway and ours. At one time marvellous enough to elicit wonder, their attempts to capture the fluid gestures of life part of our journey to motion pictures, but today the oversized nineteenth-century technology suggested to a modern viewer a place indeed inhabited by ghosts. Fashionable silhouettes of bygone eras illustrated by artist Ruben Toledo were eternally rotating, processed by the viewer, offering a brief moment of companionship before turning back around, pulled by unseen forces, to continue their ceaseless journey. They appeared unaware or uncaring of the visitors' existence, seeking, moving towards something we cannot conceive, or merely trapped by our never-ending fixation, like memories that habitually, but without warning, resurface and then fade.

Nearby the visitor encountered a wall of raw wood, as though one had walked onto a construction site; it framed a pastiche of clothing memories, some clear and sharp, and others retaining only the essence of the garment. Clark segmented the body of the garment and interspersed the fractured pieces with equally disjointed illustrations, creating an exquisite corpse[5] of flat and shaped, illustrated and sewn, seen and unseen, an adult-sized mix-and-match children's book the viewer had wandered into where one could swap out heads, bodies and limbs, their own assembly of self suddenly called into question. The garments depicted as interchangeable parts reminded the viewer how easy it was to flip a page to change the look or in some cases the body entirely, suggesting our modern dressing method of recombining separates. The unfinished building materials indicated a space where decisions had yet to be finalized, pages could yet be turned to construct a different body, and asked us to pause a moment and reconsider what defines each garment and each body part and how we learned to combine them.

In another section titled '*Curiouser and Curiouser*' Clark imagined a cabinet of curiosities where adult clothing resides with children's clothing and with the clothing sewn for porcelain dolls and printed for paper ones. A space where adult clothing is weighted equally with toys and play. Dressing again becomes dressing up and identity is explored through imaginative combinations indulged before societal restrictions were imposed. The viewer re-entered the space of childhood where clothing was a tool of fantasy and storytelling, a free space to imagine possibilities. This suggestion of childhood and play returned the viewer to their relationship with clothing where its potential for driving imagination was limitless and reactivated memories of touching and dressing the bodies of dolls, fingertips brushing over the surface of the fabric, hands manipulating the buttons and snaps, and creating stories for the dolls while slipping their garments over their heads. 'Textiles – arbiters of sensuality – help form the stuff of memory in general' (Kwint, 1999: 13). The positioning of clothing sized for adults next to the dolls and their clothing gives permission to see the clothing one is wearing as a means of storytelling and a powerful space of imagination.

Other tools of seeing throughout the exhibition forced the viewer to bend, peer and peek to see the garments by situating them behind a low portal in a wall, reflected in a convex mirror, distorted by a lens or separated from the viewer by the enforced distance of partial walls fencing the garments in. These tools of play and illusion again created opportunities for imagination, forced the visitors to stop and look and make an effort while looking. The different viewing portals open a space to consider, to pause and think; these extra moments engage the brain as though presented with a game or a puzzle to solve. The clothing is reintroduced as an item of play or wonder and the connection to it becomes more than just a covering for modesty or protection, but fully embraces the power of clothing to stimulate our imaginations and represent our complexities.

As though now participating in a *dérive*, in the next room the viewer was again confronted by movement, this time mechanical rather than spectral, as three large interconnected platforms shaped like gears rotated on the floor. Resembling the inner workings of a giant's pocket watch, the gears supported a series of garments from disparate time periods. As the platforms rotated, each garment was brought out of its time and into the proximity of other garments removed from their natural flow in time, each rotation made new visual connections, the shrinking of distance effectively bending time back on itself, each detail or silhouette seen anew through unanticipated time travel and visual associations. 'Curating, through its ruthless selection inevitably creates new patterns of chronology ... the motif is no longer a linear platform but loops, cycles, labyrinths, trees. It also encourages us to read time backwards, to read it from where we are standing, always in the present' (Clark, 2008: 162). The labyrinth of Borges mechanized and unceasing in its joining and tearing asunder of relationships created through its impersonal churning, but also in illuminating the fresh and unexpected relationships the rotation of the gears made possible.

To further disorient daily bodily relationships to clothing and enable new orientations, Clark worked with sculptor and artist Naomi Filmer to develop a series of body parts, moulded on human limbs and curves, resolutely real but detached, and placed on the abstracted bodies of Stockman dress forms. Dress forms, a tool of the work room, have often been employed in fashion exhibition to suggest the making process of a garment or to represent a neutral body. Here the dress forms open the idea of the unformed, the incomplete and take our minds to the spaces of creation, not of clothing but the creation of the body and how we hold memories of bodies; the length of a neck, a hand supporting a mask, the curve of a chin are moments of brief reality highlighting gesture and the human. These distinct features remind the viewer the smooth geometric shapes of the dress forms represent human bodies, their bland perfection and repetition replace our variety and subtlety. Although the hard casts resting on the canvas covered abstractions are incomplete copies of human flesh, we recall that once they started out as human, too. Their gestures are familiar, but in being severed from the whole we see them more specifically than we did as part of a human body, we see them with focus, and that frozen gesture, that captured moment, connects our memories of bodies and gestures to their scattered fragments and the garments on display.

In 2010, several years after *Spectres* introduction, Clark was approached by the Simone handbag manufacturing family in South Korea to acquire and curate a collection of historic and modern handbags and install them to create a new museum in Seoul. The majority of the museum's now expansive collection of objects were displayed in walls of glass and dark wood cabinets and pull-out drawers reminiscent of nineteenth-century display cases or a luxury aficionado's walk-in closet, but to highlight some of the handbags Clark would return to the importance of gesture. Different bags require different hand and arm positions to make sense of their shape and their intended relationship to the body, a subtlety of gesture elusive with the use of prefabricated mannequins.

Clark achieved this specificity by selecting a hand pose appropriate for each bag and creating a plaster cast of an empty hand in that position. Although the plaster is as rigid as fiberglass mannequins, the preserved gesture captured a moment of humanity. Caroline Evans wrote for the catalogue, 'We are all technicians of the pose. The invisible notation of a life, poses and gestures leave no footprint yet they are the heartbeat of everyday action' (Clark, 2012: 232). The bags were then displayed in balance with the volume of a body and that most impermanent yet individual aspect of fashion, the pose, was captured in time. From that specific gesture, focused just on the hand and the arm, we pay close attention to the body's relationship to the object. The hand is ghostly but human, the creases of skin show points of tension and energy. The act of holding is made visible.

Partial garments were created for these abstracted body forms and their hyper-real limbs, suggesting a full ensemble, but stripped down to focus on the spot of holding. On a mannequin dressed to hold a chatelaine from the 1900s, elements of hand-crocheted lace radiated from the point of connection between hand and bag, blending to nothing, as though a handbag gives life to the parts of the body and garment it comes in contact with. The bag activates the body through its presence and viewing the part brings the whole into clarity. Once again Clark relies on our knowledge and memory as essential elements of the exhibition. She focuses intently on a gesture. That intimate focus works to spark images and recollections tied to gesture, specific and personal, from each individual's memories. The viewer is brought in as an element of the installation by supplying the humanity from their own experiences.

Soundless dialogue

Following the pursuit of understanding through acts of memory access and the reorientation of vision, Clark moved a step further away from the traditional manner of garment display in her exhibition 'The Concise Dictionary of Dress' conceived with psychoanalyst Adam Phillips. The parameters of the exhibition were a list of words jointly decided upon, passed back and forth, and defined by Phillips. The selected words were used to delineate not only ways of defining ideas about dress through objects but to guide the ways of exhibiting clothing. In their essay for the catalogue examining the role of a dictionary, they state,

> There are no clothes without words about them; but some words can have clothes, material, about them. Words for clothes and clothes for words. Each with their respective histories. Clothes designers at their best, like lexicographers, are among the most remarkable historians in the culture, endlessly renewing an inheritance that is always fading, always going out of fashion. (Clark and Phillips, 2010: 15)

Their choice to focus on words highlights the similar roles words and clothing can play in our lives, memories and identities and how garments and fashion can define how we wish to be seen. Those definitions, like language, are shaped by our personal experiences and tell the stories of our cultural and personal histories. The provided definitions were neither direct explanations nor descriptions of the garments and fragments; instead they were tangential, like something glimpsed from the corner of your eye that you cannot quite focus on fully while looking at the garment, but is inextricably bound to it. The definitions' constructed language revealed an indirect path to viewing and knowing the objects. After viewing the exhibition, educator and researcher Michal Lynn Shumate wrote, it 'challenged the viewer to think, not about a dress, but to think about thinking about dress, about the role of dress in memory' (Shumate, 2013). Functioning in a Socratic spirit the exhibition offered a silent dialogue, a repartee between word and image, and guided the viewer gently as they constructed their contributions.

Clark, building on her deep history with archives and ideas of visibility and the hidden, constructed The Concise Dictionary of Dress exhibition to be only accessible by guided tour. Visitors were led through the storage of the Victoria and Albert in Blythe House, to visit eleven carefully constructed stations, each representing ideas of dress through a word, its definitions and carefully constructed tableaux. Blythe House, a former post office, was repurposed by the government as museum storage, and the site currently houses storage for the V&A textile and fashion collections among others. In discussing Blythe House, Clark noted, 'Stored objects are also stored moments of personal and cultural memory' (Clark and Phillips, 2010). I imagine also the poetics of letters once traveling through, fleeting personal memories, was not unimportant. Three times an hour, seven viewers were guided to the different sites within the building to visit each unique space of installation nestled among the carefully packed and organized archive of dress and fashion. The words opened modes of understanding to bring bodiless garments to life in our minds. Clark and Phillips again, 'Clothes, another language of ours, another of our codes, another of the forms our histories take, keep changing, like words, but faster; and, like words, everybody uses them, and, whether they are conscious of it or not, everyone has their own style, just as everyone has their own vocabulary' (Clark and Phillips, 2010: 19). Clothing is a visual language, and just as language formed of words, we use it to communicate, not only relying on a common understanding but also applying our own personal inflections. Our idea of self shapes our choice of clothing and our reading of others.

To define the word 'plain', garments were mounted on forms draped in white Tyvek, the protective fabric of the archive, their iconic silhouettes pronounced by the specificity of the anchoring straps binding the covering. The ghostly sheet-covered garments were missing only eye holes to become fashionable Halloween costumes. One might have wondered if the referenced garments were even under the wraps, and if so, what bodies were present, or were they absent as well? And then perhaps wondered, does it matter? These shrouded forms were staged to memorialize the space of an exhibition. A hypothetical exhibition of Balenciaga and its use of space, both the space taken up by the garments and the negative space defined between the garments, is preserved. Clark explains, 'Space is so fetishized in storage facilities that it would never occur to anyone to store space. But in storing it, I am proposing to store a curatorial project' (Clark and Phillips, 2010: 113). The decisions of the exhibition maker and how she saw the garments in relationship to one another and to the viewer are preserved. The visitors were confronted by the three-dimensional space the garments occupy and how it relates to the space our bodies occupy and we begin to more clearly see our comparable volumes and know the garment bodies through our awareness of the space inhabited by our own bodies.

At another stop along the tour through the archive, Clark revisits the cabinet of curiosities, an association through proximity and arrangement, with the word 'essential'. Here photographs of sculptures and plaster casts from the V&A's collection suggesting draped garments from Ancient Greek sculptures sit next to pages from James Laver volumes, a commissioned stamp featuring a flowing Madeline Vionnet garment and a stone carving of the soft folds of a Sophia Kokosalaki dress; they were presented together on a two-dimensional plane, but not as collage; rather each element was isolated by a border, each its own distinct and discreet memory. These images of gathered and draped fabric preserved in stone, in photos, in print, show the timelessness of the draped silhouette, evolved from early dialogues between the human body and the fluidity of fabric, carved in stone by ancient cultures and recurring regularly in and out of fashion throughout history. The repetition through a multitude of cultures and times etching the form and motion on our collective knowledge. But no fragment of fabric is displayed within this assemblage. What we know to be soft and fluid is repeatedly presented flat and hard, our minds tasked to translate that representation until even in stone we see and feel the fabric and how it drapes against our form and moves in reaction to the movement of the limbs beneath. We understand the flow of the fabric in spite of the mediums in this grouping, this collection of images and surfaces repeat and repeat the classic folds defined by the body underneath until we access the proximal knowledge in our memory of touch.

The word 'pretentious' was illustrated by the outlines of dresses carved in wax by sculptor Simon Ings as though the fabric garment was a rigid and hard form and the space it took up when on a body could withstand the pressure of the heavy casting liquid to create replicable impressions, every soft fold an immobile wrinkle in the wall. Garments trapped in time, seemingly evaporated, only their shells remaining, fossils of ephemeral fabric. But ephemeral fabric supported by the imagined mass of an unseen body, the space reserved for a body resisting deflating or erasure as though a deep breath had just been inhaled and then was held in stillness until the wax solidified around it, creating a hollow three-dimensional reflection, a mirror of the space in which we see ourselves. In removing the actual object from view, the visitor is confronted by absence and compelled to imagine what is now gone. By asking the visitor to imagine, to use memory and association, language and their own presence, they could approach a wholeness of understanding the garment. By removing the volume of the body but retaining the form, or empty space of form, the viewer filled in the absence with the necessary information and connected themselves, and again their bodies, with each breath, to the clothes. These reliefs work on a level beyond the invisible mounts that support clothing with sculpted air; by removing the body and the garment, the loss of both is felt, we stare into an abyss, but one with which we are familiar. We are transported completely from the here of the space we are in to the there of our memory and fill in the emptiness with our knowing. Instead of working to disguise absence of the body in exhibition, Clark heightens it, opening a space for our bodies in relation to the clothing addressed by the display. Even though the garments upon which the impressions were based hung nearby, the hollow emptiness of the exquisitely detailed wax demands we fill it. These thought exercises perhaps even questioned the body of humanity in building and the culture that birthed ideas of both spoken and written language and the visual and tactile language of clothes. This perhaps is a defining aspect of a type of post-postmodern garment exhibition, one where neither the garment nor the body need be present if the exhibition maker can construct ways to make the viewer's knowledge and presence essential, constructing an exhibition of the mind.

Clark approaches the display of garments in the museum space through a multitude of faculties and pathways to access memory, inviting us to see differently, to sit with our personal and cultural past, to awaken the lingering memory of touch and the fleeting memory of motion, like shadows in a cave, and disorients us so we see something familiar as new again, freed from assumptions and ingrained beliefs. Stewart clearly illuminates the significance of that access, 'Memory is the animation of the past necessary to our orientation in the future' (Stewart, 1999: 36). Clark's exploration of bodies not only stimulates 'I remember' but 'I remember and I know', a virtual reality not achieved through technology but by relying on the power of our minds to acquire, store and recall the idea of a thing and the associations of touch, the emotions inherent to haptic knowledge. Enchanted by the exhibition *Spectres*' approach to displaying dress, Christopher Breward wrote, 'its lyrical, sketch-like content was immediately understood and appreciated by fashion professionals and students ... I hope to see more of this provocative boundary pushing – this attempt to grapple with fashion's shifting nature head-on' (Breward, 2008: 91).

In response to the question 'Does one need a body to bring a garment to life and why?' Clark replied, 'This question is of course at the heart of curating dress, due to its inescapable relationship to the body. I suppose for me "bringing to life" is not necessarily a priority – if by this we mean the re-enactment of history, or the proximity to its original use or look – but instead I use dress to talk about other things' (Clark and Phillips, 2010: 110). Instead of trying to reanimate the clothing and rely on mimicking or hyperbolizing the human form, she embraces the absence of a body and asks us to know the garments in other ways and as a way to know other things. Through that stimulation/activation of knowing in other parts of our brain, we can access the physical reality in our memory of experience, we can connect what we have known and have felt with what we are seeing, and our memories of how it felt both physically and emotionally complete the exhibition. Offering something more than the didactic modern exhibition and the spectacle-laden focus of many postmodern exhibitions, Clark chooses another pathway, one where knowledge and history are important, but arousing the individual experience as much as the common understanding, one where the emotion of garments is accessed not through awe but by memories stimulated by disrupting the expected and established methods of display. Clark both reminds us of what we consciously understand and compels us to remember what is buried, she invites us to feel garments with our emotions, look at the stories that haunt them and touch them again with our past experiences rather than our hands. She builds a post-postmodern space out of the fragmentation of previous approaches, a space that allows each individual to determine its final form. Her exhibitions guide us to layer our awareness of our bodies in the past and our bodies in this moment to create spaces of knowing in which we blend the visible but untouchable with our haptic memories into a whole that reconstructs the absent body.

Notes

1   In the *Yohji Yamamoto: Dream Shop* exhibition at Mode Museum, Antwerp, in 2006, garments were displayed on mannequins and racks and some were available to be tried on in the gallery. This was only possible with the permission and support of the designer. But was it a blurring of the lines between the goals of a museum and the goals of commerce? Or a realistic acknowledgement that fashions, like all works on display in a museum, are available for the right price? This type of presentation is only achievable when displaying contemporary clothing from a fashion house of necessary size and financial resources to supply the stock of garments to be touched and worn/damaged, and it is an experience accessible only to those bodies that fit within the selected garments. And in a full-on embrace of commerce, the *Virgil Abloh: Figures of Speech* exhibition, Museum of Contemporary Art, Chicago, 2019, included a controlled entry pop-up shop of the designer's work and extended to a companion Louis Vuitton pop-up shop across town.

2   *The Fashion World of Jean Paul Gaultier: From the Sidewalk to the Catwalk*, June 2011–June 2016, Montreal Museum of Fine Arts (Montreal, Dallas, San Francisco, Madrid, Rotterdam, Stockholm, New York, London, Melbourne, Paris, Munich and Seoul); *Hollywood Costume*, October 2012–January 2013, Victoria and Albert, London.

3   *American Woman: Fashioning a National Identity*, May 2010–August 2010, Costume Institute of the Metropolitan Museum of Art, New York City; Pleasure Gardens, May 2010–present, Museum of London.

4   Since 1999 The Victoria & Albert Museum has been running a programme, Fashion in Motion, where contemporary designers are invited to show a collection on live models in the space of the museum. Although this method of presentation does bring movement and human bodily support to the garments on display in a museum, visitors are not invited to touch the garments, nor try them on. The show only happens once, so unless the visitor has access to admission, and is available at the time of the show, they remain at a distance. Shows are archived in video and accessible online, but while the garments in the show are often on display in the museum for a period of time, they are not necessarily available for viewers at the same time the online video is accessed, nor are the garments necessarily acquired by the museum. The show, the garments and the video are discrete elements that can be reassembled by a researcher or an enterprising patron, but are not presented as a whole in one time to constitute a singular experience of knowing. What is the value of showing, essentially, a museum-sponsored fashion show and using the space of the museum as a venue? Who does it benefit? What is its legacy and accessibility? Questions worth exploring.

5   Exquisite corpse games allowed the creation of the connected but unexpected. Played by members of Dada artist circles, paper was folded into sections and each section would be illustrated by a different person who could not see but a hint of the previous illustration, creating a linked but absurd figure or drawing. Simplified, results could be compared to a type of children's flip book where a reader can mix and match various heads, bodies and legs.

References

Breward, C. (2008), 'Between the Museum and the Academy: Fashion Research and its Constituencies', *Fashion Theory: The Journal of Dress, Body & Culture*, 12 (1): 83–93.

Clark, J. (2004), *Spectres: When Fashion Turns Back*, London: V&A.

Clark, J. (2008), 'One Object: Multiple Interpretations, Judith Clark: Considering the Coats', *Fashion Theory: The Journal of Dress, Body & Culture*, 12 (2): 158–69.

Clark, J. (2012), *Handbags: The Making of a Museum*, New Haven: Yale University Press.

Clark, J. (2019), (exhibition maker, Judith Clark Studio), in discussion with the author. 11 January.

Clark, J., and A. Phillips (2010), *The Concise Dictionary of Dress*, London: Violette.

Clark, J., A. Haye and J. Horsley (2014), *Exhibiting Fashion: Before and After 1971*, New Haven: Yale University Press.

Evans, C. (2003), *Fashion at the Edge: Spectacle, Modernity and Deathliness*, New Haven: Yale University Press.

Greenblatt, S. (1991), 'Resonance and Wonder', in I. Karp and S. D. Lavine (eds), *Exhibiting Cultures: The Poetics and Politics of Museum Display*, 42–56, Washington: Smithsonian Institution Press.

Kwint, M. (1999), 'Introduction: The Physical Past', in M. Kwint, C. Breward and J. Aynsley (eds), *Material Memories: Design and Evocation*, 1–16, Oxford: Berg.

Martin, R., H. Koda and Metropolitan Museum of Art (1993), *Diana Vreeland: Immoderate Style*, New York: Metropolitan Museum of Art.

Palmer, A. (2008), 'Untouchable: Creating Desire and Knowledge in Museum Costume and Textile Exhibitions', *Fashion Theory: The Journal of Dress, Body & Culture*, 12 (1): 31–63.

Pantouvaki, S., and D. Barbieri (2014), 'Making Things Present: Exhibition-Maker Judith Clark and the Layered Meanings of Historical Dress in the Here and Now', *Catwalk: The Journal of Fashion, Beauty and Style*, 3 (1): 77–100.

Scaturro, S. (2010), 'Experiments in Fashion Curation – an Interview with Judith Clark', *Fashion Projects* (3). Available online https://www.fashionprojects.org/blog/676 (accessed 15 January 2019).

Shumate, M. (2013), 'The Concise Dictionary of Dress' and the Language(s) of Fashion Exhibition', paper presented at the *Benjamin, Barthes, and Fashion* Conference, Manchester, UK, 28 June.

Springgay, S. (2003), 'Cloth as Intercorporeality: Touch, Fantasy, and Performance and the Construction of Body Knowledge', *International Journal of Education and the Arts*, 4 (5). Available online http://ijea.asu.edu/v4n5/ (accessed 18 January 2019).

Steele, V. (2008), 'Museum Quality: The Rise of the Fashion Exhibition', *Fashion Theory: The Journal of Dress, Body & Culture*, 12 (1): 7–30.

Stewart, S. (1999), 'Prologue: From the Museum of Touch', in M. Kwint, C. Breward and J. Aynsley (eds), *Material Memories: Design and Evocation*, 17–36, Oxford: Berg.

Wilson, E. (1993), 'Fashion and the Postmodern Body', in J. Ash and E. Wilson (eds), *Chic Thrills: A Fashion Reader*, 3–16, Berkeley: University of California Press.

9

THE POST-POSTMODERN FASHION EXHIBITION

Dennita Sewell

Over the past decade, changing social patterns driven by global crises, climate change, unstable political regimes and advances in digital technology are creating a shift in the prevailing social conditions. Speculation that the waning postmodern era is being supplanted by a new epoch is a hotbed for new theoretical work that seeks to give a vocabulary and understanding to this new post-postmodern mode. In 2012, popular culture scholar Alan Kirby published an essay *Digimodernism: How New Technologies Dismantle the Postmodern and Reconfigure Our Culture* that identified five theories – Altermodernism, Hypermodernity, Performatism, Automodernity and Digimodernism – that he considered were the forerunners of scholarly discourse about these social, political and economic shifts and their impact on culture and aesthetics. Using Kirby's work as a starting point, fashion scholar Marcia Morgado examined the relevance of each theory to fashion industry practices in her article, *Fashion Phenomena and the Post-Post Modern Condition: Enquiry and Speculation* (2014). This chapter uses the theories and ideas put forward by Kirby and Morgado to assess fashion-related curatorial activity in museums.

When postmodernism was at its height in the late 1980s and 1990s, fashion's stature in the art world rose as the networks among contemporary art, fashion and commerce moved from a state of shared influences to becoming comingled. In 1983, Diana Vreeland's exhibition, *Yves Saint Laurent: 25 Years of Design*, at The Metropolitan Museum of Art got the ball rolling as the institution's first exhibition on a contemporary, living designer and made a mark with its significant attendance and press given to its gala events (Donovan, 1983). Over the last decade, fashion exhibitions have assumed a leading position in museum programming by generating record-breaking attendance numbers and garnering wide-scale, celebrity-filled press giving greater significance to their cultural contributions and reach. Notably, *Alexander McQueen: Savage Beauty* at The Metropolitan Museum of Art (4 May–7 August 2011) became one of the top ten most visited exhibitions in the museum's history, reflecting a broadening cultural interest in fashion.[1] The unprecedented success of that exhibition was a catalyst for the dramatic shift in traditional perceptions about the value, role and expectations of fashion in cultural institutions that finally muffled the persistent question, 'Is fashion art?'

Another important consideration for this analysis is how the larger shifting cultural conditions have disrupted the fashion system from the design process to supply chain logistics to where and how clothes are made to consumer habits and desires. These shifts are, in turn, impacting changes in fashion curation practices including the stewardship of permanent collections to what is being exhibited to how it is interpreted and how visitors are accustomed to interacting with fashion. The editorial 'Gone Global: Fashion as Art?' by Suzy Menkes (2011) reinforces these connections, 'The explosion of museum exhibitions is only a mirror image of what has happened to fashion itself this millennium. With the force of technology, instant images and global participation, fashion has developed from being a passion for a few to a fascination – and an entertainment – for everybody.' Against this backdrop of change, the following sections, one on each of the five theories, give examples of fashion exhibition curation practices that support the idea of a shifting post-postmodern ethos.

Altermodernism

In *The Radicant* (2009), Nicolas Bourriaud defines the new ethos in terms of 'altermodern' artists working in the context of mass globalization and the overproduction of objects and information. Weary from this bombardment, individuals have begun to sway towards local, national, natural and environmentally ethical practices and the increased acceptance of diversity that Morgado connects with fashion's increased focus on sustainable production practices and expanded range of the fashion image (2014: 316). While these have long been the concern of conscious forward brands such as Eileen Fisher, Stella McCartney and Patagonia, in recent years, they have become increasingly important to a broader spectrum of consumers. Notably, the Rana Plaza disaster in 2013 focused widespread public attention on fast fashion and its negative humanitarian and environmental impact.

The Future of Fashion Is Now (11 October 2014–18 January 2015) at Museum Boijmans Van Beuingen featured the work of 'the latest generation of fashion designers' from 'renowned houses to the up-and-coming' and explored their perspectives on 'innovative solutions and fresh designs at the cutting edge of fashion and art' (Museum Boimans Van Beuningen, 2014). Sustainability, futuristic technologies and the social value of clothes emerged as common themes. Curator Jose Teunissen explains how Bourriaud's Radicant theory served as a guide point for thought, 'Like the altermodern artist, today's fashion designer is someone who brings together a collection of heterogeneous elements to which he or she imparts meaning in an ever-changing context: "in the infinite text of the world"' (Teunissen et al., 2014: 18). Examples of work in the exhibition included a Zen garden designed by Viktor&Rolf messaged with a plea to move more slowly and with greater spirituality, hand-knitted works by Pyuupiru that give the wearer individual identity and lace patterns grown on the roots of strawberry plants by Carole Collet.

Since 2017, a number of fashion exhibitions addressing sustainability issues key to altermodern practices have appeared. *Scraps: Fashion, Textiles and Creative Reuse* (23 September–16 April 2017), co-curated by Susan Brown and Matilda McQuaid at the Cooper Hewitt Smithsonian Design Museum, featured the work of three eco-conscious makers: Luisa Ceverse, founder of Riedzioni in Milan; Christina Kim, founder of dosa in Los Angeles; and Reiko Sudo, managing director at NUNO in Tokyo (Figure 9.1). Inspired by the recent acquisition of a work by Kim, the exhibition gave the co-curators a platform to discuss widespread concerns about the fashion industry's role as a major generator of environmental pollution (McQuaid, 2018). McQuaid explains, 'The world around us plays a part in what we show and there is a desire to be relevant' (2018). An interactive blog series, *Scraps Stories*, on the Cooper Hewitt's website disseminated information

Figure 9.1 An installation view of 'Scraps: Fashion, Textiles and Creative Reuse' at the Cooper Hewitt Smithsonian Design Museum, New York. Photo by Matt Flynn. Courtesy of Smithsonian Institution.

and sources for sustainable textiles and fashion in a dynamic interaction with the public. According to visitor feedback McQuaid received, guests were inspired by the exhibition's message of reuse and the important role that everyone plays in the effort to reduce waste (2018).

In London, *Fashioned from Nature* (21 April 2018–27 January 2019) at the Victoria and Albert Museum placed sustainability in a historical context. In the exhibition catalogue introduction, Edwina Ehrman, senior exhibition curator, states, 'The narrative of *Fashioned from Nature* was prompted by today's widespread concerns about environmental damage and also by the V&A's collection of fashion and textiles, which includes many objects acquired because they exemplify particular materials and techniques, and which often stimulate new questions when viewed through the lens of present-day environmental preoccupations.'

Hypermodernity

In his essay *Time against Time or the Hypermodern Society* (2005), Giles Lipovetsky puts forward a theory that describes our times as a hypermodern culture which has replaced the desire to create a 'radiant future' with the 'euphoric present'. Using the principals of fashion as a metaphorical construct, he describes an anxiety-filled society fuelled by excess, overabundance, frivolity and irrationality in terms of hypercapitalism, hyperconsumption, hyperindividualism and so forth. Two sections of the essay, 'The Past Revisited' and 'Memory in the Age of Hyperconsumption', address the current phenomenon for the creation of new museums, museum-type institutions and anniversary-related activities that honour and celebrate subjects and events of all kinds (Lipovetsky, 2005: 56–62). Lipovetsky positions this activity, 'The more our societies are dedicated followers of fashion, focused on the present, the more they are accompanied by a groundswell of memory.' The 'value attributed to the past' has moved into an 'infinite' realm and acquired increased economic value (2005: 59). Morgado connects these ideas with the gross overproduction of fashion goods, excessive decorative design details and consumers' obsessive pace for shopping for throwaway clothes (2014: 319–20).

Lipovetsky's 'frenzied vogue for the past' (2005: 61) is demonstrated in the seventieth anniversary of the House of Dior which was celebrated with a series of monumental activations including the unveiling of a new, state-of-the-art archive, multiple exhibitions organized by a range of institutions accompanied by comprehensive books and catalogues, special events and a variety of social media activations. It was kicked off with a grand celebratory opening for the blockbuster exhibition, *Christian Dior: Designer of Dreams* (5 July 2017–7 January 2018) at the Musée des Arts Décoratifs in Paris organized by Olivier Gabet, the

Figure 9.2 An installation view of 'Christian Dior: Designer of Dreams' at the Musée des Arts Décoratifs, Paris. Photo by Travis Hutchison. Courtesy of Triptyque.

Museum's director and Florence Müller, Avenir Foundation Curator of Textile Art and Fashion, Denver Art Museum (Figure 9.2). While the exhibition subject was rooted in the slow hand of couture traditions and enduring legacy of the house, the extravagant multi-sensory experience and grand scale installation sprawled over 3,000 square meters of the 1905 Gaston Redon designed Northwest wing of the Louvre like a luxurious fashion theme park. The grandiosity of the original Beaux-Arts interior was amplified with a flood of high-tech video projections and coloured lighting effects that created a magical backdrop for the more than three hundred haute couture designs, countless accessories, atelier toiles, documents, illustrations, photographs, magazines and videos. This arousing, sensory experience positioned the historical memory of Dior heritage in a glamorous fashion wonderland. This is just one of many celebratory exhibitions organized around the world that year to honour Dior. While each institution brought their own perspectives, unique works, publications and museum store merchandise to the project, collectively, they demonstrate the pleasures hypermodern society derives from these grand commemorative experiences.

Performatism

In 'Performatism, or the End of Postmodernism' Raoul Eshelman describes the new epoch as a complexly new replacement of postmodernism (Eshelman, 2008). Central features of performatism as summarized by Morgado are: simple-minded subjects who have authorial power, theistic plotlines, transcendence, double framing and locked frames. Other key ideas include a shifting point of orientation from pessimism and its association with emptiness, absence and dysfunctionality to psychological or fictional states of good or transcendence linked to states of love, fulfilment and resurrection and so on (Morgado, 2014: 321). Eshelman explains, 'we find in performatist works a tendency to invest in characters with far ranging authorial prerogatives. Accordingly, characters are endowed with the ability to manipulate time, space and causality for their own benefit' (2008: 6). Morgado finds parallel examples to Eshelman's thesis in fashion phenomena in the short film *Electric Holiday*, produced for a Christmas 2012 window display created as a collaboration between Barneys and the Walt Disney Company (2014: 322). The film featured Disney characters in the roles of fashion industry celebrities wearing cartoon versions of couture designs in a Paris runway setting. Amusing, delightful and uplifting, the film is set in the double frame of Minnie Mouse in the middle of a dream and ends with Micky Mouse giving her a kiss and a Lanvin dress that she puts on as her 'real' self and sends her into a state of transcendence. Morgado draws forward additional Performatist qualities in the 'erasure of distinctions between fashion and art', and to 'novel transgendered appearances' and 'constructedness of sex' in the work of artist Vanessa Beecroft and the mixed gender appearance of Marc Jacobs in a portrait by Francois Nars (Morgado 2014: 323–5).

Performatist ideas can be found in the curatorial practice of double-framing of fashion designs with runway show videos or animations that seek to transcend the museum and transport the viewer into the context of a fashion show or the mind of a couturier. For example, in *Balenciaga: Shaping Fashion* (27 May 2017–18 February 2018) at the Victoria and Albert Museum, the exhibition team, led by curator Cassie Davies-Strodder, used x-ray photographs and animated dress patterns of some of Cristobal Balenciaga's iconic designs to 'reveal his mastery of pattern cutting, draping and manipulation of fabrics' (Victoria and Albert Museum, 2017). The animations begin with an imaginary pen that draws the outline of each pattern piece which are then 'stitched' and drawn together to create a three-dimensional depiction of the process of constructing the design. With an average running time of 1 minute and 25 seconds, these interpretive animations mesmerize visitors, most of whom no longer have a connection with making clothing. The animation distils the process of making a couture level garment that would, in reality, take many hours of time, specialized tools and the skill of many hands to make into a brief, simplified impression.

Another example can be seen in the holograms of faces projected onto mannequin heads that were the marvel of *The Fashion World of Jean Paul Gaultier: From Sidewalk to Catwalk* (17 June–2 October 2011) at the Montreal Museum of Fine Arts exhibit curated by Theirry-Maxime Loriot. Upon entering the exhibition, visitors were greeted by a mannequin with a lifelike, 'talking' image of the *enfant terrible* designer's face flanked by a benevolent order of 'singing' mannequins with projected faces of the provocateur's transgressive, transgender, multicultural disciples wearing Gaultier signature designs. Further into the exhibition, a revolving catwalk transported museum guests into the front row of a Gaultier fashion show. Gaultier, as the central character of this performative work, becomes its theist author and transcends 'the context around him'. The fashion designs, based on subversions of traditional notions of masculinity and femininity, multi-ethnic sources and pop culture, espouse his narrative. The exhibition 'makes strange the border between life and art' and supports the proposition that performatism can be expanded to explore new meanings of fashion as an art and the constructed assumptions of the institutions that house it' (Morgado, 2014: 323).

Automodernity

In *Auto-Modernity after Postmodernism: Autonomy and Automation in Culture, Technology and Education*, Robert Samuels explores the implications of how the advancing use of technology is shaping the way 'digital youth' think and learn and their implications on educational methodologies and identity. Samuels encourages institutions to reimagine a more tolerant and open view of how today's digitally minded youth work in a continuous, multitasking flow, often with multiple devices, between individual, private and public spheres, and individual and collaborative paradigms (2008: 231). Morgado finds connections with these assertions in wearable technology's many iterations of smart textiles, fibre-optic threads, infused fabrics and the like. Other parallels include the blurred lines between the human and the machine in cyberpunk and steam punk appearances that are usually described as a blend of neo-Victorian and neo-Edwardian styles with cyber-technology (Morgado, 2014: 328).

Automodern expression can be seen in the work of the Dutch fashion designer Iris van Herpen. The concepts she develops and her work are formed by hybrid blends of art and science, artificial and organic and precision of chaos (van Herpen, n.d.a). The vision for her Spring 2019 couture collection explains this viewpoint, 'For "Shift Souls", I looked at the evolution of the human shape, its idealization through time and hybridization of the female forms within mythology. Specifically, the imagination and the fluidity within identity change in Japanese mythology gave me the inspiration to explore the deeper meaning of identity and

Figure 9.3 An installation view of 'Iris van Herpen: Transforming Fashion' at the Phoenix Art Museum, Phoenix. Photo by Ken Howie. Courtesy of Ken Howie Studios.

how immaterial and mutable it can become within the current coalescence of our digital bodies' (van Herpen, n.d.b). The making of her designs often combines highly technical computational techniques to create hypercomplex laser cut pieces that then require countless hours of handwork to assemble into the final garment. In 2015, Mark Wilson, chief curator at the Groninger Museum and Sarah Schleuning, curator decorative arts and design at the High Museum in Atlanta, co-organized *Iris van Herpen: Transforming Fashion* (7 November 2015– 15 May 2016) that travelled to multiple venues in the United States and Canada including Phoenix Art Museum (24 February–13 May 2018). The clothes were presented on mannequins in a straightforward, uniform pose that van Herpen's studio coated in Dragon Skin, a high-performance silicon rubber, brushed over crackled paint that resulted in an eerily skin-like surface. The humanoid look of the mannequin wearing van Herpen's other-worldly designs merged the craft of couture construction with digital technology and a surreal view of the human body in automodern expression (Figure 9.3).

We can see the seeds of automodern ideas in the exhibition *New Nomads* (11 May–21 July 2002) that I organized at the Phoenix Art Museum featuring prototypes from Royal Philips Electronics research labs that explored experimental concepts in wearable electronics with potential to support human's health, safety and pleasure functions. The Phillips prototypes were the work of a collaborative team made up of psychologists, fashion designers, textiles scientists and consumer product designers that drew upon the diverse knowledge of these specialists to drive innovation. An evolved view of this movement can be seen in the exhibition, 'Access + Ability' (15 December 2017–3 September 2018) that presented products, projects and services developed for people with disabilities (Cooper Hewitt, 2017). In support of Samuels's argument to update education for automodern learners, when the digital generation, who naturally learn and work collaboratively, soon grow into leadership positions, innovation has the potential to flourish and further solidify the potentials of what the new post-postmodern era will become.

Digimodernism

Alan Kirby's work, *Digimodernism: How New Technologies Dismantle the Postmodern and Reconfigure Our Culture*, identifies the advent of digitalization as the singular impetuousness of the shift towards new cultural and artistic forms (2009: 50). He identifies digimodernism's dominant features as: onwardness (ongoing), haphazardness (going in multiples directions), evanescence (hard to capture), reformulation (hybridized meanings) and anonymous, multiple and social authorship (including pseudonymity) (Kirby, 2009: 52). Morgado identifies the following fashion parallels: the haphazardness of contemporary appearances, the imaginative variations of Japanese street style, the proliferation of decorative cases that morph personal technology into a fashion accessory, the growth and influence of fashion blogs and the recent collaborations between designers and mass market retailers (2014: 330).

The exhibition *blog.mode: addressing fashion* (18 December 2007–13 April 2008) at The Metropolitan Museum of Art presented sixty-five costume and accessories dating from the eighteenth century to the present in its Costume Institute galleries and invited the public to comment on them along with curators Harold Koda and Andrew Bolton through a blog on the Museum's website. Koda explained, 'Fashion, both a reflection and an expression of a zeitgeist, is open to a wide range of interpretations' (Metropolitan Museum of Art, 2008). Whimsical headings for each of the works 'Let Them Eat Cake', 'The Birth of Venus' and 'Crocodile Rock' broke down hierarchical barriers between the curator's official text and the personal judgements made by individuals. The exhibition and blog present Digimodern traits in an ongoing conversation about the works that veered in multiple directions through multiple authors with varying levels of expertise. Furthermore, the openness of the subject allowed the curators to be more playful and seemingly haphazard in choosing what was actually a carefully constructed selection of works.

From different perspectives, Digimodern conditions can be found in *Items: Is Fashion Modern?* (1 October 2017–28 January 2018) at the Museum of Modern

Figure 9.4 An installation view of 'ITEMS: Is Fashion Modern?' at MoMA, New York. Photo by Martin Seck. Courtesy of The Museum of Modern Art, New York/Scala, Florence.

Art organized by Paola Antonelli, senior curator, and Michelle Millar Fisher, curatorial assistant in the Department of Architecture and Design (Figure 9.4). For the first time in more than seventy years, the institution took on the subject of fashion inspired by its seminal exhibition, *Are Clothes Modern?* (28 November 1944–4 March 1945) conceived of by architect and social historian Bernard Rudofsky. *Items* was a 'profuse' exhibition which involved years of research and travel, and a myriad of collaborative think tanks that drew together more than 350 works from numerous institutions and private collections (Antonelli and Fischer, 2018). The minimal installation design featured black and white graphics that categorically numbered the alphabetically listed 111 'items' examined in the exhibition. Planar white platforms and pedestals uniformly served as presentation stages for the diverse range of loosely ordered objects drawn from both high and low fashion put forward as the 'paragons of design' that shaped style in the twentieth and twenty-first centuries. Digital era platforms were used to engage audiences through Instagram challenges and podcasts featuring a range of designers, makers, historians and educators. Marketing advertisements featured 'real' people rather than glamourized fashion models. Connections to Digimodern ideas including 'multiple authorship', 'haphazard visual effects, random mixes of garment styles and personal commentary' are demonstrated in the mix of both upscale and downmarket brands, mounting of the works on various types of forms, and the loose flow of the relationship among items in the installation. In a *New York Times* review of the exhibition, art critic Roberta Smith offered: 'At times the word "fashion" in the show's title almost smacks of false advertising: It might better have been called "Clothes Are Us, and Us and Us" or "Personal Style, Crowdsourced"' (Smith, 2017: C13, C20). The answer to the question Is Fashion Modern? may well be 'no' – it is Digimodern – at least in the context of the *Items* exhibition.

Conclusion

Ultracontemporary (27 October 2018–24 March 2019), a fashion exhibition in Phoenix Art Museum's Ellman fashion design gallery, was organized as a result of a windfall opportunity to collect a series of new works for the permanent collection through the successful fundraising efforts of Arizona Costume Institute, a museum organization that supports fashion design and a project supported by trustee Doris Ong (Figure 9.5). While the parameters were open for what would be purchased, the opportunity to advance the fashion design collection forward with a series of significant contemporary works that captured the spirit of the changing cultural ethos characterized by cultural upheaval, political unrest and technology-driven disruptions seemed important. From aggressive slogan-emblazoned designs that championed protest to hyper-feminine clothing that seemed to represent a state of numbness and denial, fashion designer's responses to the cultural climate presented over the 2016–18 collections were wide ranging.

The final list of works acquired were selected for their point of view of the forward edge of conceptual work in fashion as art and how they expressed key cultural aspects important at that moment in time and included works by Alessandro Michele for Gucci, Rei Kawakubo for Comme des Garçons, John Galliano for Maison Margiela, Yeohlee Teng, Stephen Jones and Iris van Herpen in collaboration with Julia Korner, Walter van Bierendonck and Carol Collet. Displayed in a multimedia installation, the platforms, which accommodated just one object each, were configured from a series of 6 × 12 foot rectangles slashed diagonally at different angles to create complementary pairs of varying geometric shapes. Forming a metaphor for the state of disruption that the fashion designs were made in, the platforms pairs were arranged in the gallery with a degree of separation that created the tension of them falling apart but were close enough so that the original whole shapes could be surmised.

Elements of all five theories on post-postmodernism discussed above can be found in *Ultracontemporary*. Altermodern traits of social and environmental sensitivity were brought forward in Carol Collet's biomanufactured 'Biolace', demonstrating the growing importance of sustainable practices as a priority

Figure 9.5 An installation view of 'Ultracontemporary' at the Phoenix Art Museum, Phoenix. Photo by Ken Howie. Courtesy of Ken Howie Studios.

in our society. Hypermodern fashion logic is seen in the Gucci ensembles that celebrate the youthful perspective of nostalgic styles which were excessive in their mixture of colours, fabrics and accessories. And, especially, in the nearby projection of the accompanying campaign film by Glen Luchford that depicts models transported by the sheer pleasure of wearing clothes in the narrative of a Gucci-filled wonderland. Performative double framing, blurred distinctions between fashion and art, and challenges to cultural categories of gender appeared in the scarves by Walter van Bierendonk that featured various artists' depictions of the designer's face worn like masks by runway models as a live Pertchen band performed pagan ritualistic music intended to 'heal the world'. Automodern commentary on the 'radical restructuring' of public and private realms and the integration of digital devices in John Galliano's design for Maison Margiela dramatized the tension of his 'ongoing study of seductions in the millennial era' (Freidman, 2018: Styles 1). Julia Korner's framed digital renderings of her collaborative design, 'Eleventh Dress', with Iris van Herpen provides another automodern example. Digimodern ideas were expressed in the ample inclusion of video as integral to the installation design and to the extent that it supplanted the need for extended text. This was especially seen in the complementary formats of a short film and virtual reality film, 'Yellowbird New York: A Work in Progress', by film-maker Travis Hutchison about Yeohlee Teng's process of making of a museum commissioned work through the suggestive pairing of images and music but did not include oral or written explanations.

The analyses in this chapter may not provide definitive proof of the arrival of a new post-postmodern epoch, but they do support pause for thought about the contribution of fashion exhibitions to the cultural zeitgeist of the twenty-first century. In the more than two decades that I have worked in art museums as a fashion curator, I have observed these cultural institutions search for ways to shed their stigma as cabinets of historical curiosities and, like public libraries, seek relevancy among new systems for learning and forms of entertainment that compete for people's time and support. For many of these institutions, fashion has become an important contributor to the successful achievement of attendance goals and audience development by drawing visitors from a wide range of new sectors to the museum. Some of this success can be seen in the examples of this chapter and the way that fashion exhibitions can rapidly respond to the pulse of the cultural zeitgeist. There are so many more important exhibitions organized by my colleagues around the world that would serve the discussion of these theories if space allowed. I am optimistic that these examples will only contribute to the increased understanding that fashion is seen as art through this new lens of post-postmodernism.

Note

1   See E. Wilson (2011), 'McQueen's Final Showstopper', *New York Times*, 31 July: 1; Metropolitan Museum of Art (2011), '661,509 Total Visitors to Alexander McQueen Put Retrospective among Top 10 Most Visited Exhibitions in Metropolitan's History', press release, Metropolitan Museum of Art, 8 August. Available online https://www.metmuseum.org/press/news/2011/mcqueen-attendance (accessed 13 October 2018).

References

Antonelli, P., and M. Fischer (2018), *ITEMS: Is Fashion Modern?*, New York: Museum of Modern Art.

Donovan, C. (1983), 'Salute to Yves Saint Laurent', *New York Times*, 4 December: Section 6, 157.

Eshelman, R. (2008), *Performatism, or the End of Postmodernism*, Aurora, CO: Davies Group.

Freidman, V. (2018), 'Couture in a Tug of War', *New York Times*, 8 July: Styles 1.

Kirby, A. (2009), *Digimodernism: How New Technologies Dismantle the Postmodern and Reconfigure Our Culture*, London: Continuum.

Lipovetsky, G. (2005), *Hypermodern Times*, Cambridge: Polity Press.

McQuaid, M. (2018), Interview by Dennita Sewell, 14 December.

Menkes, S. (2011), 'Gone Global: Fashion as Art', *New York Times*, 4 July. Available online https://www.nytimes.com/2011/07/05/fashion/is-fashion-really-museum-art.html (accessed 20 September 2020).

Metropolitan Museum of Art (2008), ' "Blog.Mode: Addressing Fashion" Sparks Dialogue at Metropolitan Museum's Costume Institute', press release, Metropolitan Museum of Art. Available online https://www.metmuseum.org/press/exhibitions/2007/blogmode-addressing-fashion-sparks-dialogue-at-metropolitan-museums-costume-institute (accessed 4 June 2020).

Morgado, M. A. (2014), 'Fashion Phenomena and the Post-Modern Condition: Enquiry and Speculation', *Fashion, Style & Popular Culture*, 1 (3): 313–39.

Museum Boimans Van Beuningen (2014), 'The Future of Fashion Is Now', Museum Boimans Van Beuningen. Available online https://www.boijmans.nl/en/exhibitions/the-future-of-fashion-is-now (accessed 26 November 2018).

Samuels, R. (2008), 'Auto-Modernity after Postmodernism: Autonomy and Automation in Culture, Technology, and Education', in T. McPherson (ed.), *Digital Youth, Innovation, and the Unexpected*, 219–40. Cambridge, MA: MIT Press.

Smith, R. (2017), 'Well-Dressed Artifacts: Transforming Art Galleries into Fashion Runways at MoMA', *New York Times*, 6 October: C13, C20.

Teunissen, J., H. Nefkens, J. Arts and H. Voet (2014), *The Future of Fashion Is Now*, Rotterdam: Museum Boijmans van Beuningen.

van Herpen, I. (n.d.a), 'Vision', *Iris van Herpen*. Available online https://www.irisvanherpen.com/about (accessed 2 June 2020).

van Herpen, I. (n.d.b), 'Shift Souls', *Iris van Herpen*. Available online https://www.irisvanherpen.com/haute-couture/shift-souls (accessed 20 October 2018).

Victoria and Albert Museum (2017), 'Balenciaga: Shaping Fashion', Victoria and Albert Museum. Available online https://www.vam.ac.uk/exhibitions/balenciaga-shaping-fashion (accessed 28 October 2018).

10
COUNTER-FASHION AS CRITICAL PRACTICE
The Rational Dress Society

This chapter is an argument for decoupling capitalism and fashion. Victor Margolin calls the designed world the 'product milieu' (Margolin, 2018), drawing attention to the ways in which our environment is shaped and directed by the work of designers. Fashion is the design of subjects themselves, the vehicle through which we encounter those around us. Given the pressure that contemporary fashion faces, the intractable relationship between fashion, environmental devastation and human rights abuses, we, the members of the Rational Dress Society, believe that counter-fashion offers an urgent corrective to a system on the verge of collapse. Fashion designers and artists are uniquely positioned to respond to this crisis. It is not enough to critique existing systems or report on conditions. It is only from within the practice of design itself that alternative models can be pursued. We believe that fashion can be redefined as a practice outside, and even antithetical to, the dictates of capitalism, market forces and consumer culture. Contemporary counter-fashion practitioners are drawing on historical examples of revolutionary, utopian and political dress to imagine alternative futures, new ways of being with each other and the environment, and the mobilization of social solidarities and collective desires. Counter-fashion offers a way forward, a collective reimagining of our relationship to dress.

We are not used to thinking about the potential of fashion outside of the realm of consumer culture and the everyday realities of shopping. In Western (European- and American-influenced) society, fashion and capitalism appear as nearly synonymous terms. From its inception, fashion has been closely tied to industrial production and global exchange. The invention of the mechanical sewing machine during the Industrial Revolution fuelled the birth of the factory system and the garment industry. Fashion is defined by its relationship to continuous stylistic change (Helman, 2008). This change takes the form of trends that require systems of mass manufacture in order to sustain themselves.

It is difficult to conceive of fashion outside of the context of capitalism since it is a direct expression of that economic system.

Fernand Braudel explains in *Civilization and Capitalism*: 'I have always thought that fashion resulted to a large extent from the desire of the privileged to distinguish themselves, whatever the cost, from the masses who followed them, to set up a barrier' (Braudel, 1982). Seen in this light, fashion first emerged as an industrial technology for preserving class, race and gender hierarchies by visually differentiating social groups. Its rapid changes meant that only an elite few could afford to keep up with trends. Although recent developments in fast fashion have made garments more affordable, these underlying tendencies towards social division remain. The young and stylish are positioned against the old and poor. Consumers who want lower prices are at odds with the factory workers who make their clothes. Fashion is continually drawing lines between winners and losers in the global market.

The shifting, cyclical nature of fashion means that it is reduced, in our imaginations, to cycles of production and shopping. In such a closed system, there is little impetus for rethinking the liberatory potential in our clothes. In her essay 'Other Fashion Systems', Kate Fletcher describes the naturalization of the relationship between fashion and consumption: 'the prevailing consumerist fashion style and story appear "natural" to our way of thinking and behaviour: it is normal to access and engage with fashion primarily by exchanging money for product; it is expected that these same products will look dated and stylistically incongruous in six months; it is usual to discard rather than repair' (Fletcher and Grose, 2012).

Fast fashion

Reilly and Hawley (2019) note the complex relationship among conditions between consumers as a sign of post-postmodernism and conceive of 'micro-trends' as a result of hyperconsumption and hyper-mass production. Recent changes in the garment industry, characterized by the rise of fast fashion companies like Zara, H&M and Forever 21, have accelerated our usual relationship to fashion. Over the past twenty years, the traditional industry calendar, in which clothes are produced on a six-month, seasonal cycle, has been supplanted by the production schedule of global supply chains. Now, garments can go from conception to store racks in just two to three weeks as companies compete to bring consumers volumes of cheap clothes at faster rates. This new production cycle puts increasing strain on labour as workers are pushed to meet shorter production deadlines. The company Zara produces 1.23 million garments per day (TradeGecko, n.d.). When factories cannot meet the production demands of industry, they employ a complex system of subcontractors and sub-subcontractors, which renders oversight and regulation difficult. The result is a system of ever-faster production, in which garment workers are forced to operate in unsafe and inhumane working conditions. Lipovetsky ([1987] 1994) argues that mass production, marketing strategies and shifting consumer identities have created a 'mania for consumption' (32).

This increased production requires a reciprocal increase in consumption. In order to compel consumers to purchase greater quantities of clothes, fast fashion companies employ a strategy of planned obsolescence. According to publicly available industry standards, fast fashion garments are designed to retain their value from no more than ten wash cycles (Joy et al., 2012), locking consumers into a pattern of continuous buying and discarding. These clothes are so cheap that it is no longer economical to repair them, or to buy second hand. The pressures on the environment are significant; the vast majority of these garments end up in landfills (Wicker, 2017). In addition, Morgado (2014) notes the practice of fashion companies destroying old stock in order for it to not reach the secondary market.

Fast fashion companies sell clothes by invoking the language of democracy, celebrating the new affordability of trends. In this logic, fashion is equated with freedom of expression. Fast fashion celebrates the availability of previously unaffordable trends as a public good, an overcoming of the old hierarchies that have defined fashion. We are finally free to fully express ourselves through dress, we have endless choices in the retail environment, money no longer limits our access. What this rhetoric obscures is the ways that fast fashion and consumer culture limit choice. We may be able to pick out one of a dozen mass-produced garments, but we find ourselves unable to choose a different system altogether. Consumers who work in low-paying fields in which wages have not kept up with cost of living increases (Gilson et al., 2017) can't afford quality clothes, and they are locked into buying and continuously replacing cheap garments out of necessity. A relatively small choice, like picking out a tank top or sweater, is offered as a replacement for a more meaningful choice – buying less, buying locally produced garments, buying beautifully made clothes, sewing our own clothes, repairing out clothes instead of replacing them. The conflation of freedom with the limited choices one makes in the retail environment has the effect of individualizing and narrowing the field of consumer action. Systems of abuse, designed to perpetuate incommensurate power relations, are transformed into acts of self-expression. Fletcher argues, 'The prevailing system is the result of intentional, political choices, and, as such, consumerist fashion is revealed as a power structure, rather than an expression of our desire for dressing ourselves in multiples of cheap garment' (Fletcher and Grose, 2012). Fast fashion leverages our desire for expression against us, locking us into systems that promise freedom while constraining the field of our actions to realm of shopping.

In Hal Foster's 2004 essay 'Design and Crime', he describes a transition in the ways that mass-manufactured objects are conceptualized and sold to consumers. In the early days of industrial production, the standardization of the commodity object was the quality that made it desirable; the Model T's appeal was in its sameness. As supply chains grew increasingly complex and flexible in the late twentieth century, the terms shifted. Now, it is Zara's ability to produce the effect of mass-produced customization that explains its appeal. Using Bourriaud's (1998/2002) concept of altermodernism, Morgado (2014) suggests that mass customization or the ability for consumers to create 'unique' products form preset choices supplied by the brand, as a sign of post-postmodernism. In addition, the consumer is subjected to a marketing tactic that Foster calls 'perpetual profiling'. An individual walks into a store and, presented with a wide variety of cheap garments, they are able to pick out one, or two, or fifteen items that seem to speak to their specific desires and persona. Next week, if their identity shifts, their garments can change accordingly. Fast fashion means that not only are a much wider variety of styles available but stores can completely turn over their inventory in a period of two weeks. No subculture is too niche; industrial capitalism speaks to the consumer in increasingly intimate terms. Foster names this condition 'self-interpellation', a 'hey, that's me' effect in which the consumer feels an identification with a commodity object, hailing themselves into the late capitalist production apparatus (Foster, 2003). Thus, these practices align with Lipovetsky's (2005) thesis on hyperconsumption and Morgado's (2014) subsequent extrapolation of wastefulness in the fashion industry.

Counter-fashion

Clothes are the interface between individual and society, and as such they are an important tool in the political imagination. To recognize oneself and to be recognized in the public sphere is at the heart of our participation in fashion. Writing about the utopian history of early Israeli kibbutz-wear, fashion historian Anat Helman defines counter-fashion as the act of dressing to signal a shared ideology (Helman, 2008). Movements in counter-fashion mobilize clothes to produce political solidarity. Artists and designers have often worked together to identify the political possibilities inherent in garment design. In the late 1920s, Soviet designer Varvara Stepanova and Italian Futurist Thayaht produced experimental garments that imagined new futures. In the 1960s, the American designer Rudi Gernreich's space-age unisex designs influenced the second wave of the feminist movement.

We propose counter-fashion as a necessary strategy for developing alternatives to the current fashion system that produces microtrends (Reilly and Hawley, 2019) and fosters hyperconsumption (Lipovetsky, 2005; Morgado, 2014) using dubious manufacturing practices.

The mainstream fashion industry is deeply beholden to the model of continuous, exponential growth that their investors demand. They have effectively sold this growth model as a public good and an inevitability. But Foster asks, 'What happens when this commodity machine – now conveniently located out of view from most of us – breaks down, as environments give out, markets crash, and/or sweatshop workers scattered across the globe somehow refuse to go on?' With rising climate change and growing pressure on the factory system (as evidenced by the Rana Plaza disaster of 2014) we believe that collapse is imminent. The re-emergence of counter-fashion in the field of visual art and experimental design presents a way forward, a space to propose alternatives to mainstream fashion that are not subject to the same economic models. Counter-fashion is a tool for mobilizing human desire to produce new social bonds. It is this engagement with desire, the capacity for clothes to produce group identification, that suggests a path forward, a proactive decoupling of fashion and capitalism.

Practice

For the last several years, we, the members of the Rational Dress Society, have been producing JUMPSUIT, an open-source, ungendered monogarment to replace all clothes. Over the course of our research, we have encountered many artists and designers who are also working to create new counter-fashion, garments that help us to reflect critically on our relationship to consumption and suggest alternatives. What follows is a brief overview of three contemporary counter-fashion projects. New York-based artist Fawn Krieger, Chicago-based designer Sky Cubacub and Rotterdam-based designer Marloes ten Bhömer provide instructive examples of the ways that artists and designers are currently engaged with experimental and utopian dress, drawing on the history of counter-fashion to produce clothes that explore new models of production and dissemination.

Fawn Krieger's project *OUTFIT*, which she has been making since 2016, is a line of unisex garments inspired by the history of East German mail order catalogues (Figure 10.1). These are simple garments, whose modular patterns suggest both workwear and the history of experimental, geometric designs that come out of constructivist experiments of the early twentieth century. The patterns for *OUTFIT* are available to be ordered through the mail for a $5 fee. The designs are simple enough to be sewn by beginners; *OUTFIT* is a garment that can be readily adapted and engaged with on the level of production. The large pockets, plain fabrics and dark colours are practical, oriented towards use and activity. Krieger talks about her work in terms of mobilizing soft power,

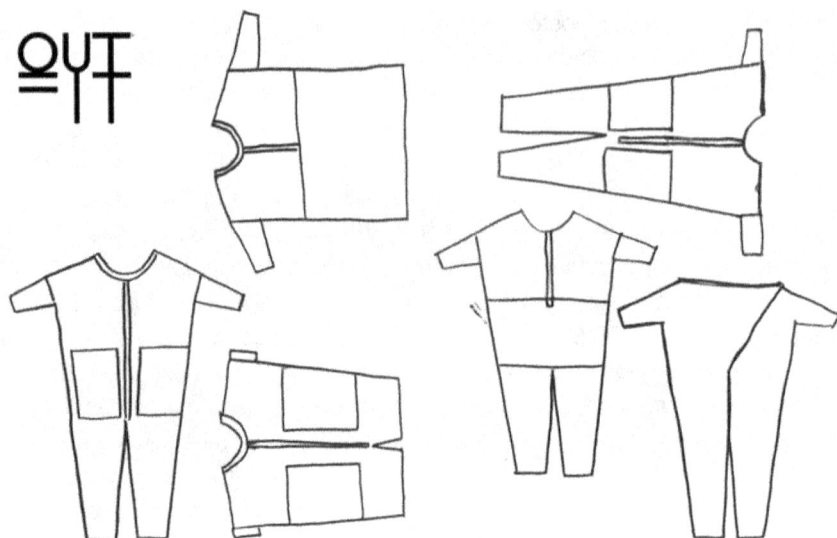

Figure 10.1 Fawn Krieger, *OUTFIT*, 2016.

envisioning the home and domestic life as a propagandistic space. 'OUTFITS are designed for working bodies moving through urban spaces from morning till night' (Krieger, n.d.). This is a politics of daily routines, memory and affect. Unlike mainstream fashion, which prioritizes change and stylistic innovation, Krieger's *OUTFIT* is historical, tied to past social formations, lost values and collective ways of living. Often, counter-fashion and utopian dress is figured in futuristic terms, but OUTFIT makes a space for genealogical design practice that embraces anachronistic models of dress, forgotten utopias that might be rehabilitated to meet the demands of the present.

If Krieger's work draws from the past, Sky Cubacub's *Rebirth Garments* takes up the language of the future, using performance fabrics, metallic ornamentation and neon colours to make a line of garments that draws on science fiction and pop culture (Figure 10.2). Cubacub describes the philosophy behind *Rebirth Garments* as 'clothes for the entire spectrum of gender and ability', or *Queer Crip Dress Reform* (Cubacub, 2015). Cubacub's garments are not meant for mass production; they are tailored to the specific needs of each client. Each garment is the culmination of a series of interviews and personal fittings. The vibrant aesthetic follows a principle of 'radical visibility', a critique of the cultural dictate to hide or minimize physical differences that do not adhere to the gender normative, racist and ableist standards of mainstream culture (Cubacub, 2015). In radical visibility, garments are designed to celebrate and emphasize differences between wearers.

Figure 10.2 Sky Cubacub, *Rebirth Garments*.

Marloes ten Bhömer is an experimental shoe designer whose work crosses boundaries between critique, satire and experimental manufacturing processes. ten Bhömer's wide-ranging project, *A Measurable Factor Sets the Conditions of Its Operation*, takes women's high heel shoe as a site of analysis (Figure 10.3). Traditionally, high heel shoe design is a highly standardized process in which a variety of pre-made, modular parts (e.g. heels of different shapes and designs) are plugged into other component parts that make the shoe's structure. This process streamlines industrial manufacturing and maximizes profit, but renders high heel shoe design a static field, resistant to innovation. In the case of women's heels, this manufacturing technique is particularly problematic because it incentivizes designers to reproduce already-existing, sexist high heel designs that inhibit movement, perpetuating stereotypes of women as physically dependent and helpless. In response, ten Bhömer produces a body of speculative work that makes an analytical argument for change while simultaneously proposing an alternative. Her work begins with an appropriation video that collects instances of women's heels breaking in popular media, often as a plot point that renders the female characters vulnerable, waiting to be rescued by a male protagonist or offered up as prey for a variety of monsters. In this taxonomy, a link is made between the high-heeled female subject and qualities of passivity and submission. The high heel is a fetish object that immobilizes the female body, rendering its wearer dependent and inert (ten Bhömer, n.d.).

Figure 10.3 *Bluepanelshoe*, Marloes ten Bhömer, 2015.

ten Bhömer further explores this dynamic through a series of videos, shown in a clinical, laboratory environment, that document women walking in high heels on a variety of surfaces. Shot in slow motion, this video suggests both scientific study and fetish film, fluctuating between assessment and parody. Ultimately, this video work, combined with further kinematic and anatomical studies, forms the basis for a series of prototypes – a proposal for a new taxonomy of high heel show that rejects factory formula design. ten Bhömer uses rapid prototyping technology to develop a shoe design based on a constellation of foot-to-ground contact points. This new shoe, called *Bluepanelshoe*, has its basis in motion, proposing a model for female footwear that imagines women as active participants in social and political life, literally de-objectifying its wearer.

We have offered these examples of contemporary counter-fashion because we believe that the current moment calls for a re-evaluation of fashion itself. Fashion has often been dismissed as the embodiment of the worst elements of consumer culture, elitism and social division – with good reason. But it is fashion's close relationship to capitalism that makes it ripe for intervention. If fashion and capitalism are intertwined, to change fashion – to test out alternatives – might also change capitalism. It is from within the field of fashion design, not outside it, that the work of imaginatively un-making capitalism must occur. This is the work of counter-fashion in late capitalism.

References

Bourriaud, N. ([1998] 2002), *Relational Aesthetics*, trans. S. Pleasance and F. Woods, Dijon, France: Les presses du réel.

Braudel, F. (1982), *Civilization and Capitalism 15th to 18th Century: The Structures of Everyday Life*, Berkeley: University of California Press.

Cubacub, S. (2015), 'A Queercrip Dress Reform Movement Manifesto', *Rebirth Garments*, 22 April. Available online http://rebirthgarments.com/radical-visibility-zine (accessed 29 November 2018).

Fletcher, K., and L. Grose (2012), *Fashion and Sustainability Design for Change*, London: Laurence King.

Foster, H. (2003), *Design and Crime (and Other Diatribes)*, London: Verso.

Gilson, D., M. Mechanic, L. McClure, J. Harkinson, D. Gilson, K. Butler, A. Kroll, F. Echavarri and P. Levy (2017), 'Overworked America: 12 Charts That Will Make Your Blood Boil', *Mother Jones*, 25 June. Available online https://www.motherjones.com/politics/2011/05/speedup-americans-working-harder-charts (accessed 22 February 2018).

Helman, A. (2008), 'Kibbutz Dress in the 1950s: Utopian Equality, Anti Fashion, and Change', *Fashion Theory the Journal of Dress Body & Culture*, 12 (3): 313–39.

Joy, A., J. F. Sherry, Jr., A. Venkatesh, J. Wang and R. Chan (2012), 'Fast Fashion, Sustainability, and the Ethical Appeal of Luxury Brands', *Fashion Theory*, 16 (3): 273–96.

Lipovetsky, G. ([1987] 1994), *The Empire of Fashion: Dressing Modern Democracy*, trans. C. Porter, Princeton, NJ: Princeton University Press.

Lipovetsky, G. (2005), *Hypermodern Times*, Cambridge, MA: Polity Press.

Krieger, F. (n.d.), Outfit. Available online http://www.fawnkrieger.com/outfit.html (accessed 29 November 2018).

Morgado, M. A. (2014), 'Fashion Phenomena and the Post-postmodern Condition: Enquiry and Speculation', *Fashion, Style & Popular Culture*, 1 (3): 313–39.

Reilly, A., and H. Hawley (2019), 'Attention Deficit Fashion', *Fashion, Style, and Popular Culture*, 6 (1): 85–98.

Margolin, V. (2018), *The Politics of the Artificial: Essays on Design and Design Studies*, Chicago: University of Chicago Press.

ten Bhömer, M. (n.d.), 'Marloestenbhomer', http://marloestenbhomer.squarespace.com/ (accessed 15 August 2019).

TradeGecko (n.d.), 'Zara Supply Chain Analysis – the Secret behind Zara's Retail Success', *Inventory Management Software*. Available online https://www.tradegecko.com/blog/zara-supply-chain-its-secret-to-retail-success (accessed 2 January 2018).

Wicker, A. (2017), 'The Earth Is Covered in the Waste of Your Old Clothes', *Newsweek*, 16 March. Available online http://www.newsweek.com/2016/09/09/old-clothes-fashion-waste-crisis-494824.html (accessed 2 January 2018).

11

ENTROPY, FASHION AND POST-POSTMODERNISM: AUTO-ETHNOGRAPHY OF A BOOK EDITOR

José Blanco F.

'Fashion has a function: to let people walk through fields of possibilities … sacralizing every form of diversity, [and] feeding indispensable self-determination skills.' Alessandro Michele as quoted by Nicole Phelps

I, Book Co-editor

Is there even such a thing as post-postmodernism? Do we need a neologism to describe every single 'moment', new ethos or paradigm shift? Why have we so obsessively tried to describe our lives and our artistic expressions as a succession of movements, as never-ending dialectics? Can post-postmodern theories give us the freedom to stop thinking linearly? Working as a co-editor on this book has been fun (yes, indeed), a lot of work (most certainly) and challenging (undoubtedly). In the past two years or so, I have often asked myself: Why on earth am I working on this book? The most common answer: Not just the eye has to travel, the mind most excruciatingly has to do so as well. So, when Andy proposed this project I decided to accept the challenge. Inspired by Marcia Morgado's (2014) essay we set out to look for signs of post-postmodernism in the wild and open field of fashion studies or among those from other fields researching fashion. Are the various concepts that have been suggested as substitutions for or developments after postmodernism part of the fashion theory discourse? Now that we have survived postmodernism, can we just move on? Apparently, no.

David Rudrum and Nicholas Starvis in their introduction to *Supplanting the Postmodern: An Anthology of Writings on the Arts and Culture of the Early 21st Century* (2015) compare postmodernism to a river that has subsided and is no longer in spate. The authors acknowledge the difficulty and lack of consensus on how to account for this downturn and the fact that the term 'postmodern' simply became too broad. There is no agreement, they believe, on whether postmodernism ended or not, or if we even need to announce its death. Rudrum and Starvis admit the fact that no ideal term exists to substitute postmodernity and argue against the use of 'post-postmodernism' as a catch-all term. They further argue that the term post-postmodernism lacks specificity which renders it useless (2015: xxi). It does not clearly reflect a specific interest to be 'post' or to actually depart from postmodernism in order to pursue what postmodernism established in different directions or by other means. Moreover, they believe, there is also no certainty on whether the term post-postmodernism intends to create new departures from the death of postmodernism (2015: xxi). With no ideal term in hand, Andy and I forged ahead with the imperfect yet most encompassing moniker available as many others before us have done. We continue hoping that a better term would eventually appear. In the meantime, post-postmodernism is what we have to work with.

I marched on with Andy, writing a call for chapter proposals, selecting chapters, writing a proposal for the publisher, editing chapters, going back and forth with authors not just on concepts and editorial changes but also on … please send contributions in a timely manner. And here we are; you have the book in your hands and, no doubt, by now you have enjoyed the wonderful and diverse contributions by a group of brilliant authors. Through the editorial process, the most important question for me was: Why and how does this matter to me, to José? This final chapter attempts to answer that question.

I came from Costa Rica to the United States to attend graduate school in the late 1980s. From the moment of my first encounter with some art criticism and literary theories that were new to me, I struggled with the idea that I was supposed to accept as fact that a bunch of French male philosophers could explain my own life better than I could. It became a personal mission to escape the stronghold of frameworks set out by these philosophers and perpetuated in academia. How do I retrieve what is of value from those theories while also trying to move away from narratives that can be coercive and respond mainly to privileged spaces occupied by mostly white male writers of a certain social status? I felt that the only way to fully engage with these theories was by focusing on the individual, by each of us asserting our identity over theories of the past and present, by putting personhood over labels and by accepting the freedom of breaking away from all frameworks: negative and positive, oppressive or not, social or individual.

It is, for instance, in what I consider a post-postmodern concept per excellence, genderfuck, where we see the individual making an effort to question and subvert accepted notions of gender as well as social expectations of gender roles by claiming and forging an identity that does not fit the structures and concepts set forward by either modernism or postmodernism. It is no coincidence that fashion and appearance management are among the most useful tools at the disposal of anyone interested in engaging in genderfuck practices. As Alessandro Michelle claims in the epigraph of this conclusion, fashion's function in post-postmodern times may be to allow us to explore possibilities beyond any previous constraints; that very personal exploration should, then, allow us to create true diversity – one centred on the individual and not in the groups the individual belongs to.

I have elsewhere applied a phenomenological approach to discuss my lived experience and creative authorship in selecting my underwear (Blanco, 2014). That autoethnography piece allowed me to explore the meanings created by my interaction with my underwear through the years. Any observation I made in that piece about how my underwear choices have been shaped by my cultural context, socio-economic status and relation to my own body and sexuality also reveals how my lived experience with dress and fashion has been a journey from modern to post-postmodern experiences. I was born in the 1960s as Costa Rica solidified its status as a global modern democracy following our 1948 civil war and the abolition of our army. I grew up in a society striving to become modern, to be part of global 'civilized' societies. Besides the fact that my parents were working class and there was a very limited amount of clothing pieces I could afford, my identity as a Costa Rican man was fully defined by modernist parameters, a cultural and literal essentialism of myself that I had little room to change if I wanted to join the aspirational 'modern' world of Costa Rican urbanites. Later in the 1980s I became an immigrant when I moved to the United States to attend graduate school in Los Angeles, California. I was immediately confronted with professors, courses and research arguing that the grand narratives I enthusiastically studied in Costa Rica were no longer relevant since postmodernist theories had handicapped their validity and significance. As a young scholar in training, I was surprised by the fact that I had been accepted for graduate school outside Costa Rica, precisely because of my robust educational background structured around modernist and – as I know now – colonial discourses. Simultaneously, it felt somewhat liberating to be able to question the meaning that had been assigned to my identity in an eager modernist society back in Costa Rica. These revelations made me aware that Latin America had always been – to a certain extent – postmodern, that I was the result of hybrid cultures and that embracing said complexity would allow me to better understand my own identity. I started figuring out the different parts of my identity: a gay man, an immigrant, a documented immigrant, a Latino, a gay Latino, a Catholic and a 'million' more micro-labels. Postmodernism taught me that my identity was merely a collection of floating signifiers, an array of simulacra, of something I was in the past and something someone else thinks I am, was or could be at any given point. How do I dress to be? Which aspect do I embrace in my appearance management? What do I give up? It was not fun to talk about identity within postmodern frameworks.

I survived postmodernism; I made it to the 2000s and remained an individual. Or, as Lipovetsky (2005) suggests, postmodernity receded without any clear indication of what happened to us. I am no longer able to explain my identity, style and fashion choices using either modernist or postmodernist approaches. Metamodernism, one of the concepts used for analysis in some chapters on this volume, introduces the idea of oscillation 'between a modern enthusiasm and a postmodern irony, between hope and melancholy, between naïveté and knowingness, empathy and apathy, unity and plurality, totality and fragmentation, purity and ambiguity' (van den Akker and Vermeulen, 2010: 5–6). I find dress, fashion and appearance management among the easiest and often more effective tools at my disposal to assert myself as an individual and, yes, oscillate. When I see that I have agency, that I make choices, fears of homogenization begin to dissipate. I can choose which part of myself I want to express and I enjoy the ability to always go back to a previous expression of self or try something else. I can let go of the irony and confusion and say: Oh yeah, I am all of that, every single piece of it in every single moment and all of it all the time. In the 2010s, as I began to better understand theories of intersectionality as applied to myself, I was able to better converse with my students about non-monolithic identities. I became free from the tyranny of having to explain 'what' I am; I can just be. Instead of defining myself and my wardrobe choices by one single identity, I began searching for communities that would allow me to be who I wanted to be and dress how I wanted to dress whenever I wanted to.

I, Radicant

The search for the above-mentioned communities meant that, as proposed by Bourriaud (2009), I was interested in transcending cultural codes and building an identity that was no longer rigid, distancing myself whenever I wanted from identity politics. I became a nomad, a wanderer, an immigrant with strong roots, belonging here and there and everywhere, always a tourist even within my identity; free to constantly experiment with clothes, hairstyles; dressing one way to go teach and another way to go out to the gay bar. I am not saying that I, or anyone else, did not do that before; I am simply stating that I do it now without guilt or reservation. 'Apollo and Dionysus', I tell my husband every now and then when I use the same tote bag to carry candles, chimes and talking pieces for the peace circle conversations with my students during the day and snacks and water for the 4 a.m. exodus from the gay bar.[1]

Appearance management is an extremely valuable tool to express deeper personal transformation or even just the oscillation from Apollonian to Dionysian energies in one's life. Dress can also signal a shift from over-reliance in traditional values and strict societal guidelines and structures to a more democratic system of respect for the individual. As a social media meme states, what if 'tradition is just peer pressure from dead people'? Iqra Shagufta Cheema argues in her chapter in this volume that 'post-postmodernity requires its subjects to constantly question, rediscover, and refigure the foundations of their identity'. She believes that this is what some Muslim women are accomplishing by exploring multiple identities through dress, albeit the fact that their counterparts from older generations seem to believe that authenticity is fixed at a point in history. Nigel Lezama explains in his chapter that in post-postmodern times consumers can become free from their habitus – as defined by Pierre Bourdieu's theories, which were central in fashion studies during the late postmodernist period. Hypermodernity, Lipovetsky indicates, implies a weakening of 'regulative power of the collective institutions' (2005: 55). That is to say, in post-postmodern times we can choose personhood over labels, social expectations and style tribes. Lezama further argues that 'the power of dominant culture and its habitus have waned as the impact of democratic and individualistic ideology is experienced more and more profoundly in social practices, albeit through the tightening grip of late capitalist and neoliberal ideology on the cultural sphere'. Indeed, I am not claiming that fashion, by providing individuals with agency in defining their exterior identities, is an all-liberating force, but that – for some of us – it can be an invaluable tool.

At some point in the 2010s I got tired of being peripheral and having to make an effort to 'represent' who I was, particularly from an ethnic point of view where I was expected to constantly perform the 'Latino' character in everyone's script. I grew up in Costa Rica unashamedly wanting to be a punk rocker, loving superhero movies and desperately wishing to one day visit Disneyland. When I arrived in the United States in the late 1980s, however, I had to learn how to dance salsa and merengue to comply with expectations or else risk being labelled a 'bad' Latino. I yearned to be part of the modernist global culture I had studied back home and at no point did that make me feel 'less' Costa Rican. I eventually understood, based partly on my encounter with postmodern theories, that said yearning derived from colonialist narratives. Living through a constant questioning of why I liked the things I liked, however, was exhausting. Bourriaud describes this: 'Through a kind of double negation or reverse deafness, the postmodern scene endlessly re-enacts the rift between colonizer and colonized, master and slave, keeping to the frontier – its object of study – and thereby preserving it as such' (2009: 14). If Bourriaud is right, then in post-postmodern times I can effectively reclaim my modernist self. I can say without shame that Chekov and Ibsen are my favourite playwrights and that I am absolutely mesmerized by the work of Charles James and Elsa Schiaparelli. Further, without specifically trying to 'decolonize' myself, I can also freely say how much I love the work of playwright Lauren Yee and the fashion designs of Mary Katrantzou and Erdem Moralioglu, while also not feeling embarrassed that I did not mention a single person of Latin American descent in the two sentences above. I venture as an individual, carrying my singularities, resisting standardization when I must, but also welcoming the opportunity to join a global culture, because the world I live in is simply and unescapably global.

Bourriaud (2009) further argues for a process of 'creolization' which involves acclimatization, cross-breeding of heterogeneous influences and even cultural authentication managed ever so carefully to prevent cultural appropriation. 'It is roots that make individuals suffer; in our globalized world, they persist like phantom limbs after amputation, causing pain impossible to treat, since they affect something that no longer exists' (Bourriaud, 2009: 21). I have, in my identity and my appearance, treasured my roots as a Costa Rican but I no longer aim to re-enroot myself in a singular identity. I am happy to grow my roots and add new ones. My roots are constantly in motion as they are part of a very complex identity that I feel now freer to accept than I ever had in the past. Managing my appearance, I aim to take what is valuable from my intersectional identities, pack it in my messenger bag with a few basic garments and explore my 'laboratory of identities' (Bourriaud, 2009: 51). I do not want to be a guest in anybody else's appearance rules anymore; so, I don't care if that older Southern white woman at a fancy museum event tells me that my shirt and my tie do not match, because I can tell her: 'Well … we don't do that anymore.'

I, Hypermodernist

Is fashion a key to life and identity? Hardly, but as I argue above, it is a darn good tool for many of us. Lipovetsky (2005) believes that fashion facilitates individuality and democratization by allowing us self-expression. Hypermodern fashion is indeed Bourriaud's 'laboratory of identities', a self-conscious identity that leads, perhaps, towards a more fleshed personhood, a hyperindividuality. This is not to say that fashion is not loaded with problematic issues. Fashion as a phenomenon and as an industry thrives on social injustice, exclusivity and elitism. In this volume, Abigail Glaum-Lathbury and Maura Brewer of the Rational Dress Society problematize the connections between fashion and capitalism and argue for the need for immediate changes and decoupling capitalism and fashion, a work, they believe, must come from within the fashion industry. This is a challenge that we must face more than ever in a post Covid-19 world.

Laura Lanteri (2020) asks if fashion can regain its relevance after the global pandemic crisis as consumers cling to what we deem essential and veer away from the industry's 'lure into impossible aspirational dreams of never-ending consumption' (19). Lanteri adds: 'The dynamics that have driven the exorbitant financial and commercial growth of the industry are the very same forces that – exasperated by a global pandemic of unthinkable proportions – are now possibly risking its extinction' (19). The system was already on the verge of collapse but fashion, as I argue here, can be transformative and meaningful. Lanteri believes that 'fashion and luxury will have to change because the audience they used to have are not there anymore. Fashion is no longer simply a monologue, and customers are emerging as much more powerful voices in this dialogue. They are shouting' (19).

The notions of hyperconsumption and hyperindividuality seem inseparable from the idea of capitalist consumerism. Like many others, due to a lack of proper financial capital, I can hardly ever afford expensive brands and slow or handmade fashion, or even eco and ethical brands. I resort to a combination of fast fashion global brands (Top Shop, Uniqlo, Zara, H&M, WE, Cotton On, etc.) and a few aesthetically consistent or 'classic' pieces – particularly suits – that I have deemed worthy of investment. As I dream of buying high-quality designer suits, it becomes clear to me that there is an irony implied in the fact that slow fashion, bespoke suits and couture pieces turn out to be the most responsible and sustainable choices and that, simultaneously, their consumption implies the adoption of a capitalist system of fashion exclusion, excess and overabundance. Although I would hardly classify myself as a hyperconsumer in Lipovetsky's terms, it is clear that the wide range of available commodities allows me to play with identity. Gucci is certainly out of my expense reach, but in more limited and frugal ways, I embrace the aesthetic and cultural heterogeneity that – according to Nigel Lezama's chapter in this book – Gucci makes available to post-postmodern consumers. In post-postmodern fashion choices, personhood comes before any cultural and subcultural normative; style is hybrid and perennially changing if you want it to be so. Hypermodernity prioritizes the individual and therefore options abound not just in clothing but in music, streaming services, transportation and lodging options. I surf through fashion and dress codes just like I surf, as a bilingual speaker, through language codes.

Can fashion truly help 'un-make' capitalism as the members of the Radical Dress Society contributing to this volume believe? Are my efforts better placed in a drastic change of my wardrobe? How do I operate within a system where, if I want my clothes to fit properly, I need to have money to pay for custom fitting and tailoring? I have been telling myself for years: when I have money, I will stop buying fast fashion. In order to operate in my laboratory of identities, it seems I need access to a larger number of commodities and fast fashion provides that flexibility. I wonder if fast fashion, unfortunately, is the very essence of post-postmodern style for those of us with little or no access to Gucci, Vetements, Tom Ford and Supreme.

I, Performatist

I was not familiar with Eshelman's work until we started working on this book. I became fascinated with his concept of theist works of art where 'in terms of reader response, performatist narratives must create an ironclad construct whose inner lock or fit cannot be broken by the reader without destroying the work as a whole' (Eshelman, 2008: 20). This concept of theism helped me understand how the fashion designer was supplanted at many fashion houses by the post-postmodern role of creative directors; individuals who are continuously aiming to provide not merely a collection of clothes but an aesthetic and, often, ideological frame for their potential customers. Chapters in this book analyse how the work of Alessandro Michele, Tom Ford and Demna Gvasalia is done from an all-encompassing theist or auteur perspective, where, as consumers of either fashion or fashion as art, we are presented with a full narrative and a branded lifestyle from these creative directors. Could I ever walk out of my house on a direct-from-the-runway Gucci look? If so, then my entire appearance would have been defined from shoes to headgear by Michele. The only way I could ever wear Gucci without sacrificing my identity would be by refusing the entire frame provided by the creative director's specific collection, the current and past meaning of the brand, the way the garment was presented on the runway, including freeing the clothes from the model's body and taking one or two pieces from the ensemble and transposing them to my body. I have to, as Eshelman suggests, destroy the whole work as it was performed by the original creator to escape or transcend the conceptual frame and then engage critically with the work in order to make any substantial use of any purchased pieces.

As Grant Johnson in his chapter about Tom Ford indicates, we have become increasingly more comfortable with recognizing fashion designers as creative authors as we have done with film directors and those who do both, like Ford himself. Fashion films, which enjoyed a period of great popularity in the early 2000s, were precisely aimed at seeing fashion as part of wider creative efforts to build a brand. The nomenclature change from fashion designer to creative director is significant in the sense that creative directors are now outwardly involved with brand awareness and marketing. These frames, however, can be destroyed by individual consumers not simply interested in the aesthetics of the product and the meaning assigned by its creator but, more specifically, on their own performance of the product.

Caroline Bellios argues in her chapter that exhibit maker Judith Clark goes beyond the 'didactic modern exhibition and the spectacle-laden focus of many postmodern exhibitions' to present a frame that the exhibit's visitor can engage with as an active participant from a departure point of common knowledge and history. That initial frame, however, goes beyond and presents the objects as an 'exhibition of the mind' which accesses and is accessed by our memory. This happens precisely because of the unexpected way in which the objects are displayed and, specifically, the enhancement of body absence. Performatism proposes that the split concept of sign and strategies of boundary transgression that dominated postmodern thought is being replaced by a unified concept of sign and strategies of closure (Eshelman, 2008: 1). In this context the observer or consumer of the work and the work itself – as created by Alessandro Michelle for Gucci in his capacity of creative director, Judith Clark as exhibit maker or José Blanco F. as an individual with free agency dressed for an event at a museum in Chicago – become part of an 'endless regress of referral that has no particular fix point, goal, or center' (Eshelman, 2008: 1). Performatist framing means that the reader or viewer receives a work that has a meaning defined by a theist author as part of a finished creative effort; yet we can shift or transcend that framing with an outer frame that goes beyond the original intent. Our reaction is part of a collective approach to the author's proposal and yet, we are at liberty to subjectively interpret the creator's work. It is at this point when, I feel, we return to the territory of how, as an individual, I reaffirm my personhood and play with my identity using garments that were perhaps designed for a different purpose or meaning but because the garment has no essence in itself – albeit the creator's original intention – I can redefine it, reframe it and reconstruct it at will. Those who read my framing or performance of said sartorial choices will, in turn, have the ability to accept or reject my new framing of the objects. The hand of the creator is always there, but in this sort of 'transcendent functionalism', I build a new framework for the piece in function of my performed identity or identities and with the freedom to always return to a different frame. Eshelman explains: 'Just because we slip in and out of complex sets of overlapping roles doesn't mean that we get hopelessly lost in them, or that fact and fiction are *really* equivalent, or that the *possibility* that something can be fabricated means that our everyday faith in it must be vitiated' (2008: 11).

Finding new personal meaning in apparel choices is a true rupture with postmodernism. Moreover, sometimes our wardrobe identity changes are ritualistic and acquire deep meaning. Speaking to a few friends who are drag performers, I have come to understand the 'sacredness of drag', the importance of not just the final product but also of the process of creating a new narrative that is built by switching or modifying your appearance. As Eshelman argues, 'a good formal definition of the "performance" in performatism is that it *demonstrates with aesthetic means the possibility of transcending the conditions of a given frame* (whether in a "realistic," social or psychological mode or in a fantastic, prenatural one)' (2008: 12, emphasis original).

I, Oscillator

Time is fleeting, so is memory. Welcome to post-postmodernity. I do oscillate, frame and reframe myself, accept novelty and ephemerality for as long as I feel like, but I have my eyes open and always on the prize: myself. Hyperindividualism has allowed me to better define my own social and gender position and actively question others' desires to label and box me. I belong to many groups, subgroups, subcultures, fan groups, taste cultures and so on, and I function properly (for the most part) in each, partly because I carefully select what I wear to each space and time. Style is not static, neither is identity.

Vermeulen and van der Akker (2010) argue that there is no modern or postmodern; notions co-exist and so in a post-postmodern experience, oscillating is the secret. I like thinking about post-postmodernism not as a condition, theory or a series of theories, and certainly not as a moment in time. I like thinking about post-postmodernism as an experience, as a living choice to centre on personhood. As I am writing these final notes, I came across an interview with Aaron Philip in *Out* magazine. Philip first describes herself: 'I'm a Black woman in a wheelchair, who is trans, and I want to be respected for that' and then argues,

> personhood should be recognized over anything else, and that should be profitable in fashion. It's inaccurate to think people are all just white, tall, able-bodied, skinny, beautiful, cisgender models and that clothes should only be tailored to those sizes and body types. The world is moving in a direction where everyone wants to be seen for who they are without having to compromise. (Philip, 2019: 9)

I am not limited by any labels or style tribes, I can put on a harness and go visit my good friends at Jackhammer in Chicago (hey guys!), or put on a baseball hat and a blue top to go see the Chicago Cubs play at Wrigley field, dress up in a suit and tie for the Driehaus Design Initiative fashion show or go 'trendy' to an event at Chicago's Museum of Contemporary Art. I am all of that, more than all of that and none of that, but I want to claim the right to define myself while also reclaiming my own story.

The *Metamodernist Manifesto* argues that '[we] must liberate ourselves from the inertia resulting from a century of modernist ideological naivety and the cynical insincerity of its antonymous bastard child' (Turner, 2011). An oscillatory movement between polarities, Turner argues, can propel all of us into action. In terms of fashion, appearance management and identity, I see this as an opportunity to explore my personhood finally liberated from the grasp of French philosophers. Postmodern irony and relativism serve very little to a generation facing enormous challenges not only to their way of living, our political systems and our planet but also to our right to our own identity, our microidentity, our personhood. The manifesto goes on to explain that 'existence is enriched if we set about our task as if those limits might be exceeded, for such action unfolds the world'. There shall be no rules on how to create post-postmodern fashion or be a post-postmodern fashion designer or create and nurture a post-postmodern identity. We just are what we are and do what we do guided by nothing but ourselves. The metamodernists advance the idea that 'today, we are nostalgists as much as we are futurists', and thus we move into a future that is wide open and yet well-grounded on our nostalgia for the past and our roots. Afro-futurism and indigenous futurism, for instance, have presented a vision of the future that is inspired by science fiction and technology while also utilizing practices, aesthetics and even ideologies from the past: a more intriguing approach than a mere desire to 'decolonize' your already-lived personal or communal history.

Decolonizing, an overused academic term du jour in the late 2010s, ignores the true injustice of the colonial powers – mainly the occupation and exploitation of other people's lands – and assumes that 'decolonizing' will free us if we extricate the past from our identity and the ways we express it, including dress. I do not feel that I need to decolonize myself. The work should concentrate on making my personhood and surroundings more democratic in order to comprehend what the over-reliance on grand narratives and the subsequent total dissolution of those narratives never allowed me to discover about myself: José. What are the facts – not the theories and ideologies – that formed who I am today? I oscillate and, therefore, I dig deep into the many aspects of who I am. Turner ends his manifesto by stating: 'Thus, metamodernism shall be defined as the mercurial condition between and beyond irony and sincerity, naivety and knowingness, relativism and truth, optimism and doubt, in pursuit of a plurality of disparate and elusive horizons. We must go forth and oscillate!' (2011).

I, Entropic Being

I have been obsessed with the notion of entropy – a concept in thermodynamics that measures the level of disorder in any given system – since I was a first-year college student. I was thrilled when I read in the *Metamodernist Manifesto* that 'all things are caught within the irrevocable slide towards a state of maximum entropic dissemblance' (Tuner, 2011). Is entropy what defines post-postmodernism? Is the postmodern spirit of fragmentation merely augmented by the number of new theories announcing the end or the death of postmodernism without a clear term or set of characteristics to define what comes next?

Lipovetsky (2005) had already indicated that hypermodernity was typified by the acceleration of movement and change. I consume; therefore I am. I consume again, therefore I am again, and again, and again and continuously enjoy the pleasure linked with change. We are presented every day with more information and goods than we can handle, all delivered through an ever-increasing number of networks. We are constantly inspired, or perhaps required, to question our identities, rediscover ourselves in both our past and present and, then, reconfigure our identities for the present and future.

Rudrum and Starvis (2015) continue the analogy of postmodernism as a river that has subsided by arguing that, if we bring together all the 'competing' terms suggested to supplant post-postmodernism, they constitute a 'delta effect' where the river of postmodernism splits and diverges into different streams and along different courses all stemming from 'the once-mighty postmodern river' (2015: xiii). The state of post-postmodern theory is indeed an entropic one. Perhaps postmodernism dissipated or expanded into an infinite number of ideas, theories, explanations, experiences – an entropic process in full chaos. Postmodern fashion allowed for fragmentation and experimentation and – whatever experience follows it – post-postmodernism, as named in this book, has allowed me to claim allegiance to my individuality, hyperindividuality, personhood. Thus, the result for me and others may be a great constellation of individual ways to express identity through dress and fashion. Experiences and expressions of identity are constantly changing, old ones can be renewed, new ones can be discovered and any can be discarded as part of the entropy of identity in the twenty-first century.

Note

1   I am referencing the philosophical duality of Apollo and Dionysus which is more closely associated with Friedrich Nietzsche who in *The Birth of Tragedy* (1872) argues that the union of these two forces is responsible for the rise of dramatic poetry (a Dionysian impulse encased in an Apollonian structure). The Apollonian can be described as a tendency towards order and formality while the Dionysian aims to challenge that established order by promoting an aesthetic of disorder or entropy. Apollo is associated with beauty, moderation, balance, meaningful coherence, simplicity and a classic wisdom that works well within social laws and parameters. Dionysus, on the other hand, appears through intoxication, boundary dissolution, stylistic experimentation and the creation of an incoherent reality in direct opposition with order.

References

Blanco, F. J. (2014), 'Revealing Myself: A Phenomenological Approach to My Underwear Choices through the Years', *Critical Studies in Men's Fashion*, 1 (2): 117–31.
Bourriaud, N. (2009), *The Radicant*, trans. J. Gussen and L. Porten, Berlin: Sternberg Press.

Eshelman, R. (2008), *Performatism, or the End of Postmodernism*, Aurora, CO: Davies Group.

Lanteri, L. (2020), 'Fashion's Great French Revolution', *Women's Wear Daily* (11 May): 19.

Lipovetsky, G. (2005), *Hypermodern Times*, Cambridge: Polity Press.

Morgado, M. A. (2014), 'Fashion Phenomena and the Post-Postmodern Condition: Enquiry and Speculation', *Fashion, Style & Popular Culture*, 1 (3): 313–39.

Phelps, N. (2019), 'Spring 2020 Ready-to-Wear: Gucci', *Vogue*, 22 September. Available online https://www.vogue.com/fashion-shows/spring-2020-ready-to-wear/gucci (accessed 2 November 2019).

Philip, A. (2019), '50 Radical Ideas for Queer Liberation: Idea No. 46: The Fashion Industry Will Be More Accessible to Queer Folks, Trans Folks, Disabled Folks, And Beyond', *Out Magazine*, 27 (9) (June–July): 94.

Rudrum, D., and N. Starvis (2015), *Supplanting the Postmodern: An Anthology of Writings on the Arts and Culture of the Early 21st Century*, London: Bloomsbury.

Turner, L. (2011), *Metamodernist Manifesto*. Available online Metamodernism.org (accessed 2 November 2019).

Vermeulen, T., and R. van den Akker (2010), 'Notes on Metamodernism', *Journal of Aesthetics & Culture*, 2 (1). doi:10.3402/jac.v2i0.5677.

INDEX